PATRICK FRASER TYTLER

ENGLAND
UNDER THE REIGNS OF
EDWARD VI. AND MARY

VOLUME I

Elibron Classics
www.elibron.com

Elibron Classics series.

© 2005 Adamant Media Corporation.

ISBN 1-4212-0876-8 (paperback)
ISBN 1-4212-0875-X (hardcover)

This Elibron Classics Replica Edition is an unabridged facsimile
of the edition published in 1839 by Richard Bentley,
London.

ENGLAND

EDWARD VI. AND MARY.

LONDON:

PRINTED BY SAMUEL BENTLEY,
Dorset Street, Fleet Street.

G. P. Harding, del.

W. Greatbach, sc

KING EDWARD 6ᵀᴴ

*The Original by Holbein in the Collection
of Lord Northwick.*

London, Published by Richard Bentley, 1839.

ENGLAND

UNDER THE REIGNS OF

EDWARD VI. AND MARY,

WITH THE

CONTEMPORARY HISTORY OF EUROPE,

ILLUSTRATED IN

A SERIES OF ORIGINAL LETTERS

NEVER BEFORE PRINTED.

WITH HISTORICAL INTRODUCTIONS AND BIOGRAPHICAL
AND CRITICAL NOTES

BY PATRICK FRASER TYTLER, ESQ.
AUTHOR OF "THE HISTORY OF SCOTLAND," ETC.

IN TWO VOLUMES.

VOL. I.

LONDON:
RICHARD BENTLEY, NEW BURLINGTON STREET;
Publisher in Ordinary to Her Majesty.
1839.

PREFACE.

THE following letters, with very few exceptions, have been selected from Her Majesty's invaluable collections of manuscript original letters preserved in the State Paper Office.* In this great depository of historical truth, it is perhaps known to some of his readers that the Author, with the permission of the Government, has been for many years engaged in the collection of materials for his History of Scotland ; a work which has occupied more than fourteen years of his life, and which he hopes, at no distant period, to bring to its conclusion. These labours necessarily led to the perusal and transcription of a large portion of the English and foreign manuscript correspondence in that national collection, and it was impossible not to be struck with the new and valuable light which was thrown by its stores upon English and Continental history. So important, indeed, are these stores, and yet so little are they known or appreciated, that the Au-

* The Author has to acknowledge the polite permission of the Right Hon. Lord John Russell, Secretary of State for the Home Department, to transcribe and publish these letters.

thor believes he does not overstate the fact when
he asserts that no perfect History of England, either
civil, ecclesiastical, or constitutional, can be written
till this collection is made accessible by catalogues
to men of letters. But leaving this subject, upon
which he will never cease to hope that something
may at last be effected by the country, it occurred
to him that an experiment might be made by print-
ing a selection of such letters as illustrated a small
portion of European history, and making an attempt
to present them to the public in a more popular
form than has yet been done.

Such is, shortly, the history of this Work. It remains only to say a few words regarding the plan upon
which it has been written, so far as it varies from
that adopted by the Author's respected predecessors
in the same field. Hitherto all the "Collections
of Original Letters" with which he is acquainted,
valuable as they have undoubtedly been to the historian and the antiquary, have possessed few attrac-
tions for the general reader; and the reason seems
obvious. They presuppose in any one who takes up
the book a full acquaintance with the history of the
period which they illustrate, a familiarity with an
ancient and repulsive orthography, and an intimate
knowledge of the lives and characters of the personages by whom and to whom they are written.

Is it too much to say that these qualifications are
rarely possessed,—that even the best-informed reader
will often find himself at fault? With a view to ob-

viate such objections, the present Work has been divided into periods, each of them prefaced by short historical Introductions; slight biographical sketches are given of those illustrious statesmen and scholars who pass in review before us; and occasional critical discussions are introduced where the letters were calculated to throw new light on obscure or disputed passages of English history, or supplied unknown or important facts in the lives of eminent men. Lastly, it has been judged right to render these letters intelligible to general as well as antiquarian readers, by abandoning the ancient mode of spelling.

Upon this point, of retaining or dismissing the antique dress of historical documents, much has been written; and there are scholars, for whose opinion the Author has sincere respect, who will think such an innovation almost equivalent to a literary felony. But, without entering into detail, he must say that after serious consideration, and long familiarity with ancient letters in every variety of orthography, he has not been able to discover in what possible way their historical value is injured by the change.

Devonshire Place,
February 26, 1839.

CONTENTS

ORIGINAL LETTERS,

ILLUSTRATIVE OF ENGLISH AND CONTINENTAL HISTORY.

INTRODUCTION TO PERIOD FIRST.

1546-7—1549.

CONTEMPORARY PRINCES.

England.	France.	Germany.	Spain.	Scotland.	Pope.
Edward VI.	Francis I.	Charles V.	Charles V.	Mary.	Clement VII.
	Henry II.				Paul III.

As it is my wish to render these letters instructive to the general reader as well as useful to the historian and the antiquary, it will be necessary to give a brief sketch of the state of England and the Continent at the period when they commence. This seems expedient, because they detail events, and contain political reflections, which are not only of English but of European interest; by which expression I mean simply to state that this Work involves illustrations of the history of France, Italy, and Germany, as well as of England. Indeed, it is evident that such of these letters as have been

B

selected from the correspondence of English ambassadors at foreign courts, must contain more of foreign
than of domestic history; but then it is such a portion of foreign history as throws light upon the relations of England with the great Continental powers
at an important period of their and her annals.

The letters relative to England, commence with
the death of Henry the Eighth, and the accession of
Edward the Sixth, under the protectorate of his
uncle, Edward Seymour, Earl of Hertford, shortly
afterwards created Duke of Somerset; and the portion of history which is illustrated in the First Period, is the interval between the death of Henry,
Jan. 27th, 1546-7, and the deposition of the Protector Somerset, Oct. 12th, 1549.

The great events under the ministry of Somerset
stand so prominently forward, that we easily recognise them; we meet first with the war in Scotland, undertaken for the purpose of compelling
that nation to give their infant queen in marriage
to Edward, and next with the full establishment of
the Reformation, through the active agency of
Cranmer. Looking to our foreign policy, the
Council is seen occupied with negociations for
the confirmation of our pacific relations with
France and the Emperor Charles the Fifth: and
these are soon succeeded at home by the jealousies arising against the government of the Protector; the conspiracy of his brother, the Lord
Admiral, whose object it was to wrest the supreme

power out of his hands; the great rebellions in Norfolk and Devonshire; and, lastly, by that extraordinary revolution which took place in the Council of State, when a majority, led by the Earl of Warwick, deposed Somerset, and compelled him to purchase his life with the complete sacrifice of his power.

If from England the eye is turned to the Continent, we find that France had just seen expire its favourite sovereign, Francis the First, 31st March 1547; whilst his son, Henry the Second, at the age of twenty-nine, succeeded to his hereditary throne. At the same period, Charles the Fifth, by far the ablest and most powerful monarch in Europe, had consolidated his empire, and, uniting the power of the old to the resources of the new world, threatened to become an absolute dictator in Europe. In Germany, Ferdinand, King of the Romans, brother to Charles the Fifth, had been repeatedly compelled to defend his dominions against the invasions of the Turks, who, under Solyman, one of their greatest princes, were become highly formidable; and in the Netherlands the regency was in the hands of Mary, Queen Dowager of Hungary, sister to Charles the Fifth, who had been placed by that monarch in this high office. Italy, as is well known, was at this period separated into a variety of independent states, amongst whom a leading part was acted by the Genoese, who, under the famous Andrew Doria, had risen into great power; whilst the papal throne was occupied by Paul the Third, (Alexander Farnese,) who, during the latter years of his life, which terminated in 1549, had been so devoted to France, that Charles the Fifth used to say, if his body were opened, they would find three fleurs de lis upon his heart. Last of all, in Scotland, which, although a small and remote power, exercised a considerable influence at this moment, the regency, during the minority of Mary, Queen of Scots, had been entrusted to the Earl of Arran, the nearest heir to the throne. His power, however, was scarcely equal to that possessed by Mary of Guise, the Queen-mother, widow of James the Fifth, and sister to the Cardinal Lorraine and the Duke of Guise.

Such were the principal sovereigns of Europe at this period; and, in extent of dominion, none, it is evident, could compete with the Emperor. The rise of this extraordinary power in the house of Austria was unlike the common career of greatness; it had been peaceable and bloodless; it was achieved by a series of fortunate marriages, the well-known epigram being no less pointed than true:

> Bella gerant alii; tu, felix Austria, nube.
> Nam quæ Mars aliis, dat tibi regna Venus.

It was marriage which brought to Austria the Low Countries; Maximilian, son of Frederic the Second, having espoused Mary of Burgundy, heiress of the last Duke of Burgundy. Again, it was the marriage of Philip the Handsome, son of this Maximilian, to Joanna, Infanta of Spain, which brought to her son, Charles the Fifth, the immense Spanish succession,—Spain, Naples, Sicily, Sardinia, and Spanish America (1516). To these were added, on the death of Maximilian, Charles's grandfather, the extensive dominions in Germany belonging to that monarch; and, to consolidate this vast power, it only remained that its possessor should be elected to the empire,—an event which took place in 1519.

Yet, even then, the star of the house of Austria was still in its ascendant. In 1521, Ferdinand, Charles's brother, espoused Anne, sister to Lewis, King of Hungary and Bohemia. Lewis being slain in the battle of Mohatz (1536), these twin kingdoms fell to Ferdinand in right of his wife; and it is worthy of notice, that in this same year Charles resigned to Ferdinand his hereditary dominions in Germany. The two brothers became thus the founders of the two great branches of the house of Austria; that of Spain having its origin in Charles the Fifth, and that of Germany in Ferdinand. Last of all, Charles himself having married the Infanta, daughter of Emanuel, King of Portugal, acquired by this alliance (not indeed in his own person, but in that of his son, Philip the Second,) the entire kingdom of Portugal. This last accession, however, did not occur till long after the period when these letters terminate—in 1580.

Can we wonder that so immense an empire, centering in one family, and casting into shade every other power, should have alarmed the princes of Europe ; that they should have become impressed with the idea that Austria aimed at universal dominion ; and that a determination to resist its power, and prevent its further growth, should have become, in their minds, one of the great principles of action ?

This jealousy, which had been deeply felt by Francis the First, and which, indeed, mainly guided the course of his policy, was awakened in his son, Henry the Second, about the time when these letters open.

But, besides the struggle between the European princes and the ambition of the house of Austria, there was another and still greater moral conflict in progress at this moment, which was felt with more or less violence in every kingdom of Europe ; I mean the contest between the principles of the Reformation and the ancient faith of the Romish church. In Germany, the doctrines of Luther had been adopted by a large portion of the princes and free towns in the empire ; and, in 1530, they had not only presented to the Emperor the noted confession of their faith, known by the name of the Confession of Augsbourg, but had bound themselves to each other in a covenant of mutual belief and mutual defence,—the famous league of Smalcald. Into the history of this league, and of the progress and fortunes of the Protestant confederacy from 1530 to 1546, it does not belong to this work to enter. From the first origin of the union, it was regarded by the Emperor with the most jealous eye; but his wars with the Turks, his expedition against the Barbary pirates, and his great struggle with Francis the First, prevented him from bringing against it that strength which he well knew was necessary for its destruction.

Having at length, however, concluded a peace with France in 1544, and secured himself, as he imagined, against the hostilities of the Ottomans, Charles began gradually to develope those formidable projects for the subjugation of the Protestant princes, the extirpation of their alleged heresy, and the consolidation of one great spiritual and temporal dominion, which there is reason to believe he had been long secretly maturing.

Already he had artfully prepared the way by sowing dissension and jealousies between the Romish and the Protestant princes of the empire; he had hailed with pleasure their growing hatred; and when, in 1546, he avowed his resolution to direct his arms against the chiefs who had united at Smalcald, and to compel them to the reception of the ancient faith, the German princes who were attached to Rome, eagerly embraced his cause, and blindly enrolled themselves in a service which soon proved to them an iron yoke. Nay, Charles artfully and successfully worked upon the selfishness of the Protestants themselves. Maurice, head of the Albertine branch of the house of Saxony, and one of the most remarkable men of his time, had long looked with envious eyes on the possessions of his cousin, John Frederic, the Elector of Saxony; and he lent his powerful aid to the Emperor, trusting that, if he were victorious, the estates of the fallen Elector would be bestowed upon him as the price of his assistance. On the other hand, Charles was joined by Albert, Margrave of Brandenburgh, a fierce and turbulent spirit, who only breathed freely amid the smoke of war, and who, although professedly a Protestant, had no objection to the plunder of his brethren.

The general Council, which, contrary to the remonstrances of the opponents of the Romish church, had been summoned for the termination of the contests in religion, having assembled at Trent, in Dec. 1545, Charles, in a diet held at Ratisbon, in June 1546, commanded the Protestants to submit to its decrees. They replied by reproaches, exposed the partiality of this spiritual tribunal, and demanded the cause of his great military preparations. His answer left no doubt upon their minds that the armament would be directed against themselves; and, making a precipitate retreat from Ratisbon, they flew to arms. The Duke of Wirtemberg seized the passes of the Tyrol; whilst John Frederic, and the Landgrave of Hesse, at the head of an army of ninety thousand men, advanced upon

Ratisbon. It was a critical moment for the Emperor, who, forsaken by his usual caution, seems to have precipitated matters when he was little able to make head against his enemies. His utmost force was nine thousand men; but with this retreating behind Ratisbon, and soon after falling back upon Ingoldstadt, he fulminated against the Elector and the Landgrave of Hesse the ban of the empire; they met it by a declaration of war, and advanced against his entrenchments. At this crisis, had the Elector followed the advice of the Landgrave, and stormed the imperial camp, Charles must have been undone. But treachery had divided the Protestants; many of their officers had sold themselves to the enemy; they opposed the proposal for an attack: the critical moment passed; before it could be recovered, reinforcements had arrived from Italy and the Low Countries, and the Emperor was saved. 1546.

It was now his turn to assume the offensive; and whilst Maurice, by an attack on Saxony, had compelled John Frederic to separate the Protestant army and defend his own dominions, Charles, in a successful campaign against the Duke of Wirtemberg and the imperial towns of the higher Germany, forced them to renounce the league of Smalcald, submit to his authority, and pay a heavy fine. It remained only to turn his arms against John Frederic, the Elector of Saxony, who by this time had defeated Duke Maurice. This victorious chief found himself attacked by two armies at once; by the Emperor on the side of Bohemia, and by Albert of Brandenbourg on his Franconian frontier. Over Albert he gained a complete victory in the battle of Rochlitz, March 2nd, 1547; and, had not treachery again entered his army, he might have been equally successful against his imperial enemy; but betrayed by his officers, who intercepted all intelligence, he divided his force, and, at the head of a corps of eight thousand men, was surprised, defeated, and taken prisoner by Charles, in the famous battle of Mulhberg, 17th of April, 1547. Soon after, Wittemberg opened its gates to the conqueror; and this unfortunate prince, who, as leader of the league of Smalcald, had tamed the pride and lowered the flight of the imperial eagle, was glad to purchase his life by the sacrifice of his honours, his patrimonial dominions, and all but his religion, to the will of the Emperor. On this last point he was firm, and steadily refused submission to the decrees of the Council of Trent.

Nothing now remained for Charles but to deal with the Landgrave of Hesse, upon whose part all resistance would have been vain; and he, having capitulated on the condition of enjoying his liberty, was, by a disgraceful fraud of Granvelle, prime minister to the Emperor, shut up in prison; a proceeding which, although originating with the minister, reflected great discredit upon his master the Emperor. June 1547.

Having thus completely destroyed the league of Smalcald, Charles entered Augsbourg in triumph, assembled a diet, invested Maurice with the electorate and duchy of Saxony, and proceeded to the settlement of all religious differences; and here his dictation was as despotic as at the head of his armies. A temporary formulary of the faith was drawn up, which was named the INTERIM. It was declared to be binding on all parties, both Romanist and Protestant, till a general council should have fixed the articles of religion upon an immovable foundation. In all essential points, it was agreeable to the doctrines of the Romish church; yet such was the power of the Emperor, that the majority of the Protestant princes were compelled to accept it. Some chiefs and towns, however, still resolutely refused submission; and, amongst these exceptions, the most noted was the magnanimous John Frederic, the captive Elector of Saxony, and the cities of Constance and Magdebourg. These last were immediately put under the ban of the empire, and war declared against them. 1547.

In this same year, the Emperor carried an important measure into execution. The seventeen provinces of the Low Countries were united to the Germanic body, and placed under the protection of the empire; not only without consulting the Princes and the Estates, who were most concerned in the change, but contrary to their wishes and to the feelings of the people. Nor was this all—for, in 1549, having triumphed over all his enemies, he returned to Brussels, carrying along with him the chiefs whom he had made captive. Having then sent for his son Philip, the Prince of Spain, he, with great solemnity, installed him as Sovereign of the United Provinces.

Whilst such were the triumphs of Charles the Fifth in Germany, he had succeeded, by a plot which reflects little honour upon him, in obtaining possession of Parma and Placenzia in Italy. These principalities had been conferred by Paul the Third upon his natural son, Peter Louis Farnese, who had transmitted them to his son Octavio. This prince, whose profligate and tyrannical conduct had made him an object of hatred to his subjects, was murdered by a party of his nobles; and, at the moment when his body was cast into the street and torn in pieces by the populace, six hundred Spanish soldiers appeared at the gates of Placenzia, and took possession of it in the name of the Emperor, whilst another detachment made themselves masters of Parma. 1547. It was openly asserted that Charles had encouraged the conspiracy. In proof of this, an appeal was made to the appearance of his troops at the very conjuncture when they were needed ; and Paul the Third, indignant and eager for revenge, entered into a negociation with Henry the Second of France, and declared his determination to recall the French into Italy. The Pope, at the same time, determined to transfer the General Council, which for three years had held its sittings at Trent, to Bologna, where he trusted it would be less under the power of the Emperor; and he entered into negociations with the Dukes of Urbino, Ferrara, and Mirandola, to induce them to unite against the murderer of his grandson.

These projects, however, were as yet pursued in secret, although the French monarch eagerly embraced them. Henry's preparations were not yet ripe for war with the Emperor, his great anxiety being to recover Boulogne from the English. This he was on the eve of accomplishing, when that conspiracy broke out against the Protector Somerset, which ended in his disgrace, and with which the first portion of these letters concludes.

These remarks will, it is hoped, prepare the reader to enter into the spirit and meaning of such letters as occur from January 1546-7 to October 1549. With regard to the religious history of this period, in England, I have purposely abstained from adding many inedited letters to the mass of printed materials which has been accumulated by the labours of Strype, Fuller, Fox, Burnet, and other writers.

PERIOD THE FIRST.

1546—1549.

HENRY THE EIGHTH died at Westminster, on Friday the 28th of January 1546-7, at two o'clock in the morning.* Parliament was then sitting, but the King's death was kept secret for nearly three days. On Monday, the 31st of January, the Commons were sent for to the House of Lords; and the Lord Chancellor Wriothesley acquainted them with the melancholy event, scarcely able to speak from tears.

He then requested Sir William Paget, Secretary of State, to read to the Parliament such parts of the late King's will as related to the succession, and the system by which the realm was to be governed during the minority of his son; and on the same day Edward the Sixth was proclaimed and conducted to the Tower of London. The Parliament was then declared to be dissolved by the death of the sovereign; and the members were licensed to depart, except the peers, whose

* Earl of Sussex to his Countess. Printed by Strype. Ecclesiastical Memorials, vol. ii. part 1, p. 19, and at greater length, by Ellis, vol. i. First Series, p. 137.

duty it was to be present at the coronation.*
The two following letters, the first from the Earl
of Hertford, shortly afterwards created Duke of
Somerset, to Sir William Paget, the second from
the same nobleman to the Council, are valuable,
because they contain some account of what took
place in the obscure interval between the King's
death and the public notification of that event by
the Chancellor,— a portion of secret history not to
be found elsewhere.   Even the MS. Council-books
of Edward the Sixth do not commence till the 31st
Jan., being the Monday after the King's death.
It will be observed, that the first letter is written
between three and four in the morning of the 29th
January, little more than twenty-four hours after
Henry expired.

THE EARL OF HERTFORD TO SIR WM. PAGET.

Orig. St. P. Off.   *Domestic.*   29 *Jan.* 1546-7.

" This morning, between one and two, I received
your letter.   The first part thereof I like very
well ; marry, that the Will should be opened till a
farther consultation, and that it might be well considered how much thereof were necessary to be
published ; for divers respects I think it not convenient to satisfy the world.   In the meantime I
think it sufficient, when ye publish the King's
death, in the places and times as ye have appointed, to have the Will presently with you, and to show

* Carte, vol. iii, p. 197.

that this is the Will, naming unto them severally
who be executors that the King did specially trust,
and who be councillors; the contents at the breaking up thereof, as before, shall be declared unto
them on Wednesday in the morning at the Parliament house; and in the mean time we to meet
and agree therein, as there may be no controversy
hereafter. For the rest of your appointments, for
the keeping of the Tower, and the King's person,
it shall be well done ye be not too hasty therein;
and so I bid you heartily farewell. From Hart-
ford, the 29th of Jan. between three and four in the
morning.   Your assured loving friend,

"E. HERTFORD."

"I have sent you the key of the will."

Endorsed. " *To my Right loving Friend, Sir William Paget,
One of the King's Majesties Two Principal Secretaries.
Haste, Post haste, Haste with all diligence, For thy life, For
thy life.*"

Edward the Sixth, at the moment of his father's
death, was at Hertford, not Hatfield, as has
been erroneously stated.* Immediately after the
event, his uncle the Earl of Hertford, and Sir
Anthony Brown, hastened to this place, from
whence they conveyed the young King privately
to Enfield, and there they first declared to him
and the Lady Elizabeth the death of Henry their
father. Both of them heard the intelligence with

---

* Sir J. Mackintosh. Hist. of England, vol. ii. p. 248, misled by Holinshed.

tears. " Never," says Hayward, " was sorrow more sweetly set forth, their faces seeming rather to beautify their sorrow, than their sorrow to cloud the beauty of their faces."* The following letter is written by the Earl of Hertford from Enfield.

THE EARL OF HERTFORD TO THE COUNCIL.

Orig. St. P. Off. *Domestic.* January 30th, 1546-7.

" Your lordships shall understand that I the Earl of Hertford have received your letter concerning a pardon to be granted in such form as in the schedule ye have sent, and that ye desire to know our opinions therein.

" For answer thereunto, ye shall understand we be in some doubt whether our power be sufficient to answer unto the King's Majesty that now is, when it shall please him to call us to account for the same.   And in case we have authority so to do it, in our opinions the time will serve much better at the Coronation† than at this present.   For if it should be now granted, his Highness can show no such gratuity unto his subjects when the time is most proper for the same ; and his father, who we doubt not to be in heaven, having no need thereof, shall take the praise and thank from him that hath more need thereof than he.

* Life of Edward VI. in Kennet, vol. ii. p. 271.

† The course here suggested was followed.—Hayward in Kennet, vol. ii. p. 272.   A general pardon was granted at the young King's coronation.

" We do very well like your device for the matter; marry, we would wish it to be done when the time serveth most proper for the same.

" We intend the King's Majesty shall be a-horseback to-morrow by XI of the clock, so that by III we trust his Grace shall be at the Tower. So, if ye have not already advertised my Lady Anne of Cleves of the King's death, it shall be well done ye send some express person for the same.

" And so, with our right hearty commendations, we bid you farewell.

" From Enwild (Enfield) this Sunday night, at a XI of the clock.

    " Your good lordships' assured loving friends,
            " E. HERTFORD.
            " ANTHONY BROWNE."

Short as are these two letters, they furnish us with some important facts, which are new to English history, and throw light on what may be justly called the salient points in the policy of Hertford and his party,—their proceedings in the interval between the King's death and its being communicated to Parliament. It has been observed by Sir James Mackintosh,* that, in our own time, the delay of three days before taking any formal steps relating to the demise of the sovereign, would be censured as a daring presumption; but neither this writer, nor any of our historians

---

* History of England, vol. ii. p. 247.

who had before, or who have since treated of this reign, were aware how far more daring was the conduct of Hertford and his associates than the mere concealment of Henry's death. Their leader had the Will in his private keeping. This is proved by the emphatic postscript, " I have sent you the key of the Will." And the fact increases the suspicion which hangs over this extraordinary document. They opened it before the King or the Parliament were made acquainted with the late King's death; they held a consultation what portions of this deed were proper to be communicated to the great Council of the nation. Hertford himself deemed some parts of it not expedient to be divulged; and when Parliament and the nation yet believed Henry to be alive, the measures which were to be adopted under the new reign were already secretly agreed on by a faction to whom no resistance could be made. It is worthy of remark also, that Hertford, although still bearing no higher rank than one of the Executors of the late King, is consulted by them as their Superior, and already assumes the tone and authority of Protector, another proof that all had been privately arranged amongst them.

The next letter introduces to us the celebrated Gardiner, Bishop of Winchester, in a collision which took place, a week after Henry's death, between this prelate and my Lord of Oxford's players.

I suspect this is one of the earliest notices of a company of players kept by any nobleman or private person. At least in Mr. Collier's work * I find none earlier. There can be little doubt that, although Wriothesley, the Chancellor, had wept in parliament in breaking to the house the King's death, his feelings were not shared by the people, who were unnatural enough to rejoice on once more feeling their heads secure upon their shoulders. My Lord of Oxford's players, therefore, had advertised an entertainment in the Borough of Southwark, at the very time, it seems, that Gardiner and his parishioners resolved to have a dirige, or dirge, for his departed master. The sons of the buskin, indeed, denominated their intended piece a " *solemn* play,"—an expression, however, which is not to be understood as indicating a religious or grave pageant, suitable to the occasion, but simply a play to be got up with peculiar splendour, or, as we would say, now-a-days, with the whole *corps dramatique*. Gardiner, hereupon, in high dudgeon, applied to Master Acton, a justice of the peace. His worship was a model of cautious justice; he doubted whether he could stop the *play*, but he was sure he could stop the *people* coming to see it, when the King's body was still above ground. Under these circumstances, Gardiner addressed Sir William Paget, the Secretary of State, as he himself says, half between " game and earnest."

* Annals of the Stage, vol. i. p. 139-40. This was probably the same Earl of Oxford who is commemorated by Puttenham, in his Art of English Poetry.

GARDINER, BISHOP OF WINCHESTER, TO SIR
W. PAGET, SECRETARY OF STATE.

Orig. St. P. Off. *Domestic.* 5th Feb. 1546-7.

" MASTER SECRETARY.—After my right hearty
commendations. I sent unto you my servant yesterday, wherein as you advise I have had redress;
and now I write unto you in another matter somewhat greater, as it were between game and earnest.

" To-morrow, the parishioners of this parish and
I have agreed to have a solemn dirige for our late
sovereign lord and master, in earnest, as becometh us; and to-morrow, certain players of my
Lord of Oxford's, as they say, intend on the other
side, within this burgh of Southwark, to have a solemn play, to try who shall have most resort, they
in game or I in earnest; which me seemeth a marvellous contention, wherein some shall profess in the
name of the commonwealth, mirth, and some sorrow, at one time.

" Herein I follow the common determination to
sorrow till our late master be buried; and what the
lewd fellows should mean in the contrary I cannot tell, nor cannot reform it, and therefore write
unto [you who,] by means of my Lord Protector,
may procure an uniformity in the commonwealth;
all the body to do one thing,—in the enterring of
our old master to lament together, and in the
crowning of our new master to rejoice together;

after which followeth constantly a time of lamentation for sin, which is not to be neglected, and which I doubt not ye will, without me, consider your charge.

" I have herein spoken with Master Acton, justice of peace, whom the players smally regard, and press him to a peremptory answer, whether he dare lett them play or not; whereunto he answereth neither yea nor nay as to the playing; but as to the assembly of people in this burgh, in this time, neither the burial finished, ne the coronation done, he pleadeth to the players for the time nay, till he have commandment to the contrary. But his nay is not much regarded, and mine less, as party to players; and therefore I write unto you, wherein if ye will not, propter invidiam, meddle, send me so word, and I will myself sue to my Lord Protector.

" At my house in Southwark, the 5th Feb.

*   *   *   *   *

" Your assured loving friend,

" St. Winton."

On the accession of Edward the Sixth the Popish party were led by the Lord Chancellor Wriothesley, Earl of Southampton, and this same Stephen Gardiner Bishop of Winchester.

The fierce temper of the prelate may be understood from one of the expressions used by him in Mary's time, regarding the English exiles for religion. " I will watch their supplies," said he, " so that they shall eat their nails, and then feed on their finger-ends." Lloyd, Worthies, p. 455. " But threatened folks," adds this author, " live long ; and before the confessors were brought to that bill of fare, the bishop was eaten of worms himself." Gardiner's mind and capacity were those of no ordinary man; but his character as a Christian bishop, notwithstanding the learned and laboured eloge in the Biographia Britannica, is too deeply stained to be white-washed by the most determined efforts. That he was bold, crafty, indefatigable, and more consistent in his errors than some of his Protestant brethren were in support of truth, must be allowed.

From the following letter of Sir Wm. Paget, the Secretary of State, to the Bishop of Winchester, the prelate appears to have written to Paget under feelings of great excitement, accusing him of intruding into matters which did not belong to his place. As to the Commission alluded to in the letter, it must be recollected that Henry the Eighth, in 1539, required the bishops to receive commissions acknowledging that all jurisdictions, both ecclesiastical and civil, flowed from the King, and that they held their bishopricks only during his pleasure. Burnet, Hist. Refor. vol. i. p. 267. These commissions, on the death of Henry, the bishops were commanded to renew, or sue out again, and it is of this that Paget speaks. Burnet, vol. ii, p. 6.

SIR W. PAGET TO THE BISHOP OF WINCHESTER.

Orig. St. P. Off. *Domestic.* 2d March 1546-7.

" My Lord,

" After my right hearty commendations. I thank you for your good advices in your letter, and trust you will think, whatsoever some bodies shall (for that they want some piece of their own willfulness) unjustly and slanderously either conceive or report of me, that I neither mean nor do nipp or snatch any person, nor that unwisely I would usurp a greater power upon me than I have indeed (which is not great),—when that I could tempre* myself from using of all that which I might have used, when time served me, with the favor and consent of him from whom all our powers were derived, provoked by him often times to use it, (as he testified to divers,) and having his promise to be maintained in the same.

" In his days that dead is, (God have his soul!) I never did that I might have done. I never loved extremes, I never hindered any man to him but notable malefactors, and yet not to the extremity. I have born much with divers men, and caused divers men to be born withall; and by the judgment of mine own conscience have deserved benevolentiam of all. If any man will bear to me malevolentiam without cause, God judge between

* Restrain.

him and me. For private respects, I will not do any
thing wherein the public cause may be hindered.
And in public causes I will say and do, as I have
done always since I have been in the place, according to my conscience, without lending the same
either to life, honor, wife, children, lands, or goods; *
and yet not with such a frowardness or willfulness
but that a good man or a better conscience may
lead and rule me.

" I malign not Bishops, but would that both they
and all other were in such order as might be most
to the glory of God and the benefit of this realm ;
and much less I malign your lordship, but wish ye
well ; and if the estate of bishops is or shall be
thought meet to be reformed, I wish either that you
were no bishop, or that you could have such a
pliable will as could well bear the reformation that
should be thought meet for the quiet of the realm.

" Your lordship shall have your Commission in as
ample manner as I have authority to make out the
same, and in an ampler manner than you had it before ; which I think you may execute now with less
fear of danger than you have had cause hitherto to
do. No man wisheth you better than I do, which
is as well as to myself ; if you wish me not like,
you are in the wrong ; and thus I take my leave

* Good set words these of Master Secretary Paget's, and
yet in 1552, he was deprived of his office and fined 2000l. for
peculation. Hayward, Life of Edward Sixth. Kennet, vol.
ii. p. 319.

of your lordship. From Westminster this 2d of March 1546.

    " Your lordship's assured to command,

                          " W. PAGET."

IN the following letter we meet with JOHN DUDLEY, Earl of Warwick, created afterwards Duke of Northumberland, and one of the most extraordinary men of his times. He was the son of the well-known Edmund Dudley, who was brought to the scaffold in the beginning of the reign of Henry the Eighth for having too faithfully lent himself an instrument to royal extortion. His mother was a daughter of Edward, Lord Lisle. At his father's death John was only eight years old ; but the reversal of his father's attainder in 1511 restored him to an ample estate, and his education under the care of Edmund Guilford, one of the finest gentlemen in the court of Henry the Eighth, transformed him into so accomplished a youth, that he became the favourite of the King's favourite, Charles Brandon, Duke of Suffolk. He had now entered the high road to fortune; and began to exhibit those talents, and to be propelled by that ambition, which carried him to so giddy a pinnacle of greatness. Patronised by Wolsey, he had the good fortune not only to escape the consequences of his fall, but to ingratiate himself with Cromwell at the time that this minister succeeded to so much of the cardinal's power ; and when Cromwell, in his turn, was disgraced and executed, Dudley's bark, so far from being wrecked by the fate of his consort, caught the gales of the royal favour, and sprang forward on her way more gallantly than before.

The death of Henry found him one of the most powerful men in the country. He had been created Viscount Lisle, he held the office of Lord High Admiral, he was Knight of the Garter, and had distinguished himself so highly in the wars of Scotland and of France, that he was esteemed one of the ablest military commanders in the nation; and by the royal will he was nominated one of the sixteen executors to whom the government was entrusted. On the accession of Edward the Sixth, the Viscount Lisle appears to have taken a leading part with the faction which raised Somerset to the office of Protector; but he did not work for small wages, as the following letter, and many others preserved in the royal collections and written about the same time, very fully demonstrate. He was created Earl of Warwick, and shared largely in the spoils and grants of property with which the Council thought it proper to enrich themselves during the minority of the sovereign. At this moment, I find that his applications to the Protector, and to the Secretary of State, through whom much of the patronage of this kingly office seems to have flowed, were frequent incessant and importunate. We may now give his letter.

EARL OF WARWICK TO PAGET.

Orig. St. P. Off. *Domestic.* March 1546-7.

" Master Secretary.   Perchance some folks will allege considerations concerning the not assignment of the lordship of Warwick, saying it is a stately castle, and a goodly park, and a great royalty. To that it may be answered—the castle of itself is not able to lodge a good baron with his train ; for all the one side of the said castle, with also the dongeon tower, is clearly ruinated and down to the ground ; and that of late the King's Majesty that dead is, hath sold all the chief and principal manors that belonged unto the said earldom and castle ; so that at this present there is no lands belonging unto it, but the rents of certain houses in the town, and certain meadows with the park of Wegenock.   Of the which castle with the park, and also of the town, I am Constable, high Steward, and Master of the game, with also th'herbage of the park during my life ; and because of the name, I am the more desirous to have the thing ; and also I come of one of the daughters and heirs of the right and not defiled line.

" I will rebate part of my fees in my portion, to have the same castle, meadows, and park ; wherein I pray you to show me your friendship, to move the rest of my lords to this effect : and further to be friendly to Mr. Denny, according to his desire for the site and remains of Waltham, with certain other farms adjoining unto Jeston; wherein, as for the site of Waltham, I suppose it shall grow to a commonwealth to the country thereabouts to let him have it.

"And in case that they will not condescend to me for the lordship of Warwick, as is aforesaid, I pray you then let me have Tunbridge and Penshurst, that was the Buckingham's lands in Kent, as parcel of my portion, with also Hawlden, that was my own; and, whether I have the one or the other, let Canonbury be our portion.

"The Master of the Horse would gladly, as I do perceive by him, have the lordship in Sussex that was the Lord Laware's; which in my opinion were better bestowed upon him, or some such as would keep it up, and serve the King in the country in maintaining of household, than to let it fall to ruin as it doth, with divers other like houses; being a great pity, and loss it will be at length to the King and realme.

"Your own assuredly,

"J. WARWICK."

The first of our foreign letters opens with an intimation of the death of FRANCIS THE FIRST, transmitted to the English council by Dr. Nicholas Wotton, ambassador for England at the court of France. This monarch expired at his castle of Rambouillet, on the 31st of March 1547; his great contemporary and friend, Henry the Eighth, having died only two months before. So deeply was Francis attached to his brother of England, that he caused a funeral service to be performed for him in the church of Nôtre Dame, although Henry was separated from the communion of the Romish church. Yet this need not surprise us, when we find that, in England, the obsequies of the same bitter enemy of Rome were conducted according to the rites of the church of Rome. " The body lay in state in the chapel of Whitehall for twelve days, with masses and dirge sung and said every day, Norroy standing at the choir door, and beginning with these words, pronounced aloud, ' Of your charity, pray for the soul of the High and Mighty Prince our late Sovereign Lord, King Henry the Eighth.'" *

Francis had formed a superstitious notion that himself and Henry would die in the same year; and he received the account of his last moments as if it were a bell ringing his own knell. He made an effort to shake off the oppressive feeling by indulging in his favourite recreation of the chase, and travelling from one country-seat to another (De Thou, book 3d, sub anno 1547); but it proved fruitless, and he sank under a slow fever.

Dr. Nicholas Wotton, the writer of this and of many of the most interesting of the following

* Hayward, Life of Edward the Sixth. Kennet, vol. ii. p. 272.

letters, was at the present period resident Ambassador at the court of France. As a diplomatist, he lived much in the public eye, having been no less than thirteen times employed either as ambassador or envoy for the crown of England to foreign courts. His father, Sir Robert Wotton, was Deputy Lieutenant of Guisnes; his mother, Anne Belknapp, daughter of Sir Henry Belknapp. Having been educated for the church, we find him early patronised by Tonstall, Bishop of Durham, one of the most amiable and learned prelates of his age, to whom Wotton became official in 1528.[*] In 1530 he was appointed, by Warham, prebendary of York.[†] In 1536 he appeared as proctor for the unfortunate Anne Boleyn when she received her sentence: soon after, he assisted in the composition of the work published by command of Henry, " The Institution of a Christian Man," commonly called the Bishops' Book;[‡] and in 1538, he was nominated by Cranmer one of the commissioners of ecclesiastical dispensations.[§]

Hitherto the course of his life and of his promotion had been confined to his native country: but, in 1539, Wotton was appointed a Commissioner to negociate the marriage between Henry the Eighth

---

[*] MS. memoir of Dean Wotton, communicated to me by my friend, Mr. Holmes, of the British Museum.

[†] Lansdowne, 981. 42.

[‡] Strype's Cranmer, p. 113. 77.

[§] Lansdowne, 981. 42. Holmes, MS. Memoir.

and Anne of Cleves;* and this was his first step in a series of diplomatic missions which continued almost without interruption to the close of his life, and which we shall not fatigue the reader by enumerating.

In 1549, Wotton appears to have taken an active part in the proceedings against the Protector Somerset; from which we may presume that he was one of the faction led by the crafty and ambitious Warwick. He soon after, October 14th, 1549, became Secretary of state, in the room of Sir Thomas Smith, who was sent to the Tower with his master Somerset.†

It is no easy matter to say precisely, what were Wotton's political or religious principles; for, in an age abounding in cameleon statesmen, he caught and changed colour so dexterously, that he appears a very prince amongst them. He has been quaintly denominated by one author " the very measure of congruity;" by another, " a center of remarkables;"‡ and so far the description is correct, that he adapted himself to every government, and continued to flourish under every change. The Protector's disgrace only raised him higher under Warwick; Warwick's fall led directly to his promotion under Mary; and Mary's great favour to him appears to have proved no barrier to his being thrown into the

* Cotton MS. Vitell. B. xi. fol. 186.

† MS. Privy Council Books of Edward VI, and Ellis's Letters, vol. ii. p. 166. First Series.

‡ Lloyd, Worthies, p. 108.   Wanley's Wonders, B. v. c. 36.

most difficult and responsible employments by Elizabeth.

Of his talents as a statesman and a scholar, the reader will probably form a high opinion from the letters which are now published; but the character of that man must have been singularly accommodating, and his opinions upon the great religious subjects which then shook and divided men's minds capable of an almost indefinite adjustment to contending creeds, who could steer his vessel so dexterously in such dangerous and conflicting times. Lloyd, an author of the last century, whose work upon the statesmen and favourites of England is often inaccurate but always amusing, thus sums up his sketch of Dean Wotton: " This was that rare man that was made for all business— so dexterous! This was he that was made for all times—so complying! This was he who lived Doctor of both laws, and died Doctor of both Gospels."* I verily believe this was meant for panegyric; but it sounds wonderfully like satire.

We must now let the worthy Dean speak for himself.

MR. DOCTOR WOTTON TO THE COUNCIL.

Orig. St. P. Off. *France.* 1st April 1547. *Paris.*

" My duty to your lordships remembered. The French King departed to God yesterday, about

---

* Worthies of England, p. 110.

noon; the which thing, certain of the Council, not only with words, but much more with tears running down their cheeks apace, told a servant of mine whom I had sent to the court for certain knowledge of it. My said servant saw also the Lady Margaret the King's daughter, and Madame Destampes,* and all the rest of the dames, come forth of the castle of Rambuillers, where the King died, weeping and making great moan : and all the court departed straight thence. And the Dolphin, our new King, goeth, as I understand, to St. Germain-en-Laye.

" The last news that they had in this court from the Emperor's court, was also that the Emperor was very sore sick, and not without danger: the common voice goeth abroad, that the Constable shall be revoked again to the court. What changes may come of changes of princes and councillors, your lordships can better conceive than I. And thus Jesus preserve your lordships long in health and prosperity ! Written at Paris, the 1st day of April 1547.

" Your lordships' ever to command,

" N. Wotton."

" P.S.—Having written this letter, I thought to have sent it straight away the day of the date of it; and sending to the post, to have horses prepared,

---

* The Duchess D'Estampes, mistress to Francis the First. The Lady Margaret was afterwards married to Emanuel Philibert, Duke of Savoy.

he answered, that he was commanded to deliver horses to no man. Wherefore I have been fain to send to the court to get leave to send it."

THE second letter of Dean Wotton presents us with a picture of the state of parties and of political feeling at the court of France on the accession of Henry the Second. It is drawn by no unpractised hand ; and the historical enthusiast almost startles to find himself surrounded by those whose names have been familiar to some of his pleasantest reveries,—Henry the Second, the Constable Montmorency, Catherine de Medici, Diana of Poictiers, the lordly brothers of the house of Guise,—and many other persons almost equally illustrious.

DR. WOTTON TO THE LORD PROTECTOR AND COUNCIL.

Orig. ST. P. OFF. *France. April 6th,* 1547. *Paris.*

" MY duty to your lordships remembered. The French King, straight after his father's death, hath revoked the Constable to the court again ; who is now in as great triumph (as men say) as ever he was, if it be not more. He sent also for the third president of Paris, named the President Bertrand ; and, as I suppose, for the Cardinal Bellay, for he is at the court too. The Secretary Bayard meddleth now little or nothing : but he that was the King's secretary, he being Dolphin, named Marchmont, and another called De Nors, are the chief doers in

D 2

that office; and yet nevertheless is Bourhart among them.

"Of the younger sort of those that are at the court already, these seem to be the chief favourites: Andelot,* younger brother to Chastillon, and his brother the Cardinal of Chastillon;† the Duke of Guise's sons in a manner all, but specially these, Monsr. Daumale, the Bishop of Rheims, and the Bishop of Troyes, who, as I hear say, are all three of the council : and Monsr. D'Aumale is in very great favour, and, as some say, shall be Great Master; the which is one of the offices that the Constable had, and may spare it now, being Constable.   But in greatest estimation and favour of all, as it appeareth hitherto, either of them of the older sort or of the younger sort, seemeth to be

* *Francis Coligni, Seigneur D'Andelot,* the younger brother of the great Admiral Coligni, a zealous Calvinist, and intrepid soldier ; but grave, sombre, and silent.   He was the fourth son of Gaspard de Coligni, Maréchal de Chastillon, and Louise de Montmorency.

† *Cardinal Chastillon.*—This high-born ecclesiastic was in most things the reverse of his elder brother D'Andelot.   He was a complete courtier, soft, refined, insinuating ; yet, while he seemed born only to grace society, his eye and his emissaries penetrated into every corner of the state; and, in all political matters requiring delicacy and address, he was accounted a master.   Having been converted to Protestantism, he was deposed and excommunicated by Pius the Fourth, and soon after married.   His career after this was dishonourable and calamitous.   He deserted his sovereign, fought against him in the battle of St. Denis, and, afterwards escaping to England, was poisoned by one of his domestics.

the said Bishop of Rheims, who had the chief
ordering of the King's house, he being Dolphin;
whom I would wish to be of as good judgment in
matters of religion as I take the Cardinal de Bellay
to be; but I hear he is not so, but very earnest in
upholding the Romish blindness; and for the authority of these their brethren, it is to be thought
that the Scots shall lack neither help nor favour.
Of the Dames, Madame la Grande Seneschalle
seemeth to be highly esteemed.

" When the King departed from Rambuillet,
where the King his father died, he left there with
the dead body, the Cardinal Tournon,* and the
Admiral Monsr. de Boissy, who continue about the
corpse still. The Vidasme of Chartres hath been
with the King, and, having saluted him, is gone
home again.

" Of those that were the chief of the late King's
council, the Chancellor † only, as far as I can per-

---

* *Cardinal de Tournon.*—It was this dignitary who, when
Francis the First had almost consented to hear Melancthon
discourse on the errors of Romanism, persuaded him it would
be sinful to expose his faith to so great a trial.—Anquetil,
Hist. de France, vol. vi. p. 367; where *Perron* is erroneously
printed for *Tournon.*—He was the great confidant and chief
minister of Francis the First. He died at St. Germain-en-Laye,
in 1562. " A man," says De Thou, " who could meet with
few competitors in judgment, capacity for affairs, and love for
his country." (Book xxxiv. vol. ii. p. 324.)

† This was the celebrated *François Olivier*, one of the best
and ablest men of his time.—De Thou, (book xxiii. vol. i, p.
767.), pronounces high panegyric upon his integrity, talents,
prudence, and learning.

ceive, remaineth in authority. La Royne Blanche lieth at Poissy* beside St. Germain, and the Queen went thither to her to comfort her. I cannot perceive but that she shall be well regarded and honourably entertained.

" The voice goeth, that the King shall not be buried till that Francis the late Dolphin, who lieth beside Lyons, and, the Duke of Orleans, late deceased, be brought hither, and so shall they be buried all together ; and for because that shall require a time, the interment shall not be before Easter.†

" The late King died upon Thursday ; and, upon the next Saturday, the King played a wager at tennis at St. Germain's. A nephew of mine, Thomas Wotton, was there ; and a gentleman that talked with him said unto him, Now you will peradventure wonder to see the King play now so shortly after his father's death : and it is to be wondered at indeed, not knowing the cause why ; but, for because that the King watched three or four nights about his father before his death, the physicians have counselled him to take this exercise, lest he take some hurt of the said long watching and sitting still.

---

* *La Royne Blanche*—The Queen Dowager. Eleanor of Austria, sister of Charles the Fifth. " En France le blanc étoit reservé pour le deuil des veuves de Rois." Michelet Origines du Droit Francais. The Editor owes this explanation and reference to his friend, Mr. J. M. Kemble.

† When the funeral obsequies did take place, eleven cardinals assisted ; a sight which had never before been witnessed in France.

" I hear that, very shortly upon the King's death
they despatched a courier to their ambassador in
England. I cannot consider what that great haste
should mean, unless they would not have the Baron de la Gardie to proceed so far in the matters of
late committed unto him. The which matters (as
by the communication that he had with me appeared,) were for the common aid of the Protestants;
wherein he had large commission to proceed, and
to conclude, for the marriage of the King's Majesty with this King's young daughter, or child
rather; for the marriage of my Lady Mary's Grace
with the Duke of Vendosme; for the entering into
a further and straiter league with us, so that we
should not reserve the Emperor, nor they any other
for their part.* If he have not already made, or
make not, these overtures unto your lordships, then
cannot I think but that the said courier was sent
purposely to stay any further proceeding in it;
and, for because there hath been some variance be-

* On the 11th March 1547, two new treaties between England and France were signed; but, says Rapin, (vol. ii. p.
110,) before their ratification, Francis the First died, and
Henry the Second, who succeeded him, refused to ratify them.
Francis, in fact, died only twenty days after the treaties had
been concluded. And we learn from this despatch of Wotton,
that Henry had already prepared to follow, towards England,
a line of policy different from his father's. In the MS. Privy
Council Books of Edward the Sixth, under the date March
14th, 1547, it is stated that these treaties were delivered by
Sir John Godsalve, Knight, to be laid up and preserved in the
Treasury at Westminster.

tween the Baron de la Gardie and Petro Strozzi,*
I doubt whether from henceforth the said Baron
shall be so well regarded as he hath been, the said
Petro being in great favour with the King. As for
me, I am as unacquainted, and as far to seek in this
court now, by the means of this sudden and great
change, as he shall be whom I trust your lordships will send shortly hither to occupy this room,
whosoever he be.

" They say now in the court, that the Emperor is
recovered again, and that Strazzebourgh hath com-
pounded with him. One, that came very late from
the Emperor, saith that he is yet at Norlingen; but
the Emperor's ambassador saith that he is departed
thence, and going himself towards Saxony. As for
the news that were bruited here of Monsieur de Groninge, who should have been overthrown of the
Easterlings, the Emperor's ambassador saith that
there was no such thing. And the Emperor's ambassador saith further, that Martin Van Rosseyn is

* *Pedro Strozzi.*—Son of Philip Strozzi and Clarice de Medicis, aunt of Catherine de Medicis, Queen of Henry the Second; one of the ablest military commanders of the time, and of
great ambition. Henry the Second placed him at the head of
his army in Italy, but the measure was an unfortunate one.—
(Mezeray, vol. iv. p. 686.) His character will be found minutely
drawn in a subsequent letter of Wotton's. Strozzi was the im-
placable enemy of the house of Medici, and, instead of adopting the measures best calculated to ensure the success of the
campaign, suffered his plans to be influenced by his personal
resentment.

now joined with the said Groninge, with a good
number of men, footmen and horsemen.*

"He that made the funeral oration and the ex-
equies for the late King our sovereign lord, hath
been with me, and delivered me a copy of the said
oration in writing, with an epitaph also of his making, the which your lordships shall receive herewith.   He looketh by likelihood for some reward;
the which if your lordships think he hath deserved, and that you signify to me your pleasure
therein, I shall follow it accordingly.

"I have received your lordships' letter of the first
of this present, with the commission therein to require the confirmation and oath upon the new
treaties.   The fifth of this present, Mons. de Longuevall came hitherto Paris in the evening, and
in the morning was had to the Bastile to prison.†

----

* The lights thrown upon the character and proceedings of
Charles the Fifth are not the least valuable parts of these letters.   Monsieur de Groninge was "Josse Groeninghen," made
Governor of Zealand by Charles the Fifth.   He was slain at
the siege of Bremen some time after the date of this letter.
The reader will recollect that, in the year 1547, the Emperor triumphed over the league formed by the Protestant
princes at Smalcald, defeated and imprisoned the Elector
of Saxony, compelled the Landgrave of Hesse to a humiliat-
ing submission, and, filling Augsbourg with his Italian and
Spanish troops, proceeded to convoke a Diet in that city, in
which he bestowed provinces, and dictated articles of faith,
with a determination that none should question his decisions
either as to one or the other.

† *Nicholas de Bossut*, Sieur de Longuevall, a brave soldier,

And thus Jesu preserve your lordships long in health and prosperity.   Written at Paris, the 6th April.

> " Your lordships' ever to command,
>
> " N. Wotton."

This letter of Wotton's leads me to say a few words on the state of parties in France at the accession of Henry the Second. No prince could have come to the throne under more favourable auspices. He found his kingdom in profound peace, his finances flourishing, his army commanded by veteran and able officers who had been trained under his warlike father, and the great offices of state filled by men of talents and integrity. If he turned his view to England, not only was he protected by the treaty of Guisnes, concluded between Henry the Eighth and Francis the First, 8th June 1546, but still more effectually by the war with Scotland, which afforded sufficient occupation to that country. On the side of the Empire he could look for security to the peace of Crespy, which was signed by Francis the First and Charles the Fifth on the 18th Sept. 1544.

and much beloved by Francis the First. He was accused of having a correspondence with the Emperor; and compelled to purchase his pardon by surrendering his noble chateau of Marchez, in the Laonnois, to the Cardinal Lorraine,—"under the pretence of a sale, but, in reality, as a present." De Thou, book iii. vol. i. p. 107. Mezeray, vol. iv. p. 644.

But although at peace with England and the Emperor, it was not long before Henry (or rather his ministers, by whom he was entirely governed) evinced a determination to recover Boulogne out of the hands of the English, and to resist the ambition of the house of Austria.   His first step, as we see by Wotton's letter, was, instantly after his accession, to recall the Constable Montmorency to court, and to place the whole power of the government in the hands of him against whom he had been solemnly warned by his father on his death-bed.

ANNE DE MONTMORENCY had been brought up as page of honour to Francis the First: after having risen to a high pitch of power and wealth under this monarch, he became suspected by him in his latter years, and was banished the court shortly before his death, by the influence of his great political enemies Cardinal Tournon, the Admiral Annebault, and the King's mistress, the Duchess D'Estampes.

Although his military talents were acknowledged to be of a high order, Montmorency, was unfortunate as a general: he was often beaten, yet always ready to fight again; no reverses being able to exhaust his perseverance, or subdue his undaunted spirit.   In a court full of refinement, his manners were blamed as blunt, rugged, and austere; and he gloried, it was said, in his *sobriquet* of Cato.   We discover however nothing of this in the many interviews between the Constable and the English

Ambassador. Montmorency was a devoted Romanist, and so zealous in his religious duties that at
the head of his troops he would keep his stated
hours of prayer; but it was remarked that, if
the Provost Marshal at this moment reported any
culprit, the Constable would stop for an instant,
order him an extra dose of punishment,—and then
continue his devotions; so that it became a common saying with the men, " Heaven help us from
the Credos of the Constable!" His dying words
to his confessor have been often repeated, and too
often foolishly eulogised : " Do you imagine that
a man who has known how to live with honour
almost eighty years, does not know how to die for
a quarter-of-an-hour ?" Such was the hardy and
presumptuous Credo of the Constable.

But the power entrusted under the new reign
to Montmorency was scarcely greater than that
shared by the Bishop of Rheims, D'Aumale his
brother, and, above all, by Madame la Grande
Seneschalle. Of the Bishop of Rheims, Charles
de Guise, best known as the famous CARDINAL
OF LORRAINE, it is scarcely necessary to speak.
His abilities as a statesman, his towering ambition, and the important part which he acted in
Europe, are matters of history. His personal appearance must have been striking; a tall figure,
animated and beautifully formed features, a pierc-
ing eye, a high forehead, and the most dignified
but engaging manners, rendered it impossible for

any one not to be struck when ushered into his presence.   His ecclesiastical influence was so great that Pius the Fifth used to call him *"Il Papa tramontane."*

FRANCIS OF LORRAINE, Duke of Guise and Aumale, whose popularity with the young King made his voice, according to Wotton, so influential in the government, was the elder brother of the Bishop of Rheims. He was a staunch Romanist, and one of the greatest military leaders of his age.   His successful defence of Metz against Charles the Fifth, in 1553, created a wonderful sensation in Europe.   His *sobriquet, Le Balafré*, a word which Cotgrave humorously translates a "King Harry cut," was taken from a wound in the face which he received at the siege of Boulogne in 1545.

As for Madame La Grande Seneschalle, although not a member of the council, she governed the kingdom, if we may believe De Thou, with an almost absolute sway.   This lady, the celebrated DIANA OF POICTIERS, widow of Louis de Brèze, Grand Seneschal of Normandy, had been in her youth a woman of exquisite beauty; but she was now past forty-eight, and of course a good deal faded.   Her power however remained unwithered, and she was still the favourite mistress of a monarch who was only twenty-nine. Garnier the historian insists that their attachment was a Platonic one; but Mezeray is not so easily imposed upon.   Abrégé Chronologique, vol. iv. p. 643. "Afin," says he, "qu'on sceust qu'elle regnoit, il vouloit qu'on vist partout dans les Tournois, sur ses ameublemens, dans ses devises, et mesme sur le frontispiece de ses bastimens royaux, un croissant des arcs et des flesches, qui estoient le symbole de cette *impudique* Diane."

Her disposition, he adds, was of a most agreeable kind; but her hands were more amiable still, for they were always in her purse, and she gave away her money with the best grace in the world. De Thou, Book iii. vol. i. p. 108, in describing her wonderful power over the King, informs us that it was attributed to love potions, and magical arts,—no unfrequent subsidiaries in this age.

THE CARDINAL DE BELLAY, who is mentioned in the beginning of the letter, was a man of some capacity as a scholar, and is eulogised by Brantome as having no mean talents for war. His "good judgment in matters of religion," to use Dean Wotton's own words, can mean nothing more than that he was little of a bigot. We may form some idea of his purity of mind as an ecclesiastic from his being the patron of Rabelais.

In the "Introduction" something has been said of the great battle of Mulhberg, in which Charles the Fifth in person defeated and made prisoner John Frederic the Elector of Saxony, crushed the league formed by the Protestant princes at Smalcald, and established his power for a season both as a temporal and spiritual dictator. In the following letter from Edward Carne, the English resident at the court of the Netherlands, we obtain a slight glance of the state of affairs immediately before this decisive contest.

The reader need hardly be informed that the Lady Regent whom we meet with in this despatch of Carne's was MARY OF AUSTRIA, sister to Charles the Fifth, and widow of Louis King of Hungary and Bohemia.   She was born in the year 1503, married Louis in 1521, and was appointed by her brother Regent of the Low Countries in 1531.

The King of the Romans was Ferdinand, brother to Charles the Fifth, who was elected King of the Romans in 1531.

EDWARD CARNE TO THE PROTECTOR.

Orig. ST. P. OFF. *Flanders.* April 17, 1547. *Bruges.*

"PLEASITH your Grace to be advertised, yesternight the Lady Regent received letters from the Emperor of the 12th of this, whereby she is advertised, as I am informed, that then, th' Emperor, the King of Romans, and Duke Maurice of Saxony were together at a town called Aegra, within the country of Bohemia; and that, the same self day, the Duke of Alva marched forward toward Saxony with the Emperor's avant gard, and that the Emperor himself marched the morrow after.   They say here that he will give the battle to the Duke of Saxony; but some thinketh that too great a hazard, for they say here for truth that the Duke of Saxony hath at the least

five or six thousand horsemen, and five or six and
twenty thousand footmen, well appointed : notwithstanding, they say the Emperor hath more. And
farther I am informed, that two thousand light-
horsemen of the Bohemians be gone from the King
of Romans to the Duke of Saxony's service, which
causes them here to fear lest the Emperor should
be abused with his own men that be Almains ; but
this departing of the Bohemians is kept very privy
here.

" The Emperor hath despatched a post to Spain
with all diligence, as I hear, to send to him with all
speed more Spaniards. As touching the army before Breame (Bremen), I hear nothing since the
advertisement of the death of Monsr. de Groning,
whereof I advertised your Grace in my letters of
the 16th of this ; other· occurrents I càn hear of
none at this time. And thus do I beseech Almighty
God to conserve your Grace in long and most prosperous life, with all your's.

" From Bruges, the 17th of April 1547.

" Your Grace's most humble and
most bounden beadsman,
" EDWARD CARNE."

There are some points in English History, or
rather in English feeling upon English History
which have become part of the national belief,—
they may have been hastily or superficially assumed — they may be proved by as good evi-

dence as the case admits of, to be erroneous; but they are fondly clung to — screwed and dove-tailed into the mind of the people, and to attack them is a historical heresy. It is with these mus-ings that I approach her who is so generally exe-crated as the " bloody Mary." The idea of excit-ing a feeling in her favour, will appear a chimeri-cal, perhaps a blameable one; yet, having examined the point with some care, let me say, for myself, that I believe her to have been naturally rather an amiable person. Indeed, till she was thirty-nine, the time of her marriage with Philip, nothing can be said against her, unless we agree to detest her be-cause she remained faithful to the Roman Catholic church; nor can there, I think, be any doubt that she has been treated by Fox, Strype, Carte, and other Protestant writers, with injustice. The few unpublished letters of hers which I have met with, are simple, unaffected, and kind-hearted; forming, in this respect, a remarkable contrast to those of Elizabeth, which are often inflated, obscure, and pedantic. The distinguishing epithets by which the two sisters are commonly known, the " bloody Mary," and the " good Queen Bess," have evi-dently a reference to their times; yet we constantly employ them individually.

These observations apply, however, more to Mary the Princess than Mary the Queen. After her marriage with Philip, we can trace a gradual change in her feelings and public conduct. Her devoted attachment to Philip, and the cold neglect with which he treated her, could not fail to tell upon a kind and ardent heart: blighted hope and unrequited affection will change the best dispositions; and she whose youthful years had undoubtedly given a good promise, became disgusted with the world, suspicious, gloomy, and resentful. The subsequent cruelties of her reign were deplorable; yet it is but fair to ascribe much of them rather to her ministers than to herself: she believed it to be a point of her religion to submit her judgment to the spiritual dictation of Pole, Gardiner, and Bonner; and they burnt men upon principle. This was a miserable mistake,—bigotry in its worst sense; but we can imagine it existing in a mind rather distorted and misled, than callously cruel. No one ever accused Cranmer of cruelty; yet he insisted on burning Joan of Kent. These remarks, the reader who wishes to judge for himself should follow up, by studying Sir Frederick Madden's minute and interesting memoir of Mary, prefixed to the volume of her Privy Purse Expenses. On one point I must differ from Sir Frederick Madden; I am afraid that she *was* ugly. The following letter from her when Princess, addressed to the Duchess of Somerset, her " good Nan," exhibits her in an amiable light; interceding for two poor servants who were formerly attached to the household of her mother, and who had fallen into poverty.

PRINCESS MARY TO MY LADY OF SOMERSET.

Orig. St. P. Off. *Domestic.* 24th April 1547.

" My good Gossip,

" After my very hearty commendations to you, with like desire to hear of the amendment and increase of your good health, these shall be to put you in remembrance of mine old suit concerning Richard Wood, who was my mother's servant when you were one of her Grace's maids, and, as you know by his supplication, hath sustained great loss, almost to his utter undoing, without any recompence for the same hitherto; which forced me to trouble you with this suit before this time, whereof (I thank you) I had a very good answer; desiring you now to renew the same matter to my lord your husband, for I consider that it is in manner impossible for him to remember all such matters, having such a heap of business as he hath.

" Wherefore I heartily require you to go forward in this suit till you have brought it to an honest end, for the poor man is not able to lye long in the city.

"And thus, my good Nann, I trouble you both with myself and all mine; thanking you with all my heart for your earnest gentleness towards me in all my suits hitherto, reckoning myself out of doubt of the continuance of the same. Wherefore once again I must trouble you with my poor George Brickhouse, who was an officer of my mother's wardrobe, of the

beds, from the time of the King my father's coronation; whose only desire it is to be one of the knights
of Windsor if all the rooms be not filled, and, if
they be, to have the next reversion; in the obtaining
whereof, in mine opinion, you shall do a charitable
deed, as knoweth Almighty God, who send you good
health, and us shortly to meet, to his pleasure.

"From St. John's, this Sunday at afternoon, being
the 24th of April.

"Your loving friend during my life,

"MARYE."

We now return to the Continent, and the Emperor Charles the Fifth.

BISHOP OF WESTMINSTER TO SIR WM. PAGET.

Orig. St. P. Off. *Germany.* April 26, 1547. *Plagenetz.*

"AFTER my most hearty commendations to you.
When I had yesterday depesched John Honyngs to
have brought you such news as were here, and, for
want of post horses, he should have ridden three or
four posts with his own, (which as yet he must do;
forasmuch as, without the postmaster's letters, when
he shall come up on the posts, he can have no
horse,) he was constrained to tarry the same until
this day.

"When I had made this despatch, and dined, I
went to see the bridge, and the place where our
men passed the day before; there was such a
throng there, that a man had been better to have

passed with the baggage than with those passengers. I tarried therefore to pass there till yesterday, where I saw some part of the burned bridges, and some part of the men thereabouts slain; and where, by the way, divers did bruit that the band of Duke Frederick was five thousand footmen and two thousand horsemen.

" To make this victory the greater, an honest officer of the Emperor, that was all the night in the chase among the light-horsemen, affirmed for a truth that they were ten enseigns of footmen, and but three at the most of horsemen; which, after they were driven from the passage, were so hotly pursued with the Hungarians and Spaniards, and the light horse of the Italians, that ever gave the skirmish so hotly, that their flight could not be fast: by reason whereof th' Emperor repairing the burnt bridge of the enemy within an hour, (as is said,) and sending with great diligence all of his horsemen and footmen on, so refreshed his skirmishers, that [they] followed the enemy three leagues from the bridge, and there gave the overthrow, took the Duke, and slew his son in the entry of the wood, and, as he said, fifteen hundred of their soldiers, among whom were many gentlemen; and the other that was taken with the Duke of Saxe, is one of the Brunswick's.

" It is said that the Emperor hath sent to summon all the strong towns of the Duke's, and [it] is thought that there will be made no resistance. Here we

abide yet, consulting what shall be done. Yet I cannot hear of any other army of the Duke of Saxony
than he had here with him; saving that they say
he hath good garrisons in his towns.

"Thus much I thought good to write, having this
occasion of Honyngs' tarrying; and heartily I bid
you farewell.   From Plansenitz in Mesnia, the
26th of April 1547.

"Your assured loving friend,

" THOM. WESTMINS^r."

*The Right Hon. Sir Wm. Paget, Knight, one of
the King's Majesty's two Principal Secretaries.*

The above short letter from the Bishop of Westminster was written only two days after the battle
of Mulhberg;* and as he had examined the field,
and no doubt spoken with many officers engaged,
it is to be regretted that he has not been a little
more circumstantial in his epistle.   But bishops
were now more pacific men than in the days of
Anthony Bek, the warlike prelate of Durham
under Edward the First.—In De Thou, book iv.
c. 10, 11. vol. i. p. 136, 137, will be found a minute
and picturesque account of the battle.   Charles'
personal appearance is finely described:

—" The Emperor (says he) was mounted upon
a bay Spanish jennet, covered with housings of
scarlet silk, fringed with gold.   He wore a coat of
mail which glittered with gold, and had a scarlet

* See Introduction.

scarf over his breast, which is the honourable badge
of the house of Burgundy.   Arrayed thus, and holding a short broad-bladed javelin in his hand, he appeared not unlike the renowned Cæsar as he formerly passed the Rubicon, when, having rejected
every offer of peace, he placed his hopes in nothing
but victory."   De Thou's recital of the interview between Charles the Fifth and his illustrious prisoner
is striking.   The Duke of Alva conducted the
Elector to the Emperor : the Elector (says the
historian,) rode upon a Friesland horse, and wore
a blackish corslet inlaid with streaks of silver, with
a light shirt of ringed mail, because he was too fat
to carry heavier armour ; and thus, having his face
streaming with blood from a wound which he had
received in the battle, he was brought into the
Emperor's presence, and was going to pull off his
glove, and alight from his horse, that, according to
the custom of the country, he might give his hand
to the conqueror, when the Emperor stopt him,
The Elector then accosted him in this manner :
" Since fortune will have it so, I acknowledge
myself your prisoner, most merciful and potent
Emperor."   He would have proceeded, but Charles
breaking in, exclaimed, " Am I now then called
Emperor, who lately, in all your conversation and
even in your public papers, was styled sometimes
Charles of Ghent, and at other times the person
who assumed the title of Emperor ? "   As the other
was proceeding with his speech, and asking with

a steady countenance that he might be treated according to his dignity, the Emperor made no other answer than that he should be treated according to his desert, and with a gesture of disdain turned his back and left him.

Charles bestowed the Electorate upon Duke Maurice of Saxony, although he was a Lutheran. His aim was to convince the world that this was not a war of religion, but a contest undertaken to quiet the disturbances of the empire.

The " burnt bridges," which the Bishop mentions having examined, alludes perhaps to a circumstance which occurred immediately before the imperial army passed the river. The Spanish infantry had thrown themselves into the water, and endeavoured to cross; but were repulsed by a desperate fire. Making a second attempt, they rushed into the stream up to the shoulders, and had reached the boats of the Saxons on the opposite side, when the enemy set them on fire, cut their cables, and allowed them to drift down the current. At this instant ten Spanish soldiers stripped themselves of their clothes, and, holding their swords in their teeth, swam after the boats amid a murderous fire from the batteries on the opposite bank, seized them, and brought them in triumph to the Emperor, who employed them, along with his own, to construct a bridge on which his infantry and artillery crossed the river.* Carne, in the following

* De Thou, vol. i. p. 157. Bulkely Edition.

letter, informs Paget of the joy which the victory gave at Bruges.

EDWARD CARNE TO SIR WILLIAM PAGET.

Orig. St. P. Off. *Flanders.* 2d May 1547. *Bruges.*

" Pleaseth your mastership. (Forasmuch as I trust the same is merrily returned to the court from the country, where I heard say your mastership had been of late,) I am so bold as write this to the same, as touching occurrents here which arrived this evening very late. They be such that all the court here do wonderfully rejoice of the Emperor's late victory in Saxony, and of the taking of the Duke of Saxony prisoner ; whereof I will make no long letter unto you, because this post does bring the full news thereof from my Lord of Westminster. Both the Duke of Arskot and the President Schore sent to me the advertisements thereof immediately upon the arrival of the same to the Lady Regent, this post being then arrived hither ; or else I had incontinent despatched thither th' advertisements thereof accordingly. * * * * "

The impression made at Paris by the news of the defeat of the Elector, and the fears of the Protestants, are strikingly described in Wotton's next letter. Burgart was the Duke of Saxony's ambassador at the French court.

DR. WOTTON TO SIR WILLIAM PAGET.

Orig. St. P. Off. *France.* May 16, 1547. *Paris.*

" SIR, MY DUTY REMEMBERED.

"As I wrote to you yesterday that I would do this day, I came to Paris to speak with Burgart; and he hath no other certain accounts of his master's affairs but this : that his master was taken during the truce betwixt Duke Maurice and him, and his army was divided in divers parts and places, whereof was with him but about 10 enseignes of footmen, and about 1000 horse, his * * * † not taken; but hath now gathered together the rest of his army, and hath, as he saith, about 24,000 footmen; and in case they had (for) a head such a man as the Landgrave is taken to be, he saith they were able to fight with the Emperor, though he were stronger than he is. And he saith that the Bohemians that take part with the Protestants are in arms about 10,000 men, but he cannot wit what to say nor to think of the Landgrave; for, if he had been as earnest and constant as his master hath been, matters he supposes had been in other state than they are now. Doctor Bruno came not hither; but from Amiens took his way straight towards Argentine, as Burgart saith.

"He saith, also, that he findeth this Council here clean altered; and findeth some of them, to his opinion, much enclining to the Emperor, and others

† This word is illegible.

to the Scots. And albeit that he perceiveth that
these men begin to find fault with certain of our
doings, yet he saith that he trusteth that they intend not to proceed so far as to renew the war with
us. And considering the great inconveniences that
would come of it, if the war were now renewed,
not only to England and to France, but generally to all Christendom and specially to Germany, the which during that war no doubt were
to be all subdued to the Emperor, he wisheth much
that we might and would forbear some part of our
right (meaning thereby, not to proceed any farther
in the new building at Boulogne); the which en-
gendereth a steadfast opinion in these men's heads,
that we never intend to make restitution of it;
rather than that, for such a thing as that is, we
should put England and France into trouble again,
and suffer Germany to be without recovery subdued, and thereby make the Emperor the stronger,
and all the rest of Christendom the weaker. Of
these matters I suppose he writeth to you himself.

" The man (not without cause) is in great per-
plexity and trouble of mind, and dare not return
homewards as yet, fearing to be taken by the way.
He saith, that if he hear any thing concerning us,
he will give advertisement of it. And thus Jesu
preserve you long in health and prosperity!

" Written at Paris, the 16th of May 1547.

"N. WOTTON."

I have already given a letter from the Princess
Mary, interceding with the Duchess of Somerset
for two poor servants, who had been attached to
her mother's household. We now find her remind-
ing the Protector of his " gentle promise" to grant
pensions to those aged persons in her own household, who had served her long, and whose sands
were fast running out. Now this is amiable, and
does not look like the " *bloody*" Mary.

THE PRINCESS MARY TO THE PROTECTOR.

Orig. St. P. Off. *Domestic.* 28th December 1547.

" My Lord. I heartily thank you for your gentleness showed touching my requests late made unto
you, whereof I have been advertised by my Comptroller ; and altho' I shall leave to trouble you at this
present with the whole number of my said requests,
yet thought I it good to signify unto you my desire for those persons which have served me very
long time, and have no kind of living certain.
Praying you, my Lord, according unto your gentle
promise, that they may have pensions as other my
servants have, during their lives ; whose years be so
far passed that I fear they shall not enjoy it long.
And, hereafter, I will advertise you of the other
things wherein I moved you.

" Thus, with my hearty commendations, as well to
yourself, as to my gossip your wife, I bid you both
even so farewell ; praying Almighty God to send

you both as much health and comfort of soul and
body as I would wish to myself.

" From Beaulieu, the 28th of December.

" Your assured friend to my power,

" MARYE."

To my Lord Protector.

Whilst the Protestant princes in Germany had
received so severe a defeat from the Emperor in
the battle of Mulhberg, their cause in England
had triumphed in the complete establishment of
the Reformation; which was effected by the power
of the Protector Somerset, and the agency of Archbishop Cranmer; but into the history of this most
important moral revolution I do not enter, for
reasons already given.

The reverse at Mulhberg was for a season over-
whelming to the German princes; yet nothing
could break the undaunted spirit of John Frederick,
the Elector of Saxony. His character has been
well given by Roger Ascham, in contrast with that
of the Landgrave of Hesse, who is also mentioned
in Wotton's letter. Ascham spoke from personal
observation; and it were to be wished that his
minuteness of detail had been always imitated by
those who have written concerning great men. " I
told you at large (says this most facetious of peda-
gogues) both of the abbey with 1600 nuns, and also
the LANTSGRAVE, whom we saw prisoner. He is
lusty, well-favoured—something like Mr. Hebil-

thwat in the face; (What a pity Mr. Hebilthwat's
face has not descended to posterity!) hasty, incon-
stant, and, to get himself out of prison, would fight,
if the Emperor would bid him, with Turk, French,
England, God, and the Devil.   The Emperor, perceiving his busy head without constancy, handles
him thereafter; his own Germans, as it is said, be
well content that he is (not) forthcoming."   *   *   *

"JOHN FREDERICK is clean contrary; noble, cou-
rageous, constant; one in all fortunes, desired of
his friends, reverenced of his foes, favoured of the
Emperor, loved of all.   He hath been proffered of
late, it is said, by the Emperor, if he will subscribe
to his proceedings, to go at large, to have all
dignities and honours again, and more too.

"His answer was, from the first, *one*, and is still,
that he will take the Emperor for his gracious sovereign lord; but to forsake God and his doctrine
he will never do, let the Emperor do with his
body what he will."*

The Elector, soon after his being taken prisoner,
gave a fine instance of that constancy and sweetness
of disposition which could not be overcome by the
severest reverses.   Charles, immediately after the
battle, besieged Wittenberg; in which town, Sybilla of Cleves, Frederick's wife, with their children, had hoped to be safe, and which for a while

* English Works of Roger Ascham, by Bennet, p. 369, 370,
compared with the original.   British Museum.   Lansdowne,
98, 10.

defied the utmost efforts of the imperialists. To terrify the place into a surrender, the Emperor condemned John Frederick to death; trusting that his wife, Sybilla, would purchase his life by the delivery of the town. When informed of the sentence, he had just sat down to his favourite game of chess, and, looking up, he calmly observed, "This blow is levelled not against me, but against Wittenberg and my poor wife. Would that Sybilla could bear such news as well as I can! What is the loss or gain of a few days to a worn-out old man. To me the sentence has no terrors! Come, Ernest," said he, then cheerfully turning to the Duke of Brunswick, his antagonist at chess, and his fellow-prisoner; " come, for all this we shall not lose our game!" And he beat Ernest, and showed his usual satisfaction at his triumph. This was indeed, as Ascham says, to be " one in all fortunes."

Burgart, of whom Wotton speaks in the commencement of his letter, was John Frederick's Vice-chancellor, then at Paris as the envoy and representative of his master. He was the intimate friend of Melancthon, and had been ambassador in England in 1538.* His reasoning, as to the incipient hostile feelings of France towards England, and the calamitous consequences of a war between these two countries, in paralysing the resistance of Europe to the increasing power of the Emperor, is acute and conclusive.

* Strype's Ecclesiastical Memor. vol. i. part i.

Whilst these events were passing on the Continent, an opposition arose against the Protector Somerset from a quarter where he had, perhaps, least expected it. His younger brother, THOMAS LORD SEYMOUR, of Sudley, and High Admiral of England, imagined that he had not been sufficiently considered in that distribution of honours and estates which was made by the executors of Henry the Eighth. Being uncle to the King, he persuaded himself that his authority ought only to be second to that of his brother; and he secretly paid his addresses to the Queen Dowager, Catherine Parr, with the object of increasing his power. The Admiral was a gallant, accomplished, and, if Holbein's pencil has not flattered, a very handsome man; and Catherine, in the misguided notion that he loved herself, and not her jewels or her dowry, gave him her hand. The result was unhappy; but we shall not anticipate. The following letter of Lord Seymour was written during the courtship, when the Admiral was in the habit of privately visiting the Queen at her manor of Chelsea. Their confidante was his sister Herbert. For a letter of so early a date as 1547, it is elegantly and playfully written.

THE LORD ADMIRAL TO THE QUEEN.

Orig. ST. P. OFF. *Domestic.* 17th May 1547. *St. James.*

"AFTER my humble commendations unto your Highness. Yesternight I supt at my brother Herberd's; of whom, for your sake, besides mine own, I received good cheer; and after the same, I received from your Highness, by my sister Herberd, your commendations, which were more wellcome than they were sent.   And after the same, he waded farther with me, touching my being with your Highness at Chelsea, which I denied, being with your Highness; but that, indeed, I went by the garden as I went to see the Bishop of London's house, and at this point stood with her for a time; till at the last she told me farther tokens, which made me change colours, who, like a false wench, took me with the manner.   Then remembering what she was, and knowing how well you trusted her, [I] examined her whether those things came from your Highness, and by that knew it to be true; for the which I render unto your Highness my most humble and hearty thanks; for by her company, in default of yours, I shall shorten the weeks in these parts, which heretofore, were three days longer in every one of them, than they were under the plummet at Chelsea.

"Besides this commodity, I may ascertain your Highness by her how I do proceed in my matter, although I should lack my old friend Walter Excell.

"I have not as yet attempted my suit, for that I would be first thoroughly in credit ere I would move the same; beseeching your Highness, that I may not so use my said suit, that they should think, and hereafter cast in my teeth, that by their suit I attained your good will ; for hitherto I am out of all their danger for any pleasure that they have done for me, worthy thanks, and, as I judge your Highness may say the like, therefore, by mine advice we will keep us so ; nothing mistrusting the goodness of God, but that we shall be as able to keep out of their danger, as they shall be out of ours : yet I mean not but to use their friendship, to bring our purpose to pass, as occasion shall serve.

" If I knew by what means I might gratify your Highness, for your goodness to me, showed at our last being together, it should not be slack to de-clare mine to you again.   And to that intent, that I will be more bound unto your Highness, I do make my request, if it be not painful to your High-ness, that once in three days I may receive three lines in a letter from you, and as many lines and letters more as shall seem good unto your High-ness.

"Also, I shall humbly desire your Highness to give me one of your small Pictures, if you have any left ; who, with his silence, shall give me occasion to think on the friendly cheer that I shall receive, when my suit shall be at an end.   And thus, for fear of troubling your Highness with my long and rude letter, I take my leave of your Highness ; wishing that my hap may be once so good, that I may declare so much by mouth at the same hour that this was written, which was twelve of the clock

at night, this Tuesday, the 17th of May, at St.
James's.   *   *   *

"From him whom you have bound to honour,
love, and in all lawful things obey,

"T. SEYMOUR."

Endorsed in a contemporary hand,
  "*The L. Admiral to the Queen.*
  Of his suit for marriage."

This letter is interesting, as it proves how soon
the rivalry between the two brothers had begun, and
that Lord Seymour's towering ambition would be
content with no common share of power. Sir Henry
Ellis* has published a letter from the Queen to
the Admiral, written subsequent to their marriage,
but when the event was still kept secret. Unfortunately, it is without date. In Haynes' Collection, p. 61, is a letter, also undated, from the
Queen to the Admiral; which shows that Catherine, as well as her husband, could brave the Protector. "My lord your brother (says she) hath
this afternoon a little made me warm. It was fortunate we were so much distant, for I suppose, else,
I should have bitten him." And then she playfully
adds, as if warning her husband that he might himself happen to meet with the same kind of reproof,
"What cause have they to fear having such a
wife?"

From May 17th, 1547, to March 7th, 1547-8, I find
in the State Paper Office few letters which are of

* Original Letters, vol. ii. p. 151.

F 2

much moment in the light they throw upon the continental or domestic relations of the country.

During this interval, the French monarch, acting by the advice of his prime-minister, Montmorency, had two great objects in view: to recover Boulogne out of the hands of the English, and to weaken the Protector by succouring the Scots; but as yet his plans were not made public. At home, Somerset was occupied with the war in Scotland; and her Majesty's Collection is rich in the materials afforded to the Scottish historian. The disastrous defeat given to Scotland in the battle of Pinky, the strict alliance entered into between that country and France, the resolution to convey Mary, the young Queen, to an asylum at the French court, her betrothment to the Dauphin, and the determination of Henry the Second to send an army into Scotland, all occurred in this interval, and I have fully dwelt on these subjects in another work.*   But, although barren as to continental matters, I find in the correspondence of this interval two letters worthy of notice, from the celebrity of the persons to whom they introduce us,—the PRINCESS ELIZABETH, at this time a girl of fourteen, and WILLIAM CECIL, afterwards her prime minister.†

Everything is interesting which illustrates the early life of this great Queen; and some curious

---

* History of Scotland, vol. vi.   Edin. 1837.

† Sir Henry Ellis, in his Original Letters, vol. ii. pp. 145-148, has given us two letters of Elizabeth, when Princess, both undated, but which he places in 1547.

passages regarding her girlhood are to be culled
from Haynes' State Papers, of which Warton has
made ample use.*   At sixteen, she was evidently in
love with the Admiral Lord Seymour ; and the
romping and boisterous *badinage* which was carried on between them says little for the decorous
principles of her Governess, Catherine Ashley.
Had the same sharp eyes and scandalous tongues
which busied themselves about Mary, her rival
Queen, been as active in prying into and ex-
aggerating the early coquetry of Elizabeth, we
should have had many strange tales ; and yet an
examination of Haynes must convince us, that
although scandalous reports were circulated, of
which the Princess herself complains, † there
was no real foundation for them,—nothing but the
coarse romping of the times,—a sort of semi-bar-
barous feudal flirtation.   There is a strange eulo-
gium pronounced upon her by Bishop Aylmer,‡
who affirms, on the authority of her Italian schoolmaster, that she in her youth possessed two qualities which were incomparable when found in one
woman, —" a singular wit, and a marvellous meek
stomach."   The following is, I believe, the earliest
letter of the Princess yet published : she was now
in her fifteenth year : its penmanship is beautiful ;
and its style more simple and natural than her usual
ornate and obscure epistles.   It should be recol-

* Life of Sir Thomas Blount, p. 100, and Haynes' State
Papers, p. 96.

† Haynes, p. 89.   ‡ Strype's Life of Aylmer, p. 196.

lected, that the Queen Dowager, to whom it is
addressed, died on the 5th September 1548.

THE PRINCESS ELIZABETH TO THE QUEEN DOWAGER.

Orig. St. P. Off. *Domestic.* 1547. *Cheshunt.*

"Although I could not be plentiful in giving
thanks for the manifold kindness received at your
Highness' hand at my departure, yet I am something to be borne withall, for truly I was replete
with sorrow to depart from your Highness, especially
leaving you undoubtful of health : and, albeit I answered little, I weighed it more deeper, when you
said you would warn me of all evils that you should
hear of me; for if your Grace had not a good
opinion of me, you would not have offered friendship to me that way, that all men judge the contrary. But what may I more say, than thank God
for providing such friends to me; desiring God to
enrich me with their long life, and me grace to be
in heart no less thankful to receive it than I now
am glad in writing to show it; and although I
have plenty of matter, here I will stay, for I know
you are not quiet to read.

"From Cheston (Cheshunt), this present Saturday.

"Your Highness' humble daughter,

"Elizabeth."

Endorsed. "*To the Queen's Highness.*"

The early steps by which William Cecil, afterwards the great Lord Burleigh, ascended to such a
height of power, have been somewhat loosely no-

ticed by his biographers; and considerable obscurity hangs over his career from 1540, when he was a
young man of twenty years of age, studying law at
the inns of court, to Sept. 6th, 1550, when he became Secretary of State.*   His grandfather, David
Cecil, Esq. was Water-bailiff to Henry the Eighth,
and one of the King's Serjeants-at-Arms.   His father was Richard Cecil, Esq. Yeoman of the Wardrobe.   From these facts we may infer that he was
descended from an honest and respectable, rather
than from a " very ancient and honourable house,"
as his biographers have so often repeated.   He belonged, I think, to the gentry of the country.
The Heralds, it is true, in the palmy days of Burleigh, got up for him a handsome descent from
William Sitsilt, an intimate friend of William
Rufus in the year 1091; which pedigree (with reverence be it spoken) is said to be drawn by Camden :
yet so much doubt hangs over the effusions of
Rouge Dragons and Clarencieux's when working for
prime ministers, that, till the proofs are produced,
we may be allowed to hesitate.   His Life, by a Domestic, affirms that young Cecil, coming to court to
visit his father, entered into controversy with
O'Neill's two chaplains, and confuted them in a
Latin argument on the supremacy of the King
over the Pope.   This, he adds, was made known
to Henry, who gave him his patronage and the

* MS. Privy Council Books of Edward VI.   For reasons afterwards given, I do not consider that he was Secretary of State
before 1550.

promise of the office of Custos Brevium ; but no
date is given, and the whole story is vague.*

We know from his Journal, that, on the 6th
of May 1541, when twenty-one years of age, he
came to the Inns of court. His marriage to a
sister of Sir John Cheek took place in August
1541, and this seems to me to have been the first
thing that brought him into notice ; for, Cheek
being appointed tutor to Prince Edward in 1544,†
he must have had opportunities of befriending his
brother-in-law : and yet I suspect he did not even
then desert the law, and come to Court. The
exact year when he did so, has not yet been pointed
out by any of his biographers, and his Journal is
silent on the subject.

The following letter from Lady Browne, written
in July 1547, not six months after the accession
of Edward the Sixth, proves that Cecil was then
in some situation of confidence and power under
the Protector Somerset. The author of his life
in the Biographia Britannica, (the best critical
account of him yet written, though too indiscri-
minate in its praise,) imagines that he was Master
of Requests as early as 1547 ; but to this office he
certainly was not promoted till much later. This
clearly appears from the letters addressed to him
which I have seen in the State Paper Office ; and

---

* If true, it must have happened in October 1542, when
Cecil's age was twenty-two.—Irish State Papers, published by
Government, vol ii. p. 428.

† Strype's Life of Cheek, p. 22.

from the same source it is evident, that in 1547 he managed the whole correspondence of the Protector; probably, in the capacity of his Private Secretary. The letter of Lady Browne, at all events, establishes a fact, not before known in the life of Burleigh; that at the age of twenty-seven, he had embraced the service of the Duke of Somerset, and was not only a statesman, but in a place of high trust and influence. It is pleasant to find a letter, apparently immaterial, throwing light upon the early life of so remarkable a man.

THE LADY BROWNE TO CECIL.

Orig. St. P. Off. *Domestic.* 23rd July 1547.

" Gentle Mr. Syssyll,

" After most hearty commendations. This shall be to render you most hearty thanks, for your gentleness showed unto me at all times. Further, it may be to certify unto you, that I have unto my Lord Protector's Grace a letter, in the which I am an humble suitor to the same his Grace, for as much as I understand his Grace, doth appoint certain gentlemen and others, to go into Scotland to serve the King's Majesty there, that it will please his Grace to accept and appoint my brother to be one also amongst them. And supposing his Grace not to know my brother, I shall desire you to prefer his suit, and that by your means he may deliver my said letter to my Lord's Grace; and for your gentleness herein I shall reckon myself, as I am indeed, much beholden unto you. Thus always ready to trouble you, I will desire you to have me commended unto your good bedfellow, and so bid you most heartily to farewell. From Horsley, this Saint James's day.

  " By your assured to my little power,

Endorsed.   " ELIZABETH BROWNE."

  " *To my friend Mr. Syssyll*
   be these delivered."

Cecil accompanied Somerset in his great Scottish expedition, and was present at the fatal battle of Pinky, (Sept. 10th, 1547,) where he narrowly escaped being killed by a cannon-shot.* It was the first and last of his fields. On his return, he continued to rise in the favour of his master ; who, in the following letter, written about five months after the fight, speaks of him as "his Servant William Cecil," and in such terms as leave no doubt that he then managed much of the correspondence of the Protector. It was one of the complaints of Warwick, and the councillors who composed his faction, that Somerset was too fond of popularity, and interfered with judges and officers in their treatment of poor suitors. The letter proves that there was some ground for their assertions; but, considering the venality of justice, and the tyranny of feudal barons in those days, the accusation was rather honourable than otherwise.

 * MS. Private Journal. Life, by a Domestic, p. 10. Edited by Collins.

THE PROTECTOR TO LORD COBHAM.

Orig. HARLEIAN. 284.   19th February 1547-8.

" AFTER our hearty commendations to your good lordship. Whereas heretofore, at the instant complaint of a poor woman, we signified unto you that our desire was to have her so ordered by you as she should have no farther cause to complain ; we have since that time understood, by your letters written to our servant William Cicill, that ye intended no wrong in your doing, but in the King's behalf to make a stay for his Grace's rents : which thing being declared to the complainer, could in no wise pacify her, alleging that your lordship did her extreme wrong, being known to all the country ; the which trial she did earnestly require. And, therefore, we have written our letters for the same purpose to Sir Robert Southwell and *   *   *   *, of whom we will be certified to the full contentation of the party. Thus heartily fare ye well.

" From Somerset Place, the 19th Feb. 1547-8.

" Your lordship's loving friend,

" E. SOMERSET."

Endorsed.

" *To our very good and loving friend,*
   the Lord Cobham, give these."

I may conclude these brief notices of this early and obscure part of Cecil's life, by alluding to a letter in the State Paper Office, dated 13th July 1548,—

that is, about five months after the above to Lord
Cobham,—in which he is addressed by Sir Walter
Mildmay and others as " *Secretary* to my Lord
Protector's Grace." It must be to this office, I think,
that he alludes when he says in his Latin Diary,
under the year 1548, " *Mense Septemb : Cooptatus
sum in Officium Secretarii;*" * because I have not
found a single document in the State Paper Office
addressed to him as Secretary of State, prior to 1550.
The first notice of his being appointed Master of
Requests to the Protector, occurs in a letter of Roger Ascham to Cecil, dated 5th Jan. 1548-9, and
printed by Strype in his Life of Cranmer.†

It is time, however, to proceed with our Correspondence, and, turning to France, we find that,
although peace was upon Henry's lips, because his
preparations were not yet completed, the rumour
of an approaching war with England had become
very strong in the country. This is clearly shown
by the following letter from Dr. Wotton to Sir William Petre, Secretary of State.

SECRETARY PETRE, with whom we now meet for
the first time, was born in Devonshire, " that great
nursery of parts," to use the words of Fuller, and
educated at Exeter College. The Earl of Wiltshire
chose him as his son's tutor ; and Cromwell, meeting

---

* I am aware that this supposes him to have made a confusion between the months of July and September ; but the
Journal seems to have been drawn up, late in life, and this is
not a solitary error in Cecil's chronology.

† Vol. ii. Appendix, 38.

him at the Earl's house, detected his talents and
sent him to travel, with an allowance of 125*l.* a
year. He returned, says Lloyd, after an absence of
five years, a complete gentleman; being a happy
composition of every region, with that easy and
debonnair manner, which inspired confidence and
opened the hearts of others, whilst, beneath this,
there was a reserve and self-possession that shut
up his own.* In state affairs he was remarkable for his silence at the Council-board. When the
conferences took place for the peace between England and France in 1550, Monsieur Chastillon had
reasoned earnestly against the sum demanded by
the Protector. " Ah !" said he, " we should have
gained the last 200,000 crowns, had it not been for
the man who said nothing."

In the second letter addressed by Wotton to the
Protector, he alludes to the joy experienced at the
French court on the report of a victory gained
by the Scots over the English. The intelligence
proved to be erroneous; the Scots were repulsed, instead of having been successful, in their
attack upon Broughty Craig,—a strong fort in the
mouth of the Tay. The influence possessed by so
small and remote a kingdom as Scotland, in its relation to the other European powers, has not been
generally understood ; but many of the observations
in these letters will convince the reader of the fact,
and, indeed, a few moments' reflection would lead

* Lloyd, p. 453.

him to anticipate it. A Scottish war was always one of the best cards which France could play against England.

N. WOTTON TO SIR WILLIAM PETRE.

Orig. St. P. Off. *France.*   March 7th, 1547-8.   *Paris.*

"Sir, my duty remembered.   I was right glad to see your hand at this last letter, and longed for to see it.   I have not answered to your last letter for because I trusted to have been at home by this time; and, seeing that I trust so to be shortly, I suppose the matter requireth not so great haste but that it may stay till I come home.

"When that my Lord of Warwick, my Lord of Durham, and I, were sent hither for the ratification of the Treaty, we had the form of the ratification and the oath delivered us in writing; and therefore, if any new ratification be made, or oath given now, it were not amiss that you sent a copy of the form of that self [same] ratification and oath that was made and given then by the late French King, the which shall be a good precedent for them now.

"Lesseter, my servant, who brought this last despatch, sayeth that, all the way as he came from Boulogne to Paris, they speak all of war, and say that the French King prepareth to recover Boulogne again; but hitherto have I heard never a word of it here in Paris, nor my men at the court

hear no such communication.   And thus Jesus preserve you long in health and prosperity !

" Written at Paris, the 7th of March 1547.

" Yours to command,

" N. WOTTON."

DR. WOTTON TO THE PROTECTOR AND COUNCIL.

Orig.   ST. P. OFF.   *France.*   7th March 1547-8.   *Paris.*

" * * * THE Bishop of Rome's Nuntio that
should go into Scotland is yet at Melun ; having
not yet, as I hear, his commission or money that he
should have with him into Scotland. * * The court
is departed from Fontainbleau, and is come down
into a house of the Constable's called Eston, within
four or five leagues of Paris, where they will not
tarry long ; and it is thought that the King will
be up towards Champaign for a while. * * * Harpax showeth me that the French ambassador, Osey,*
who was despatched a good while ago to go into
Scotland, is yet in Brytaine.   He saith that a
French painter, named, as I remember, Nicholas,
who was some time in England, hath delivered to
the French King the pictures of all the Havens in
England ; and that [by] these means to land their
men easily that go into Scotland, [they] will not
stick to land them in some haven of ours, so it be

---

* Monsieur D'Oysel.—Harpax was a Scottish spy in the pay
of England.

not too far off from the Scots : but like as that may be true, so I cannot very well believe it; for that were so directly against the Treaty, that it could by no colour be excused.

"He told me also, that one about Madame la Grande Seneschale told him that the Marquis de Main, brother unto the Queen of Scots, goeth with this aid into Scotland. The Emperor's ambassador saith, that these men send two or three hundred Spaniards amongst others into Scotland : they make a great matter here of the victory that the Scots, as they say, have had upon our men at Dundee. And thus Jesus preserve your Grace and your good Lordships long in health and prosperity! Written at Paris, the 7th of March 1547.

"Yours,

"N. WOTTON."

It was a common practice at this time for royal personages to throw off their state, disperse their council, and, indulging themselves in the freedom and *incognito* of a private life, to visit and be happy with their friends. Thus we find, on the 18th of March 1547-8, soon after the date of his last letter, Dr. Wotton informs the Protector that he had not been very recently at court, " because the French King, being disposed to visit secretly his friends and acquaintance in Paris, hath been much here and hereabout, and yet disguised;" and he adds, " that there were none in a manner of the

council left at the court:" nor can we blame a
prince for his wish to escape for a while from the
uneasy pageantry of his condition, that he may
cast off the stiff buckram of royalty, and enjoy his
freedom in his doublet and hose.

But, although thus fond of his own enjoyment,
Henry the Second, or rather his ministers, Montmorency and the Guises, had many deep projects
in their heads. His warlike preparations had
already alarmed England; and, as we may perceive by the following letter of the Bishop of
Westminster, began to excite the suspicion of
the Emperor. Charles the Fifth, in the mean
time, was too much occupied with his own affairs
in Germany, to break openly with France. He
required some time to avail himself of the triumph he had gained over the German princes;
and after having imprisoned the Landgrave of
Hesse, and rewarded Maurice by investing him
with the Electorate of Saxony, he assembled a
Diet at Augsbourg, in which he compelled the Protestant princes to swear to that temporary formulary of faith, to which, under the name of the
INTERIM, we have alluded in the Introduction.

The two following letters from the Bishop of
Westminster, the first addressed to the Council, and
the second to Sir William Petre, were written at the
moment the Emperor was thus employed. Monsieur Grandvela, whom he mentions as being
over-joyed at the success of the English arms in

Scotland, was Nicolas Perrenot, at that time prime minister to Charles the Fifth, father to the Cardinal Granvelle, who was afterwards the favourite and chief minister of Philip the Second. There is some similarity between the lives of the two Cecils and the two Granvelles. The elder Perrenot, at the time of his death, had been prime minister to the Emperor for twenty years. His son, Anthony, like Robert Cecil, having been educated in matters of state under his father, was initiated into all the mysteries of political intrigue, and when the father died, the son succeeded to his dangerous office, in the same way that the Earl of Salisbury stept into the ministerial shoes of Lord Burleigh.

BISHOP OF WESTMINSTER TO THE COUNCIL.

Orig. St. P. Off. *Germany.* 27 March 1548.

" PLEASETH your honourable lordships to be advertised, that having received your letters, and perceiving by the same at large the good and prosperous success that God hath given of late to the King's majesty against his enemy in Scotland, (for the which condign praise and honour might be to him accordingly,) I declared immediately the same to Monsr. Grandvela, who by his words rejoiced thereat, and desired to have an extract of the substance of your said letters, saying that the Emperor would take pleasure to read the same ; and by the way he asked how the French, our good neighbours, did with us.

" I told him that I heard none other but that they say they will keep peace and amity with us; and yet by their ambassador's letters, which Secretary Joyse showed me, and by the bruit here, I heard that the French did send aid to the Scots both of men and money: and here I said, I marvelled how the Emperor would take it, that the French should aid his enemies, which were not comprised in their last peace with France ; and that also such as I talked with here marvelled that the French should aid the Scots their allies, and that the Emperor should not aid us again, being his allies.

" Hereto Monsr. Grandvela answered few words, like (as I judged) as though he was not desirous to talk much of that matter : and in effect, he said the French promised by word to keep peace and amity with them, like as they promised to us ; but (said he) we trust them as I think you do, and that ye may perceive by the execution done here to such captains as served the French, and ye shall shortly hear of more in Italy.* We have (quoth he) good eye to them and their doings, and with you the Emperor will not fail to keep such covenants as he is bound by his league ; and thus, with accustomed good words, we broke off. * * * "

* The Bishop alludes to the deaths of Sebastian Schertel and other officers, executed in 1548, in the Market-place at Augsbourg, by order of the Emperor.

From the following letter we may derive some light as to the " INTERIM," that noted measure which made so much noise in the history of the Reformation.

BISHOP OF WESTMINSTER TO SIR WILLIAM PETRE.

Orig. St. P. Off. *Germany.* April 3d, 1548. *Augsbourg.*

" AFTER my most hearty commendations to you. Where, heretofore, I advertised you that I heard say how the Emperor had committed to Malvenda, and others his learned men here, to devise in the matter of *Interim* some order, which peradventure the commissaries in the said Interim might be persuaded to accept ; I hear say now, that the said learned men's Device is perfected, and delivered to the Electors to view ; but kept so secret, that by no means yet I can get no copy thereof, nor certainly learn th' effect thereof.

" It hath been told to Mr. Mount, that it should reduce Religion to the old state where it was before twenty years ; except that *communicatio sub utraque specie* should be permitted to all those that would ask it, and that such priests as be already married should be tolerated, *ne ecclesiæ destituantur ministris,* and this only until the Council should determine these matters. And further it was told him, that the County Palatine, Duke Maurice, and the Marquis of Brandenbourg, have subscribed to the said learned Device ; and that the said

Marquis hath sent for Bucerus, who is here with him in his house, to persuade him (as is thought by some) also to subscribe, to the intent that the princes may have the better shine to the world in their doings.   Mr. Mount sayeth, that he hath heard, of a good author, that Bucerus, when he had seen the Interim, said that he liked it in no wise. Melancthon is also looked for to be here shortly. Master Barnardyne, talking with certain of Duke Maurice's councillors, learned by them that Duke Maurice, for his own person, will be contented to be ordered in matters of Religion as the Emperor will have him.   Altho' I could not advertise any certainty herein, yet I thought good to signify this, that ye might know as much as we can learn. * * *"

" Augsbourg, April 3d."

There are some things not unworthy of notice in this letter.   It would appear, from the terms used by the Bishop of Westminster, that Louis Malvenda, a Franciscan friar, and author of a work entitled " Lac Fidei pro Principe Christiano," acted the principal part in drawing up the " Interim." Now De Thou and Sleidan have ascribed its composition to Pflug the Bishop of Nuremberg, Michael Helding, better known as Michael Sidonius, and John Agricola, preacher to the Elector of Brandenbourg; whilst Pallavicino* and Courayer, in his learned notes to Father Paul's History of the

* Pallavicino, B. x. c. 17.   Gerdesii Hist. Reform. vol. iii. p. 203.

Council of Trent, assert that its real author is unknown.

This Formulary, although published as an Imperial Constitution, and clothed with the authority of law, was resisted by many and ridiculed by all. Wolfgang of Bavaria, and John the brother of the Elector of Brandenbourg, refused to subscribe to its doctrines, and were ordered by the Emperor to leave the Diet. Bucer, as we see, condemned it. Melancthon mildly dissented: and John Frederick, the deposed Elector of Saxony, with his sons, not only declined having anything to do with it, but promised, if permitted, to refute its articles. Lastly, to complete the mortification of the Emperor, its provisions regarding the marriage of priests were condemned by the Pope ; and, although Charles determined to enforce it, the whole affair, as a measure of conciliation, proved a complete failure.* I may here mention, to such as may be curious in investigating the history of the Reformation, that there is preserved in the State Paper Office a manuscript copy of the Proem or Introduction to the Interim, transmitted by the English ambassador to the Protector, which is different in many of its passages and provisions from that given by Goldastus in his Imperial Constitutions. As to the submission of Duke Maurice, it was the offspring of expediency, not of conviction. This ambitious and able prince was " biding his time." He wished to

* Histoire du Concile de Trente, vol. i. pp. 469-479.

lull Charles into security, whilst he was secretly preparing to resist him. His plans, and their success, will develope themselves as we proceed.

Wotton's next letter from Paris acquaints us with the active preparations in France for the succour of the Scots; and we find that Petro Strozzi, Andelot, Jarnac, and many proud knights and leaders, were buckling on their harness, and mustering their companies, to gain laurels in the struggle with England and the Protestants.

N. WOTTON TO THE PROTECTOR AND COUNCIL.

Orig. St. P. Off. *France.* 10th April 1548. *Sens.*

" * * Petro Strozzi, as far as I can perceive, is still at Nantes, preparing and setting all in a readiness. Andelot is departed from the court, and by likelihood gone into Britaine too; for they that shall go into Scotland, draw thither apace. This bearer says, that coming hitherward he overtook many soldiers, about two or three hundred, in divers companies, that were going into Britayne, to pass over into Scotland as they said. I hear that the Admiral's Band, which is of eighty men of arms, his son's Monsr. de la Humauldaye's Band of forty men of arms, Jarnac's Band of forty men of arms, and certain other Bands of men of arms, with four or five hundred light horses, shall be sent into Scotland.

" These men have not only a good opinion of Petro Strozzi, but also a good hope that he shall do some great act in Scotland; and no doubt he dare adventure as far as any man, and hath wit enough, joined with some experience, and, besides this, overmuch desire of glory and to do somewhat whereby to increase his estimation and credit in this court: for the which considerations I reckon assuredly that he will attempt great things; and so everybody saith that knoweth him, and no less is looked for of him. And thus Jesu preserve your Grace!"

"Sens in Burgundy."

THIRLBY, BISHOP OF WESTMINSTER TO SIR W. PETRE.

Orig. St. P. Off. 15th April 1548. *Augsbourg.*

"AFTER my most hearty commendations to you. How we proceed in matters of Religion, ye shall perceive by such letters as I send to my lords, with the books sent with the same. The last Tuesday I wrote not to you, for since then I was in continual hope to have such things as I now do send, and yet then could not get them.

"We say that the Emperor will remain here until that the Prince of Spain shall come hither with his sister; and that Ferdinand th' Arch Duke shall be married to her in this town.* They say that he shall bring with him eight or ten thousand Spaniards;

---

* The Bishop of Westminster erroneously writes Ferdinand for Maximilian; the father for the son. Maximilian was married to his cousin Donna Maria, at Barcelona, in Oct. 1548.

and that these princes, whose names be written in
the schedule here inclosed, shall accompany them
hither : but they say that before August he cannot
be here.

" They say also, that letters be come hither from
Lyons, signifying that Petro Strozzi is passed thereby with four thousand Italians; and that the bruit
is there that they shall go into Scotland to aid the
Scots against us.

" The Emperor's physician said also, that the
Emperor had been long in great suspicion of the
French ; but now the Imperials assure themselves
that they shall for this year live in peace.   This is
[what] they say, and *he* says; but I *say* also, that
notwithstanding I doubt [not] but that my Lord Protector's Grace of his great wisdom hath foreseen to
withstand all such danger as these bruits may bring
if they be true : yet, notwithstanding, I cannot but
wish that all things possible be done in Scotland
ere the aid come, so that, when they should come,
they might have little joy to enter there ; and that
such Forts as we have in Scotland might be so furnished that the Scots nor their aiders should be able
to recover them, for the bruit of one fort recovered,
would be sent abroad in the world, as though all
were lost of our side.   This I cannot but wish,
although I know not how it might be done.   In
fine, to come from wishing to praying, I beseech
Almighty God, who is the giver and promoter of all
goodness, to give herein such an end whereby we

may in peace glorify his name; and that the King's Majesty may long and most prosperously reign over us.   Thus most heartily I bid you farewell.

" From Augsbourg, the 15th of April 1548.

" Ye shall receive herewith a letter of A. Mont to Master Comptroller, of such news as he hath learned.

" Your assured loving friend,
" THOS. WESTMINSTER."

To those who have studied in original letters the secret history of Europe during the sixteenth century, nothing is more striking than the base perfection to which the system of " Spies," or paid informers, was carried in England, Scotland, France, Italy, and the Empire.   These emissaries swarmed in the palace, the camp, the council, the conclave; and they were often men of family and education : nay, ministers, officers, ecclesiastics of rank and influence, bribed by the rival of their masters ; and sometimes not bribed only by one party, but receiving golden encouragement from both, and pluming themselves in their dexterity in the double coinage of lies and guineas.   In the following letter we are introduced to a member of this villanous fraternity under the disguised name of " Goodman Harpax." Who he was, I have not discovered; but he appears to have been in daily communication with Andelot, whose influence at the French court was now great; and the information which he gives to Wotton is highly interesting.

DR. WOTTON TO SIR WILLIAM PETRE.

Orig. St. P. Off. *France.* April 16th, 1548.

" Sir, my duty remembered.

"Goodman Harpax hath been divers times in hand with me to lend him money; but for awhile I answered him that I had lent him some already, and, till I was paid of that, I intended to lend him no more: but thereunto at the last he said, my Lord Protector's Grace had promised him two hundred crowns by year; and that he would write to my Lord's Grace that it would please him to cause me to be paid thereof, and also to will me to deliver unto him monthly as much as he should have. And according thereunto he hath written a letter to my Lord's Grace, the which you shall receive herewith; although his name be not at it, for because, as he saith, my Lord's Grace hath divers letters of his hand and knoweth it well, and therefore, for fear of dangers, he hath not put his hand thereto. I pray you to do so much for me as to declare this matter to my Lord's Grace, and to know his pleasure, whether I shall do as he requireth in his said letter, that I may have what to answer him when he speaketh to me any more of it.

" Harpax saith, that, talking of late with Andelot, they spake by chance, among other matters, of Berteville; and Andelot asking what he did in England, and how he was esteemed, Harpax said that he was in good credit and well esteemed, and at the late battle in Scotland he had charge of certain gunners on horseback, and did good service; * whereunto Andelot said, that he must be won and brought home again. Harpax answered, that if the late French King had lived, so he should have been indeed; for he *practised* him by the means of the Baron St. Blancourt, who made two or three journeys into England for that purpose, though he made pretence of other matters, so that at the last all was agreed upon : but now, seeing the King was dead, he thought it was not so easy to recover him as it was then.

" But Andelot said yes, and whatsoever was promised him then should be performed now; yea, and 2000$^{lb.}$ tournois by year, giving him more to amend his living than he should have had of the late King; and that therefore he doubteth not but that it will right well be brought to pass. By this, and other like communication that Andelot hath

---

* *Berteville.*—By the late battle in Scotland is meant the sanguinary and fatal defeat of the Scots at Pinky, of which the Sieur de Berteville wrote a short account, which has been printed for the Bannatyne Club by one of its members, Mr. David Constable. The original, addressed to Edward the Sixth, is in the Cotton Library.

The gunners on horseback, alluded to in the letter, were probably that fine body of Spanish and Italian carabineers, which, commanded by Pedro di Gamboa, behaved with such bravery in the battle of Pinky.—Tytler's History of Scotland, vol. vi. p. 36.—They were clad, man and horse, in complete mail ; and, by their determined charge, restored order to the English army after Lord Grey's cavalry had been defeated by the attack of the Earl of Angus.—Hayward, Life of Edward the Sixth.— Kennet, vol. ii. p. 285.

with Harpax, he taketh it for a certainty that those
men that go into Scotland, and others that are in
England, and merchantmen that resort thither, have
commission to *practise* this man ; and in case they
do, he reckoneth himself assured that Berteville will
accept the offer, and be persuaded to return home.
Wherefore Harpax thinketh it very necessary that
good heed be taken to him, and specially if he be
put to the wars again ; for if he have like commission as he had, and be not well taken heed to,
Harpax saith we shall have cause to repent it.
And yet he saith, he thinketh it good that in countenance and otherwise he be as lovingly and gently entertained as he hath been, or rather better;
for so doing, and having nevertheless a diligent
eye upon him, he saith that his doings shall be the
better perceived.

" And he saith that, if his chance be to be sent
into England, he doubteth not but to find the
means to decipher this matter, and make it plainly appear to my Lord's Grace.   And this advertisement he reckoneth to be of so great importance that he esteemeth it to be worthy of a
good reward ; and by this advertisement, and the
other of the *Fires*,* he saith may well appear what
good-will he hath to do good service.   And of those

---

* In a letter, dated prior to this, which is not printed, Harpax had communicated to Wotton an invention of a particular
Fire, something similar to the Greek fire, which was to be
used by the enemy against the English.

two matters of Berteville, and the Fires, he is ever in
hand with me as often as he cometh to me; which is
oftener than I would, for of late the Constable hath
sent him twice or thrice with letters to me. He
saith also, that divers merchants that traffick into
England find the means to convey letters from their
ambassador in England into Scotland : and therefore he would advise my Lord's Grace to cause good
heed. to be taken to such merchants, and specially
to such as complain that our men have done them
wrongs, and thereby have occasion to go from one
place to another in England; for he saith that he
knoweth certainly that under pretence of such complaints, and suing for restitution of wrongs done to
them, some merchants have so conveyed letters into
Scotland by the west parts.

" Harpax saith also, that Francis, who was Mr.
Speke's man, and is now, as I hear, in the Tower of
London, at what time he was here last, laboured
earnestly to the said Harpax to bring him in speech
to De l'Aubespine,* who, seeing his earnest suit,
durst not do otherwise ; and that there the said
Francis made promise to give advertisements of all
that he could learn in England.

" Harpax saith also, that Petro Strozzi intendeth
to do great things in Scotland; whereunto he is
the more minded, partly for the great desire of
praise and glory that pricketh him, partly for to do
such service to the French King that he esteem

* Mons. De l'Aubespine, Secretary of State to the French
King.

him, and take him for the chief and most necessary
man about him, and put him in authority accordingly, and partly for the Queen's sake,* who, as
he saith, hateth our nation of all nations; for she
is exceedingly offended with us for the keeping of
Boulogne, she bearing the name of the house of
Boulogn, and being descended of that stock, and
therefore desireth nothing more than the recovery
of it again out of our hands.   And Petro Strozzi,
being her kinsman, and knowing her mind very well,
hateth us no less than she does; and not only
hateth us, but setteth little by us, and therefore
trusteth and promiseth to bring great matters about
in this journey against us; yea, and trusteth to do
so well in it, that, to have these men our friends, we
shall be glad to re-deliver them Boulogne again.

   " And for because that, as he saith, Petro Strozzi is
subtle and crafty, and will spare no money to practise and corrupt men that will be won for money
or promises, Harpax saith it were well done, to have

---

* *Catherine de' Medici,* only daughter and heiress of Lorenzo
de' Medici, niece of Clement the Seventh, born at Florence in
1519, married in 1553 to Henry the Second, then Dauphin.
Having been for a long time neglected under the reign of Francis
the First, this remarkable woman, on the accession of her husband to the throne, placed herself at the head of a party, and by
her pliant temper and profound dissimulation gradually drew
many to her service : she caressed her rival Diana, the King's
mistress, whom she detested; and whilst she really looked on
the Constable as one of her worst enemies, she stooped to
flatter his pride, and pay the utmost deference to his counsel.—
Anquetil, Hist. de France, vol. vi. p. 471.

a good eye upon the strangers that shall serve the King's Highness in these matters in Scotland.

" He saith also, that though Petro Strozzi be both hardy and crafty as any man is, yet that his great desire of glory doth often blind his wit, and make him attempt things exceeding and passing his power; as he saith that, in the last war, he offered to set upon all our navy with two galleys only. Harpax, in all his communications, seemeth to bear a great hatred to the said Petro Strozzi, for Baron De la Gardie's sake, of whose trouble and ruin the said Strozzi is chief or only cause; and he speaketh very earnestly, and sweareth that he will work by all means possible to be avenged of him, and to do him displeasure; whereupon he saith that he studieth and museth continually, as he will further declare to my Lord Protector's Grace, if he come into England.

" He saith also, that there go at this time into Scotland five or six hundred gentlemen. He saith also, that it is out of doubt that the King of Denmark* sendeth great aid of men and victuals into Scotland, to the number, as he heareth, of thirty ships, one or other; and that the French King entertaineth him with hope that his brother shall marry the Scottish Queen, though the French King intendeth nothing less indeed.

" These things, also, I pray you to declare to my Lord's Grace. And thus Jesu preserve you!

" N. Wotton."

* Christiern the Third.

HENRY THE SECOND about this time incurred great odium for his project of creating a diversion in his favour, during his wars with the Emperor, by bringing in the Turks upon Christendom: his object being to keep Ferdinand employed at home in defending his dominions against the infidels, and thus prevent him from assisting Charles the Fifth. It was this conduct which drew from Sir John Mason the pithy remark, that, if the Devil were to be had as an ally, Henry would not scruple to entertain him ; and it is to this that Wotton alludes in the following extract from one of his letters to the Protector and Council. It proves also that the French intrigues with the Sultan commenced at a much earlier period than is assigned to them by Sismondi, the latest French historian. *

N. WOTTON TO THE PROTECTOR AND COUNCIL.

Orig. ST. P. OFF. *France.*   April 20th, 1548.   *Sens.*

" * * THE gentleman whom the French King had sent to the Turk, is returned, and hath brought such answer from Le Grand Seignor, that these men show themselves to rejoice much at it ; and with the said gentleman is come hither, as I hear, the Count of Regendorff, otherwise called Monsieur De Condy, who fled away from the Emperor's court and came to the Turk. The which Regendorff is much made of here in this court. * *

* Sismondi, Hist. des Français, vol. xviii. p. 417.

The King goeth hence to Troyes, where he will make his entry about the beginning of the next month."

In the spring of the year 1548, SIR PHILIP HOBY was sent by the Protector to supersede the Bishop of Westminster as Ambassador at the court of the Emperor. Hoby had already been employed by Henry the Eighth in some foreign diplomatic missions. We shall afterwards meet with him in 1549, taking a leading part in the contest between the Protector Somerset and Warwick; and in 1552, in the capacity of a colleague of the Marquis of Northampton, when this nobleman was sent to France to negociate the marriage of Edward the Sixth to the Lady Elizabeth, daughter of Henry the Second. He died in 1558. The most interesting part of the following letter is that which relates to Melancthon's sentiments concerning the *Interim*.

BISHOP OF WESTMINSTER AND SIR P. HOBY TO THE LORD PROTECTOR AND THE COUNCIL.

Orig. ST. P. OFF. 5th June 1548. *Augsbourg.*

" PLEASETH your most honourable Lordships to be advertised that I, Sir Philip Hobby, arrived here the first day of this month, and after conference and consideration had, as well of the King's Majesty's instructions given to me, Sir P. H., as also of your most honourable letters sent to me by the Bishop of Westminster, we sued for audience to the

Emperor, and had the same granted to us this day; but by reason, this night past, the Emperor was diseased of a flux, we be now in doubt whether we shall have audience this night, or be deferred till to-morrow, and have thought good thus much to advertise your Lordships.

"Herewith your Lordships shall receive a copy of a letter concerning the *Interim*, sent from Melancthon to Carolowicius, one of Duke Maurice's Councillors. Because it was brought to us undeciphered by one of the Emperor's physicians, I, the Bishop of Westminster, suppose that they be the gladder to show it, for that Melancthon yieldeth so much to their purpose, and openeth also an unreasonable manner of dealing with him of those that were beginners of the Protestant faction; and yet, in words, they pretend to show hereby the frowardness of Melancthon, for that he will not wholly condescend to the said *Interim*.

"Mr. Mont hath been advertised that the learned men of Wittimberg and Leipsic have sent also to Duke Maurice of late their judgment upon the *Interim*; but that by no means will be showed, albeit suit hath been made therefore by such as have great friendship and familiarity with the said Duke Maurice's Councillors: therefore it is supposed that this their said judgment is not conformable to their desires here. * * *

"Whereas I, the Bishop of Westminster, have received commandment of the King's Majesty to

take my leave of the Emperor, and so with convenient diligence to return, and also to communicate
with Mr. Hobby all such things as I shall think
may conduce to his Majesty's service here, *   *
I shall not fail, to the best of my power, most
humbly and faithfully to accomplish his Majesty's
commandment herein. Thus Almighty God preserve your good Lordships! &c.

" From Augsbourg, the 25th June 1548.

" THOS. WEST^R.   PHILIP HOBY."

The Bishop of Westminster and Sir Philip Hoby
were admitted soon after to an interview with the
Emperor; of which we find an account in a letter
dated 11th June, addressed by them to the Protector. It is not, however, of much interest.
Charles wrapt himself up, as he was wont to do, in
expressions of general good-will to England and to
Edward, but refused to entangle his politics with
any promise of assisting the Protector against
France. The ambassadors had afterwards a private
audience of Granvelle, who was less guarded, and
spoke with great vehemence against the French,
and their war in Scotland. They describe the
Spanish minister as talking mildly up to a certain
point, and then bursting into a sudden rage.
" The Frenchmen (said he) brave, and think
thereby to outface the world; but I trust they
shall therewith little prevail. They have made
earnest request to have the succour of our havens

for their navy, in the aid of Scotland; but my master is therewith nothing contented, but hath answered that the Scots be his enemies, and the King of England his good brother and friend, whose league of amity he mindeth to entertain to the uttermost." *

It appears by an interesting letter of Hoby's, printed by Strype, that the Emperor used every possible method,—by intreaty, threatening, and durance,—to prevail on that magnanimous old man, the Elector of Saxony, to subscribe the *Interim*. Granvelle dined with him, treated him most gently, seized the *mollia tempora fandi*, but found him inexorable; upon which, Charles, being much moved, ordered three hundred Spanish soldiers to surround his lodging, disarmed his retinue, sent away the greater number of his servants, dismissed his Preacher, threatening to burn him unless he instantly left the country, and commanded his cooks, upon pain of being roasted on their own fires, not to cook any flesh for the Elector on Fridays and Saturdays: and yet, continueth Hoby, "there can be no alteration perceived in him in word or countenance; but he is even now as merry and as content, to the outward show, as he was at any time of his utmost prosperity."†

Our next letter carries us from Augsbourg to

---

* Bishop of Westminster and Sir P. Hoby to the Protector. June 11th. 1548.   Orig. St. P. Off.

† Strype's Memor. vol. ii. part ii. p. 396.

England. We have already been admitted to the history of the Lord Admiral's love to the Queen Dowager. Since we last met with this ambitious man, he had advanced in the road to greatness by his marriage with Catherine Parr ; an event which for a time was kept secret, but at last circumstances rendered this impossible. The Protector was at first much incensed at the presumption of his brother, but afterwards became reconciled to him. In Haynes' Collection, p. 62, we find a *naïve* letter from the Queen to her husband, the Admiral, in which, alluding to her situation, she takes it for granted that the little stranger is assuredly to be *" a little knave,"* that is, a boy. This letter, which is undated, appears to have been an answer to the following characteristic epistle from the Lord Admiral to the Queen.

LORD ADMIRAL TO THE QUEEN.

Orig. St. P. Off. *Domestic.* 9th June 1548. *Westminster.*

"AFTER my humble commendations and thanks for your letter. As I was perplexed heretofore with unkindness, that I should not have justice of those that I thought would in all my causes [have] been partial, which did not a little trouble me ; even so, the receiving of your letter revived my spirits ; partly for that I do perceive that you be armed with patience, howsoever the matter will weigh ; as chiefest, that I hear my little man doth *shake his poll,*

trusting, if God should give him life to live as long
as his father, he will revenge such wrongs as neither
you nor I can, at this present, the [turmoil] is such.
—God amend it!

" Now to put you in some hope again: this day, a
little before the receiving of your letter, I have spoken to my lord, whom I have so well handled that
he is somewhat qualified ; and although I am in no
hope thereof, yet I am in no despair.   I have also
broken with him for your mother's gift, who makes
answer, that at the finishing of your matter either to
have yours again, or else some recompense as ye
shall be content withall.   I spake to him of your
going down into the country on Wednesday, who
was sorry thereof, trusting that I would be here all
to-morrow to hear what the Frenchmen will do; and
on Monday [at] dinner I trust to be with you, as
for the Frenchmen I have no mistrust that they
shall be any let of my going with you this journey,
or any of my continuance there with your Highness: and thus, till that time, I bid your Highness
most heartily well to fare, and thank you for your
news, which were right heartily welcome to me.
And so I pray you to show him, with God's blessing
and mine ; and of all good wills and friendship I do
desire your Highness to keep the *little knave* so
lean and gaunt with your good diet and walking,
that he may be so small that he may creep out of a
mouse-hole.   And I bid my most dear and well-beloved wife most heartily well to fare.

" From Westminster, this Saturday, the 9th of
June.

   " Your Highness's most

     " faithful, loving husband,

       " T. SEYMOUR."

" *To the Queen's Highness*
 at Hantworth."

Alas for the uncertainty of human wishes, and
the hardness of human hearts! The little knave
never did *shake his poll* in anger against the Protector, or avenge his father's imagined wrongs:
first, because he turned out to be a *Daughter;* and
secondly, because death followed hard on the heels
of life,—the mother dying on the 5th of Sept. only
four days after her delivery; and this pretty blos-
som being also nipped by death in early infancy.
And as for heart, the Admiral had scarce buried
" his dear and well-beloved wife," ere he went in
his suits of woe to renew his courtship of the
youthful Lady Elizabeth, with whom he had
already carried on an extraordinary and somewhat
indelicate flirtation, as is well known to the reader
of Haynes' State Papers.*

We are made acquainted in our next letter
with Sir Thomas Smith, one of the greatest
scholars in England during the reigns of Edward
the Sixth and Mary; and, be it spoken to his

* Haynes, pp. 96-99.

honour, one of the few upright and consistent
men during that trying æra.   He was the son
of John Smith of Saffron Walden, an Essex squire
of good family; and by his mother, Agnes Char-
nock, was descended from an ancient house in
Lancashire.   Where he received the rudiments of
his education is not certain; but at the early age
of twelve he became a student of Queen's College, Cambridge, of which he was chosen a fellow
in 1531.   About this time, Smith applied himself so
enthusiastically to the acquisition of Greek, that he
became a perfect master in that noble language,
and in 1535 was appointed to read the Greek Lec-
ture ; nor is it mean praise to say of him, that, in
classical studies, he was worthy to be the instructor
of Ascham, and a fellow-labourer with Erasmus and
Cheke.   " When Smith and Cheke," says Jortin,
" attempted to correct the pronunciation of the
Greek language at Cambridge, Gardiner, the Chancellor of the University, who hated all reformation,
stuck to his *Mumpsimus,* and set forth an absurd
and an impudent decree forbidding all such innovations. * *   Much about the same time, the doctors
of the Theological faculty at Paris maintained that
quis, qualis, ought to be pronounced *kis, kalis;* they
also contended that *ego amat* was as good Latin as
ego amo." †

In 1539 Smith enriched his mind by foreign tra-

† Jortin's Life of Erasmus, vol. i. p. 386.

vel, visiting the Universities of France and Italy; and having taken the degree of Doctor of Civil Law at Padua, he returned to England about 1542, where he soon after became Regius Professor of Civil Law in the University of Cambridge. His domestic establishment at this time is quaintly described by Strype: " He kept three servants, three guns, and three winter geldings; and this stood him in thirty pounds per annum, together with his own board." *

In 1548 Smith was knighted, and became Secretary of State under the Protector Somerset, to whom he was warmly attached. In June of the same year, he was sent, with his brother-in-law, Thomas Chamberlayne, as we see from the following letter, Ambassador to the Emperor. In this embassy the Protector had two objects in view : the first, to persuade Charles the Fifth to take part with England against the French, then becoming too formidable in Scotland ; the second, to raise, with the permission of the Emperor, a body of two thousand mercenaries to serve in England. In a note to Smith's Life in the Biographia Britannica, we find a letter from him to the Duke of Somerset, dated July 19th, at Brussels, taken from the Cottonian collection. The following short letter was written immediately after their arrival :

* Strype's Life of Smith, p. 28.

SIR THOMAS SMITH TO CECIL.

Orig. St. P. Off. *Flanders.* 1st July 1548.

" Gentle Mr. Cecil, at Brussels we arrived on Friday at night : the Queen being gone to Binks on hunting, we could not speak with her Majesty, yet I trust on Tuesday or Wednesday we shall. My Lord of Westminster came a little before us to Brussels, and shortly will be in England. Here is all things quiet, without any suspicion of war either with France or any other. The Emperor, they say, sacketh still in Germany, and is very lusty. I do marvel at nothing than that all this way no man knoweth of the burning of Ard till we have told it ; so that it maketh me almost to be afraid that that was not done indeed which we saw with our eyes, both overnight the fire, and the smoke in the morning, coming from Calais.

" I long now to hear tell of my Lord of Winchester's summons ; and how he hath demeaned himself therein, and after it. * * * Have me commended to Mr. Steward, and my other friends ; and fare you well, &c.

" Yours assuredly,

" T. Smith."

The reader will remark the anxiety which Smith expresses in the conclusion of this letter to know something of the manner in which my Lord of Winchester had demeaned himself at his summons.   He alludes here to the noted Gardiner, Bishop of Winchester, who had been committed to the Tower, on the 30th June 1548, for some expressions employed in a sermon preached before the Court, in which the prelate, although he admitted the supremacy of the King, treated the Council with great contempt.* His expected examination seems to have made a considerable noise at this time.—Warwick, in a letter to Cecil, dated June 14th, thus alludes to it :

" Being desirous to hear whether my Lord hath proceeded with the *arrogant* Bishop according to his deservings, is the chief occasion of my writing to you at this time.   I did hear that his day to be before my Lords and the Council was appointed as yesterday; but, if it had been so, I suppose it would have been more spoken of : but I rather fear that his accustomed wiliness, with the persuasions of some of his dear friends and assured brethren, shall be the cause that the Fox shall yet again deceive the Lion." †

The Fox, however, whether rightfully or not, continued to be caged within the Tower; for, on the fall of Somerset in 1549, he addressed a letter to Warwick, now Duke of Northumberland, and the Council, from that prison.—" My Lords," said he, " I have continued here in this miserable prison now one year, one quarter, and one month, this

* Article Gardiner, Biog. Brit. p. 2107.
† Orig. St. P. Off.

same day that I write these my letters, with want
of air to relieve my body, want of books to relieve my mind, want of good company—the only
solace in this world, and finally, want of a just
cause why I should have come hither at all."*
This letter, says Stowe, the Lords received in good
part, laughed very merrily thereat, and said he had
a pleasant head; but they took no steps for his en-
largement, and he continued in the Tower till the
accession of Mary. It has been well observed by
the author of Gardiner's Life in the Biographia Britannica, (which, although too much of a pleading for
the Bishop, is well worthy of study,) that, according
to Bale, this Bishop of Winchester was a devil in-
carnate; according to Pits, a very angel of light.
Fox has blackened him in his coarse, and often
careless, manner; Father Parsons, on the other
hand, (in his Warn. Word, p. 34,) pronounces him
the mildest and most compassionate of men: and
thus the prelate has descended to our times in
so perplexing a masquerade, that it is impossible to
discern his true features. If we believe Poynet, his
successor in the See of Winchester, his outward
man could scarcely have been human. " This Doctor," says he, " hath a swart colour. He had
a hanging look, frowning brows, eyes an inch
within the head, a nose hooked like a buzzard,
nostrils like a horse, ever snuffing in the wind, a

* Stowe's Annals, p. 600, quoted in Biog. Brit. Article
Gardiner.

sparrow mouth, and great paws, like the devil's talons, on his feet."

Whilst Somerset, embarrassed with his war in Scotland, the incipient discontents amongst the Commons at home, and the threatened hostility of France, scarce knew where to turn for assistance; his brother, the Lord Admiral, continued his intrigues against his government. One of his great objects was to gain the affection and confidence of the young King; for which end he often supplied Edward with money, and encouraged him in the idea that he was kept in leading-strings by the Protector, stript of every privilege and enjoyment which a young monarch ought to possess, whilst all the influence and effulgence of royalty were concentrated in the person of his Governor.

In these designs to supplant his brother, Lord Seymour was assisted by John Fowler, one of the gentlemen of Edward's privy chamber. The following letter from Fowler to the Lord Admiral shows how artfully and successfully they worked.

JOHN FOWLER TO MY LORD ADMIRAL.
Orig. St. P. Off. *Domestic.* 19th July 1548.

" I MOST humbly thank your Lordship for your letter dated the 15th of this present, which letter I showed to the King's Majesty : and whereas, in my last letter to your Lordship, I wrote unto you, if his Grace could get any spare time, his Grace would write a letter to the Queen's Grace, and to you, his Highness desires your Lordship to pardon him, for his Grace is not *half a quarter of an hour alone :* but such leisure as his Grace had, his Majesty has written, here inclosed, his recommendations to the Queen's Grace and to your Lordship, that he is so much bound to you that he must needs remember you always ; and, as his Grace may have time, you shall well perceive by such small lines of recommendations with his own hand.

" News I have none to write to your Lordship, but that we have good hope that Haddington shall be able to bide this great brunt. The King's Majesty looks every hour for good news ; for, as they come, my Lord's Grace sends the letters to the King's Majesty.

" My Lady of Somerset is brought to bed of a goodly boy, thanks be to God ; and I trust in Almighty God the Queen's Grace shall have another. The King's Majesty shall christen my Lord's Grace's son. I cannot tell your Lordship whether his Grace shall go to Shene himself or not, for as yet the child is unchristened.

" I must, among other news, declare unto your Lordship that my Lord Protector's Grace is so good lord unto me, that his Grace hath given me the keeping either of the great park of Petworth, or else of Wellawynton, whether I will chuse ; and, Monday next, I intend, God willing, to go into Sussex and see them.

" I desire your Lordship, when you send me any

letters, let them be delivered to myself; trusting, also, your Lordship will provide that this shall tell no more tales after your reading; for now I write at length to your Lordship, because I am promised of a trusty messenger. And thus I commit your Lordship to Almighty God, who preserve your Lordship with the Queen's Grace, and all yours, to his pleasure! Written in haste, at Hampton Court, this 19th of July.

   " Your Lordship's most bounden,

        " JOHN FOWLER.

 " I had forgotten to declare to your Lordship concerning the money your Lordship would my friend should have: when he has need, I shall be bold to send."

The " *small lines of recommendations,*" writ with the young King's own hand, are enclosed in this letter of Fowler's. They are as follows:

 " MY LORD. Send me for Latimer as much as ye think good, and deliver it to Fowler.

        " EDWARD."

 " To my Lord Admiral."

The second is, if possible, still more laconic.

 " MY LORD. I thank you, and pray you to have me recommended to the Queen."

The minute, torn, and shabby scraps of paper on which these royal notes are written, seem to indicate the haste and secrecy which Edward was obliged to use. *

In 1548, the Protector Somerset appointed Commissioners to enquire into the abuses arising out of the decay of tillage, and the too frequent enclosing of land for pasturage ; a system by which, as it was reported, the "realm was brought to a marvellous desolation,—houses decayed, parishes diminished, the force of the realm weakened, and Christian people, by the greedy covetousness of some men, eaten up and devoured of brute beasts, and driven from their houses by sheep and bullocks." †

One of the commissioners appointed to investigate the causes of these disasters was JOHN HALES, Clerk of the Hanaper to Edward the Sixth. He is styled, by Strype, a learned and good man ; and the following letter not only justifies the character, but presents us with some interesting information, on the condition of the rural peasantry, and the state of public feeling in England at this period.‡

JOHN HALES TO THE LORD PROTECTOR.

Orig. St. P. Off. *Domestic.* July 24th, 1548.

" I MOST humbly beseech your Grace not to think that I go about to flatter you, whilst I go about to

---

* The reader will find more on this subject in Haynes, pp. 74, 75.

† Strype's Memorials, vol. i. part i. p. 145.

‡ Strype, Eccles. Memor. vol. ii. part ii. p. 351, gives Hales' Charge on Enclosures.

advertise you of that perchance shall please you. I mean no such thing: but as it is requisite that, when a man hath done evil, he should be thereof warned, to the intent he may amend his fault; even so is it convenient that, when a man hath done well, he should know it, to the intent that, confessing from whom he received the grace to do well, he may give Him worthy thanks therefore, and desire Him to continue and increase His grace in him, that he may do more good.

"The people in all the Circuit that we have passed, (and now for the first time [it] is almost ended,) who were suspected to be disobedient, and inclined to sedition, we find most tractable, obedient, and quiet, and of such nature that they may easily be brought to do any thing that is for God's glory and the King's honour.   If they had Justices of peace and Preachers that were as well minded to further God's [honour, and the King's party,] as they be desirous to receive the same, all these imaginations and suspicions of civil wars and sedition should be proved to be utterly false, and only invented to suppress God's word, if it might so be brought to pass.

"The people confess themselves most bound to God that he hath sent them such a King, in whose so tender age so much good is intended towards them; and have a great hope that the *Iron* world is now at an end, and the *Golden* is returning again. They perceive, also, your Grace's great zeal and love toward them, and neither his Majesty nor your Grace lack praise and prayers therefore. If the thing go forward, and may take place,—as, if it do not, the Realm will shortly be brought to a miserable case,—there was never King that had so many faithful and assured subjects as his Grace shall have ; nor ever governor under a King that had so many men's hearts and good-wills as your Grace shall be assured of. If there be any way or policy of man to make the people receive, embrace, and love God's word, it is only this,—when they shall see that it bringeth forth so goodly fruit, that men seek not their own wealth, nor their private commodity, but, as good members, the universal wealth of the whole body. Surely God's word is that precious balm that must increase comfort, and cherish that godly charity between man and man, which is the sinews that tie and hold together the members of every Christian Commonwealth, and maketh one of us to be glad of another.

" Your Grace, weighing what advancement of God's glory hereby shall follow,—how much the King's honour and safety shall increase,—what honour, fame, and love your Grace thereby shall achieve,—and what wealth will thereby universally grow to the whole realm ; albeit these worldlings think that it shall be but a money matter, yet am I fully persuaded, and certainly do believe in your Grace's sayings, that, maugre the Devil, private profit, self-love, money, and such like the Devil's instruments, it shall go forward, and set such a stay in the body of the commonwealth, that all the members shall live in a due temperament and harmony, without one having too much, and a great many nothing at all, as at this present it appeareth plainly they have.

" By reason that the like Commissions be not heard of in other parts of the realm, we be thought men only bent or set to do displeasure to some men in these parts. If it might please your Grace that the rest might proceed, we should avoid all slander ; and the thing being done before the Parliament, all our world then might be informed what hurt hath grown, and what is like to follow to the realm, if it be not in time resisted.

" To advertise your Grace of any specialty we thought it not good, till in our next Circuit we shall have received the *presentments;* for, hitherto, we have done nothing but given them their charge. Howbeit, we hear that there is great labour made to corrupt the jurors, and large money offered to men to sue to be sheriffs the next year; so that if any thing be now presented, yet [upon their] having the sheriffs to their friends, they may have friendly Inquests,—such as will be contented to lend them an oath or two if need shall be.

" But if the matter be handled as it hath been in time past in the Exchequer, that the King's Attorney and the King's Solicitor may put in and put out, do and undo what they list, your Grace's intent shall be frustrated, and our labours spent in vain. Thus, taking my leave of your Grace, I pray God long preserve you with much increase of honour !

" From Windsor, the 22d July 1548.

" Your Grace's most humble to command,

" JOHN HALES."

Its domestic tone, and the light it throws on the mode of *posting* in England in 1548, render the following letter interesting. Of the facetious writer himself, or the errand upon which he was sent by Cecil, I can discover no traces; still less of his old friend Mr. Trigg.

THOMAS FISHER TO CECIL.

Orig. ST. P. OFF. *Domestic.* 27th July 1548. *Stamford.*

" SIR. After all hearty commendations ; albeit I have been but ill-favoredly handled hitherto of post-horses, and specially on the post at Royston, who played a very lubberly part with me, (tho' too long to write, but understand it, I prithee, to be very lewd), I therefore promised him, and that not without some *melancholy* terms, that I would signify part of his forwardness, and trusted, as I said to him, that he should hear somewhat thereof from the Master of the Posts ; wherefore I beseech you require Mr. Mason that in some [of] his next despatches it will please him to take occasion of a quarrel of this said post on my behalf. And unless that he, and such others as he is, be sometimes remembered by the Master, in faith, neither I, nor any other that shall pass in post, can be able to make such speed as might be required of them in cases.

" Well, Sir, I am at the last here arrived, about two of the clock this afternoon, with much ado, I assure you, because of store of rain fallen this last night in these parts, (as the Devil would,) which hath so en[dangered] the way,—I mean, made it so slippery,—that a better gelding than any of these post-horses might scant be able to hold his feet. Well, I swat for fear; and, as we rode by the way, both my back and sides, with also my man and the guide, did full well mark the chafes, and now and then with head and shoulders. And at our being within four miles of this town, we were so intrapt with a *short* shower of rain and great hail, of no less than *three hours' length,* that my Lord Privy Seal's hedge at Thornhaws, not able to hold out, we made a hole to [squeeze our way thro'] from thence hither, as our garments and skins can witness; for here I am enforced to shift me, and my servant likewise, who is so pitifully arrayed with rain and plain dirt, (saving your reverence,) that, as I [hope] to be saved, I fear I shall leave him behind me, either here or at Grangemouth.

" As for thunder, hail, rain, and lightning, your country lacketh none ; I pray God continue it, so as I were rid out of it, as presently I am ready to my saddle with a lame jade. And so assuring you that your father and mother, with your son, are merry and in good health, as my old friend Mr. Trigg telleth me, God keep you. At Stamford, this Friday, at four in the afternoon, 1548, 27th July. I remembered an old housewife's proverb, that of an hard beginning cometh, I trust, a good and merry ending.

" Yours, assured to command,

" Tho. Fisher."

" I pray you let this make my hearty commendations to your bedfellow, and also Mr. Steward Jenkin ; and, amongst the rest, at your leisure, I pray you to my old wedlock Wenefield."

" *To the Right Worshipful Mr. William Cecill, Esquier,*
    Master of the Requests, *attendant upon*
    my Lord Protector's Grace."

The early ambition of the Lord Admiral Seymour to supplant his brother, the Protector, has been already noticed. It is evident, from the following letter, addressed to him by Somerset, that complaints had been made against his tyrannical conduct as early as September 1st, 1548. It shows, at the same time, that the temper with which such complaints were received by the Duke was kind and conciliating, though firm. He felt that the unscrupulous and unjust attacks of his brother upon his poor neighbours required a check, and that it was a principal duty which he owed to the high office he occupied " to receive poor men's com-

plaints ;" but he was inclined to remonstrate affectionately, and to hope for amendment rather than
to punish with suddenness or rigour. It is the
more necessary to attend to this proof of Somerset's feelings towards the Admiral, as the latest
English historian, whose high name must give
weight to his opinions, appears to have written
that portion of his work which treats of the fate of
Lord Seymour, without giving himself much trouble
to investigate the truth. From the tone he takes,
the reader would be led to condemn the Protector
as cruel, lawless, and unnatural ;* and to pity the
Admiral, as his almost unoffending victim. The
very reverse seems to have been the case.

THE PROTECTOR TO THE LORD ADMIRAL.

Orig. St. P. Off. *Domestic.* 1st Sept. 1548. *Sion.*

" After our right hearty commendations to
your good Lordship. We have received your long
letters of the date of the 27th of August, to the
particularities whereof at this present we are not
minded to answer, because it requireth more leisure than at this time we have, and therefore shall
leave it until that we shall meet, when we may
more fully declare unto you our mind in those
matters.

" But, in the mean while, we cannot but marvel
that you note the way to be so open for complaints
to enter in against you, and that they be so well

* History of England, by Sir J. Mackintosh, vol. ii. pp. 255,
257.

received. If you do so behave yourself amongst your
poor neighbours, and others the King's subjects,
that they may have easily just cause to complain
upon you, and so you do make them a way and
cause to lament unto us and pray redress, we are
most sorry therefore, and would wish very heartily
it were otherwise; which were both more honour
for you, and quiet and joy and comfort to us. But
if you mean it, that for our part we are ready to
receive poor men's complaints, that findeth or
thinketh themselves injured or grieved, it is our
duty and office so to do. And tho' you be our brother, yet we may not refuse it upon you. How well
we do receive them, it may appear in our letters ;
where we lament the case unto you, and exhort,
pray, and admonish you so earnestly as we can, that
you yourself would redress the same, that there
should no occasion be given to any man to make
such complaints of you to us.

" In the which thing we do yet persist both in
Sir John Brigg's matter and the other, that you
should yourself look more deeply of the matter,
and not seek extremity against your neighbour
and kinsman, or others the King's Majesty's subjects ; but to obtain your desire by some other
gentle means, rather than by seeking that which
is either plain injury, or else the rigour and extremity of the law, and that poked out by the
words, which, peradventure, coming to learned
and indifferent men's judgments, may receive ac-

cording to equity and conscience a more gentle interpretation than a man in his own case, as he is affectionated, would judge.

" And this we do, not condemning you in every thing we write; for, before we have heard the answer, our letters be not so. But if the complaints be true, we require, as reason would, redress; and that you should the more earnestly look upon them, seeing you do perceive that the complaints do come to us. The which thing, coming as well of love towards you as of our office, can minister no occasion to you of any such doubt as you would make in the latter end of your letters.

" We would wish rather to hear that all the King's subjects were of you gently and liberally entreated with honour, than that any one should be said to be of you either injured or extremely handled. Such is the *hard affection* we do bear towards you, and so glad we be to hear any complaints of you.

" Thus we bid your Lordship right heartily farewell. From Syon, the 1st of Sept. 1548.

" Your loving brother,

" E. Somerset."

" *To our very good Lord and brother,*
  the Lord Admiral of England."

Somerset, on the very day that he wrote in this admonitory tone to his brother, received the news of Queen Catherine's confinement; and ad-

dressed to him the following letter, which proves, I
think, how sincerely he loved him.   Could such
a letter have come from the heart that " devised
the Admiral's destruction," as Hayward would have
us believe ?*   It is evident, from an expression he
employs, that Lord Seymour had been dabbling in
judicial astrology, and was the dupe of a prophecy
that, although the first child born to him was a
daughter, it should be the forerunner " of a great sort
of happy sons."—But the delusion was a brief one.

THE PROTECTOR SOMERSET TO THE LORD ADMIRAL.

Orig.   St. P. Off.   *Domestic.*   1st Sept. 1548.

" AFTER our right hearty commendations.

" We are right glad to understand by your letters that the Queen, your bedfellow, hath had a
happy hour ; and, escaping all danger, hath made
you the father of so pretty a daughter.   And
although (if it had so pleased God) it would have
been both to us, and we suppose also to you, a
more joy and comfort if it had been this the first a
son ; yet the escape of the danger, and the prophecy
and good *hansell* of this to a great sort of happy
sons, the which, as you write, we trust no less than
to be true, is no small joy and comfort to us, as we
are sure it is to you and to her Grace also; to whom
you shall make again our hearty commendations,

* Hayward, Life of Edward the Sixth.   Kennett, vol. ii.
p. 302.

with no less gratulation of [such] good success. Thus we bid you right heartily farewell."

> " From Sion, the first of Sept. 1548.

>> " Your loving brother,

>>> " E. SOMERSET."

" *To our very good Lord and brother,*
  the Lord Admiral of England."

The daughter who is here mentioned by the Protector was named Mary, and, after the execution of her father, was delivered to the keeping of the Duchess of Suffolk, with whom she lived at Grimsthorp in Lincolnshire. She died, as we have already said, in early infancy. In Strype's Memorials we find this high character of the Queen her mother : " She was endued with a pregnant wittiness, joined with right wonderful grace of eloquence; studiously diligent in acquiring knowledge, as well of other human disciplines as also of the Holy Scriptures; of incomparable chastity, which she kept not only from all spot, but from all suspicion, by avoiding all occasions of idleness, and contemning provocations of vain pastimes." *

We have already seen that Sir Philip Hoby suc-

---

* Strype's Memor. vol. ii. part i, pp. 201-2. There are strange contradictions in Mr. Lodge's Lives or Characters of two persons so intimately connected as Queen Catherine Parr and her husband the Admiral. In the Queen's Life, he doubts whether she was ever delivered at all. " It has been commonly asserted," says he, " that she died in childbirth;" a *report* which, adverting to the fact that she had been childless in three previous marriages, might reasonably be doubt-

ceeded the Bishop of Westminster as resident ambassador at the court of the Emperor. The following letter addressed by this knight to the Lord Admiral, though verbose, is valuable from the clear and authentic view which it affords of the policy of Charles the Fifth at this period, and of the incipient jealousies and suspicions between this potentate and the French King.

SIR PHILIP HOBY TO THE LORD ADMIRAL.

Orig. St. P. Off. *Louvain.* 16th Sept. 1548.

" MY VERY GOOD LORD. After my most hearty commendations unto your Lordship. I have not since my coming hither written unto you any of these occurrents here, knowing that your Lordship hath been from time to time ascertained of the same by my letters unto my Lord Protector's Grace; which, I doubt not, have been communicated unto your Lordship: but now, lest mine over long silence might rather seem to proceed of forgetfulness than occasioned by the alleged respect, I have presently enterprised to trouble you with these lines of small importance.

" The Emperor having, as well before as since my coming to Augsbourg, spent some time in the ordering and setting forth of the *Interim,* and having

ed. In the Admiral's Life he states, without the slightest reference to his unreasonable scepticism a few pages back, " Lord Seymour was never married but to Catherine Parr, who bore him an only daughter, Mary, born in Sept. 1548."

finally brought the same to conclusion, hath travailed by sundry means to cause it to be accepted and
observed of all States and Cities of Germany : of
whom like as some, compelled thereto by necessity,
(zealing more* the regard of worldly commodity than
the bond of their conscience towards their faith and
duty,) did hereto agree and consent; so were there
other, namely, Constance, Lind, Magdeburgh, and
many places of the Inferior Germany, that utterly
refused to accept and receive the same; offering
rather their lives and goods to the extreme jeopardy
than to suffer themselves to be *spotted* with this
new kind of doctrine : which sort of proceedings
like as the Emperor nothing liked, so did he by
sundry ways attempt to redress the same; but
finally perceiving his diligence therein smally to
profit, and that neither secret practice nor open
show of gentleness could, in the winning of these
men's hearts thereto, any thing prevail,—having first
attempted by sudden surprise the winning of Constance, at which journey (as your Lordship hath I
am sure heard) he lost, besides the repulse of a
number of Spaniards sent thither for that purpose,
his master of camp, captain of the said band, named
Don Alonso Vives, the said captain's son, and sundry other, †—he began now at the length somewhat

* Zealing—anxiously regarding.

† Don Alonzo Vivas, a gallant Neapolitan officer, originally
from Spain.—In this attack of Constance, Sleidan informs us
the Spaniards lost five hundred men, and the citizens one hun-

to relent in these matters of religion ; and fearing, as I guess, that the overstrait sticking thereto might engender a further discommodity than the benefit thereof were able to countervail, willing before his removing from Augsbourg to set some stay for the establishment of that city towards his devotion, he first caused the governance of that town to be clean altered; discharging from the Council there many whom he alleged to be unmeet for that room, and placing such other in their stead as he thought good, all men that both have somewhat to lose, and are also noted to be well-willers to his proceedings. Which order taken, and many days spent in the establishment thereof, he proceeded to the settling of Religion to the contentation (as he thought) of both Protestants and Papists there ; * appointing unto them five Churches wherein, at their

---

dred ; but the Imperialists do not admit they suffered so severely.—De Thou, Book v. sub anno 1548.

* Charles, no doubt, intended to please both Protestants and Romanists, but, as is usual in such cases, he made himself obnoxious to both ; and the Pope, acutely observing this, allowed him to pursue his course unchecked by any remonstrances from Rome. Aware that the INTERIM would be attacked by all parties, his Holiness was desirous that it should be published. " The sharp-sighted old Pope," says Father Paul, " found that the Emperor had overshot himself, and that by thus engaging with all parties he would bring them all upon him." (Beccatelli's Life of Pole, by Pye, p. 66.) The instructions of the Pope to Cardinal Sfondrato were to make a slight opposition to the Interim at first, and to withdraw it at the time of its promulgation.

liberty, to preach and minister after their accustomed manner, prohibiting the Cardinal and others of his faction in that town by any means to disturb them therein, and leaving the rest of the Churches to those priests, friars, and others, that did before possess them.

" His Majesty departed thence the 13th of this instant to Ulm, where he remained only five days ; in which time he took order for the governance of that town, as he had done before at Augsbourg, and is now come hither ; from whence, after a short abode of ten or twelve days, it is supposed he mindeth to repair straight towards the Low Countries, where, being somewhat nearer home, I shall have occasion oftener to write and participate unto my friends such news as shall occur.

" Hitherto hath your Lordship heard briefly discoursed the sum in effect of the state of proceedings in these quarters since my coming hither, and now things rest partly at this stay ; Constance unreconciled to the Emperor, but, in communication thereof, Bresme, Hamburg, Dantzic, Lubeck, Saxony, and other parts of the Inferior Germany, with determination utterly to refuse the acceptation of the *Interim ;* whereat the Emperor, as it seemeth, winketh for a season till he may compass his purpose with better opportunity.

" The Bishop of Rome, nothing satisfied with the Emperor's proceedings in these matters of religion, refuseth to ratify the same by his authority whereunto he hath been by his Majesty required ; staying upon the restitution of Piacenza, which he hath by many means procured to recover, but in vain.   The Emperor resteth nothing satisfied herewith, and therefore (these matters of religion for a time set apart) proceedeth to prepare the prevention of all events, the rather for the conceived suspicion of the French amity, by the new league between the Bishop of Rome and him ; and for this respect, under pretence of the late concluded marriage between the Archduke of Austria and his daughter, he hath of Spain, Naples, and Sicily obtained two millions of gold, which he hath commanded to be received, and reserved untouched till he dispose otherwise thereof. What innovation will follow upon his son's coming to him, who is looked for about the end of October, is uncertain.

" The French King is presently, we say, here at Turin in Piedmont, where he mindeth to rest, some think, till the Prince of Spain be past Italy ; of which abode there, we be not here in this court altogether void of suspicion.

" Certain soldiers of the island of Corsica, to the number of ten, were now lately determined to have slain Don Fernando, the Emperor's lieutenant in Italy ;* whose conspiracy being discovered, and certain of them taken, they confess to have been hired hereto by Signor Octavio, Pietro Aloysius' son,

* Don Ferdinand di Gonzaga, governor of the Milanese under Charles the Fifth.

and other of the house of Farnese, encouraged thereto, as it is reported, by their head, the Bishop of Rome,—a meet enterprise for such a Prelate.

" This letter, having been written at Spires, hath been (by reason this bearer was occasioned to remain here with me till now) stayed till this present ; and since then hath occurred none other news but that th' Emperor, departing from Spires the third of this instant, made such speed in his journey as yesternight he came to this town, from whence, after a short abode of two or three days, he mindeth to repair to Brussels, where some think he will take the Diet.

" Thus fare your good Lordship most heartily well.   From Lovayne, the 16th day of Sept. 1548.
" PHILIP HOBY."

The stern and ambitious heart of Thomas Lord Seymour seems to have been little affected by the death of his wife, the Queen Dowager, which happened, as we have seen, shortly after the birth of her infant.   He had set his hopes on having a son ; and, irritated probably by the disappointment, he was even suspected of having hastened the Queen's death by the harshness with which he treated her. Thus poor Catherine Parr, who with some difficulty had preserved her head from the axe of her third husband, was killed, as it is reported, by her fourth, with a weapon sharper than any axe, — unkindness from one we love.*

* Haynes' State Papers, p. 103. Confession of Elizabeth Tyrwhitt.

The Lord Admiral now aimed at a higher mark : he renewed his secret addresses to the Lady ELIZA- BETH, and he laid a plot for accomplishing the mar- riage of the Lady Jane Grey to the young King. This amiable and accomplished lady was descended, by the mother's side, from Mary, Queen Dowager of France, sister to Henry the Eighth. Mary, as is well known, after the death of her royal husband, Louis the Twelfth, married Charles Brandon, Duke of Suffolk ; and their daughter, Lady Frances Bran- don, having married Henry Grey, Marquis of Dor- set, had the Lady Jane Grey, who became after- wards, for the brief space of nine days, Queen of England. Her engaging qualities, her learning and accomplishments, her meekness and piety, are familiar to all our readers. From an early age she had been brought up and educated by Queen Ca- therine Parr in the household of her husband, the Lord Admiral ; who, upon the death of his wife, imagining that he must break up his establishment, proposed at first to send Lady Jane back to her father and mother. It appears, however, by a let- ter in Haynes,* that he soon repented of this offer ; and, when his ambitious thoughts revived, he retained the high-born child as too rich ' a prize to be so easily parted with. " By my last letters," says he, addressing the Marquis Dor- set on the 17th Sept. " written in a time when, partly with the Queen's Highness' death, I was so

* Haynes, p. 77.

amazed that I had small regard either to myself or to my doings, and partly then thinking that my great loss must presently have constrained me to have broken up and dissolved my whole house, I offered to send my Lady Jane unto you whensoever you would send for her." He then proceeds to say, that having since better advised on the matter, and more deeply considered the extent of his power, he found he could continue his house ; "where shall remain," he adds, " not only the Gentlewomen of the Queen's Highness' Privy Chamber, but also the maids which waited at large, and other women being about her during her life-time, with a hundred and twenty gentlemen and yeomen." At the head of his house he had placed his mother, who, he assures the Marquis, will treat his daughter as if she were her own. To this request of the Lord Admiral, the Marquis and his lady after some slight hesitation consented ; and, having first paid a short visit to her family, the Lady Jane returned to his house, and there remained till the period of his execution.

The following letter was written by the Lady Jane when she was only eleven years old. It seems to have been addressed to the Lord Admiral during a brief absence from his house ; and its date is ascertained, by a contemporary endorsement, to be the 1st October 1548,—not a month after the death of the Queen. Chaloner, in his " *Deploratio acerbæ necis D. Janæ Graiæ*," alludes, amongst her other accomplishments, to the beautiful character in which she wrote ; and the exquisite penmanship of this letter, by a child of eleven years old, amply justifies his encomium.

LADY JANE GREY TO THE LORD ADMIRAL.

Orig. St. P. Off. *Domestic.* 1st Oct. 1548.

" My duty to your Lordship in most humble wise remembered, with no less thanks for the gentle letters which I received from you. Thinking myself so much bound to your Lordship, for your great goodness towards me from time to time, that I cannot by any means be able to recompense the least part thereof, I purposed to write a few rude lines unto your Lordship, rather as a token to show how much worthier I think your Lordship's goodness, than to give worthy thanks for the same; and these my letters shall be to testify unto you, that, like as you have become towards me a loving and kind father, so I shall be always most ready to obey your godly monitions and good instructions, as becometh one upon whom you have heaped so many benefits; and thus, fearing lest I should trouble your Lordship too much, I most humbly take my leave of your good Lordship.

" Your humble servant during my life,

" JANE GRAYE."

Addressed. " *To the Right Honorable and my singular good Lord, the Lord Admiral, give these.*"
Endorsed at the time. " *My Lady Jane, the 1st Oct.* 1548."

Lady Frances Dorset was easily induced to consign her daughter for the second time to the care

of the Lord Admiral.   This is evident from the
following letter.   I have endeavoured in vain to
discover on what ground of relationship she addressed him as her " *loving brother.*"   He had
married the widow of her uncle, Henry the Eighth;
but this surely could never justify the epithet.   If,
however, the point has puzzled the genealogical re-
search of so good a herald as Sir Harris Nicolas,*
it would be absurd in the author to attack it.

LADY FRANCES DORSET TO THE LORD ADMIRAL.

Orig. St. P. Off. *Domestic.* 2nd October 1548.

" MINE OWN GOOD BROTHER,

  " I have received your most gentle and loving
letter, wherein I do perceive your approved good-
will which you bear unto my daughter Jane, for the
which I think myself most bounden to you, for that
you are so desirous for to have her continue with
you.   I trust at our next meeting, which, according
to your own appointment, shall be shortly, we shall
so communicate together as you shall be satisfied,
and I contented ; and forasmuch as this messenger
does make haste away, that I have but little leisure
to write, I shall desire you to take these few lines
in good part : and thus wishing your health and
quietness as my own, and a short despatch of your
business, that I might the sooner see you here, I
take my leave of you, my good brother, for this

* Nicolas, Life of Lady Jane Gray, p. 15.

time. From my Lord's house in Broadgate, the
second of October.

"Your assured friend and loving sister,

"FRANCES DORSET."

Endorsed.

"*To my very good Lord and brother,*
the Lord Admiral."

In the course of these letters we have already
seen something of the restless ambition of the Lord
Admiral Seymour. His intrigues often detected,
and as often pardoned, became so frequent, and his
resolutions to bring about a change in the government so manifest, that it was impossible any longer
to overlook or despise them. The neglect, or in-
dulgence, of his brother had only served to fan an
ambition already too vast, and to encourage those
fierce passions which, from the first, had made him
tyrannical and domineering. He continued his secret intercourse with the servants about the young
King, over whom he maintained an undue influence:
he had gained the heart of the Lady Elizabeth, then
a girl of fifteen, who blushed when his name was
mentioned; he courted popularity, kept an almost
royal establishment, secretly amassed large sums
of money, and was so unguarded as to throw out
speeches by which it was evident he contemplated
some desperate stroke against the Protector and
his government. His practices appear to have
come to a head in January 1548-9; and after one
more vain attempt to reclaim him, upon the part of

Somerset, he was compelled by the Council to institute proceedings against his brother. The Admiral was arrested, sent to the Tower, attainted by Parliament, found guilty of high treason, and executed upon a warrant signed by his own brother. " Hereupon," says Hayward, " many of the nobility cried out upon him that he was a bloodsucker, a murderer, a parricide, a villain, and that it was not fit the King should be under the protection of such a ravenous wolf."* These assertions of the nobles, as well as the remark of the same writer, that the accusations against the Admiral consisted of frivolous and pitiful matters, seem to me to be both equally unfounded.

There can be no doubt, however, that Somerset signed the warrant for his brother's execution; a proceeding unnatural, harsh, and cruel; but, under a minor king, such a formality was probably a miserable necessity arising out of his office as Protector; and none can read the proceedings against the Admiral, as they are detailed in the same authentic record, or study the declarations of the witnesses, as they have been printed by Haynes, without being alike convinced of the guilt of this unfortunate man, and the forgiving disposition of Somerset. It was an abominable piece of tyranny, no doubt, to pass the bill of attainder without the ac-

* Hayward, Life of Edward the Sixth, in Kennett, vol. ii. p. 303.

cused being heard in his own defence; but then, let it be remembered, this was not the tyranny of the Protector, but of the law, as administered in these iron times.

The examinations of the principal witnesses against the Admiral are preserved at Hatfield, in the noble collection of manuscripts belonging to the Marquis of Salisbury. Many of these have been printed by Haynes; but others, perhaps still more curious, exist in the State Paper Office. They leave no doubt upon the mind, that he was engaged in a plot to gain possession of the King's person, supplant Somerset, and install himself in his place; and, as they throw new light on an obscure portion of our history, the reader may be pleased with some extracts.

The first is the examination of the MARQUIS DORSET, father of the Lady Jane Grey, of whom we have spoken so recently. It illustrates the history of this unfortunate lady, and discloses the object with which the Admiral desired to retain her in his house. She was to be a step in the ladder of his ambition,—the first card to be played in his game for unseating the Protector, and obtaining an unlimited influence over the Crown.

Orig. ST. P. OFF. *Domestic.* 1548.

" Hereinafter ensue such matters as have at sundry times been opened to me, HENRY LORD MARQUIS DORSET, by the Lord Seymour, Admiral of England.

" First, immediately after the King our late master's death, one Harrington,* servant to the said Admiral, came to my house at Westminster, and amongst other things showed me that the said Admiral was like to come to great authority; and that being the King's Majesty's Uncle, and placed as he was, he might do me much pleasure ; advising me therefore to resort unto him, and to enter a more friendship and familiarity with him.

" At the same time and place, the said Harrington advised me to be contented that my daughter Jane might be with the said Admiral ; whereunto if I would agree, he said he durst assure me that the Admiral would find the means she should be placed in marriage much to my comfort.   With whom, said I, will he match her ?   Marry, quoth Harrington, I doubt not but you shall see him marry her to the King ; and fear you not but he will bring it to pass, and then shall you be able to help all the friends you have.

" Upon these persuasions of Harrington, I repaired, within se'enight after, to the said Admiral's house at Seymour Place ; and there, talking with him in his garden, he used unto me at more length the like persuasions as had been made by Harrington for the having of my daughter, wherein he showed himself so desirous and earnest, and made me such fair promises, that I sent for my daughter, who re-

---

* See his Examination in Haynes, pp. 82. 84.

mained in his house from that time continually unto the death of the Queen.

" After the Queen's death I sent for my daughter
to come home to my house, where she remained with
me for a little space ; but, shortly after, the Admiral
came to my house himself, and was so earnestly in
hand with me and my wife, that in the end, because
he would have no nay, we were contented she
should again return to his house. At this time and
place he renewed his promise unto me for the marriage of my daughter to the King's Majesty; adding that, if he might once get the King at liberty,
he durst warrant me that his Majesty should
marry my daughter. And at this Sir William
Sherington travailed as earnestly with my wife for
her good-will to the return of my daughter, as the
Admiral did with me ; so as in the end, after long
debating and much sticking of our sides, we did
agree that my daughter should return ; who so did,
and remained at his house until his coming to the
Tower.

" The Admiral said unto me in December last
past, and at sundry other places and times, that he
in no wise liked the doings of my Lord Protector
and Council; and further, he said also to me in the
gallery of his house in London, that he loved not
the Lord Protector, and would have the King have
the honour of his own things, for, said he, of his
years he is wise and well learned ; and said also to
me at the same time, tho' he could not even then

do that he would wish touching this change and alteration, yet, said he, Let me alone; ye shall see I will bring it to pass within these three years.

"When I was with the Admiral at Sudley, which was in the end of summer, and also when he was at my house, which was after Michaelmas, the Admiral, devising with me to make me strong in my country, advised me to keep a good house, and asked me what friends I had in my country; to whom I made answer, that I had divers servants that were gentlemen, well able to live of themselves. That is well, said the Admiral, yet trust not too much to the gentlemen, *for they have somewhat to lose;* but I will rather advise you to make much of the head *Yeomen* and *Frankelyns* of the country, specially those that be the ringleaders, for they be men that be best able to persuade the multitude, and may best bring the number; and therefore I will wish you to make much of them, and to go to their houses, now to one, now to another, carrying with you *a flaggon or two of wine and a pasty of venison,* and to use a familiarity with them, for so shall you cause them to love you, and be assured to have them at your commandment; and this manner, I may tell you, I intend to use myself, said he. ❋ ❋ ❋

"The day of his committing, as we came from the Parliament together, going towards my Lord of Huntingdon's house to dinner, he told me that the Earl of Rutland had accused him to the Council; and after dinner, my Lord of Huntingdon and I, my brother Thomas and Sir Michael Poyntz, came with him to his house, and, walking together in his gallery, he opened such communication as had been between my Lord of Rutland and him, whereof he made a long discourse, showing himself to be much afraid to go to the Council; and said further, that he would not go unless he might have Mr. Comptroller for a pledge to remain in the custody of his servants until his return home back again.   Whereunto my brother Thomas answered, Knowing yourself a true man, why should you doubt to go to your brother, *knowing him to be a man of much mercy?* Wherefore, if you will follow my advice, you shall go to him; and if he list to have you, it is not this house that can keep you, though you have ten times so many men as you have.   And, as this communication was in hand, Mr. Secretary Smith and Mr. Baker came in; upon whose coming, I departed and went to my chamber. * * *

" HENRY DORSETT."

I have given this Examination of the Lord Dorset from the original, signed by himself, as it has been much garbled, and some of the most material parts of it left out, by Haynes, in his volume of State Papers, published from the collections at Hatfield.* It appears that Cecil had preserved abstracts of the Marquis' Confession, made by Secretary Petre ;

* Haynes, pp. 75-77.

which, perhaps with the design of screening this nobleman from being implicated in the treason of the Admiral, are so drawn up as to give a very imperfect account of what had passed between them.

The next paper, which contains a *Conversation* between Russell, the Lord Privy Seal, and the Admiral, as they were riding to the Parliament, is not only important in the light it reflects upon the plots of the Admiral, but interesting from the dramatic form into which it is thrown. It is difficult for those who have seen the beautiful apostolic-looking head of Lord Russell, by Holbein,* its mild eye and venerable expression, to believe it should belong to the swearing old Lord, who, under the name of " Father Russell," figures in the following dialogue. It is entitled

" CERTAIN COMMUNICATIONS BETWIXT THE LORD PRIVY SEAL AND THE LORD ADMIRAL."

Orig. ST. P. OFF. *Domestic.* 1548.

" RIDING one day together with my Lord Admiral, as we followed my Lord Protector towards the Parliament House, I said unto him, My Lord Admiral, there are certain rumours bruited of you which I am very sorry to hear.

" My Lord Admiral demanded what the same should be.

" I showed him I was informed he made means

---

* See Chamberlayne's Collection of Engravings from the original drawings of Holbein, in Her Majesty's collection.

to *marry* either with my Lady Mary or else with my Lady Elizabeth.   And touching that I said, My Lord, if ye go about any such thing, ye seek the means to undo yourself and all those that shall come of you.

" He asked me who informed me thereof, desiring earnestly to know the authors of that tale to me.

" I showed him I heard it of divers of your near friends, and such as bear you as much good-will, and wish you as well to do, as I do myself.

" At that time he seemed to deny that there was any such thing attempted of his part, and that he never thought to make any enterprise therein.

" I answered, My Lord, I am glad to hear you say so ; and, giving him exhortation not to attempt the matter, we finished our communication in that behalf for that present."

" CERTAIN COMMUNICATIONS BETWIXT US AT ANOTHER TIME."

Orig.   St. P. Off.   *Domestic.*   1548.

" Riding in like sort together, within two or three days following, from my Lord Protector's house unto the Parliament House, my Lord Admiral said unto me ' *Father Russell,*' you are very suspicious of me ; I pray you tell me, who showed you of the marriage that I should attempt, whereof ye brake with me this other day ?

" I answered, he should not know the authors of the tale, but that I understood it by such as bare him right good-will; and said therewithall, My Lord, I shall earnestly advise you to make no suit for marriage that way.

" He replied, saying, It is convenient for them to marry, and better it were that they were married within the realm than in any foreign place and without the realm.   And why might not I, or another, made by the King their father, marry one of them ?

" I answered, My Lord, if either you, or any other within this realm, shall match himself in marriage either with my Lady Mary or with my Lady Elizabeth, undoubtedly, whatsoever he be, shall procure unto himself the occasion of his utter undoing; and you especially above all others, being of so near alliance to the King's Majesty.

" And he being desirous to know the cause, I alleged this reason :—You know, my Lord, that although the King's Majesty's father was a prince of much wisdom and knowledge, yet was he very suspicious and much given to suspect.   His grandfather also, King Henry the Seventh, was a very noble and a wise prince, yet was he also very suspicious.   Wherefore it may be possible, yea, and it is not unlikely but that the King's Majesty, following therein the nature of his father and grandfather, may be also suspicious.   Which if it shall so prove, this may follow, that in case you, being of alliance to his Highness, shall also marry with one of the heirs of the crown by succession, his Highness may, perhaps take occasion thereof to have you hereafter in great suspect, and, as often as he shall see you, to think that you gape and wish for his death; which thought if it be once rooted in his head, much displeasure may ensue unto you thereupon. I added also, And I pray you, my Lord, what shall you have with any of them?

" He answered, that who married one of them should have three thousand a year.

" I answered, My Lord, it is not so; for ye may be well assured that he shall have no more than only ten thousand pounds in money, plate, and goods, and no land. And therewithal I asked him what that should be to maintain his charges and estate, matching himself there.

" He answered, They must have the three thousand pounds a year also.

" I answered, By G—d! but they may not.

" He answered, By G—d! none of you all dare say nay to it.

" I answered, By G—d! for my part I will say nay to it; for it is clean against the King's will.* * *

" Riding together another time, in like sort together, toward the Parliament House, my Lord Admiral said unto me, What will you say, my Lord Privy Seal, if I go *above* you shortly? I answered, I would be very glad of his preferment; and, concerning going above me, I did not care, so that he took nothing from me. Which my Lord Admiral's saying, and my answer, I declared to my Lord Chancellor immediately the same morning.

" J. RUSSELL."

The next Examination is that of SIR GEORGE BLAGGE, an accomplished courtier, whose death we shall afterwards find alluded to by Ascham in such terms as if the sun of elegance and gentleness had been extinguished.   Blagge was one of the gentlemen of the Privy Chamber to Henry the Eighth, who was very fond of him, and, for what reason is unknown, used to call him his *Pig*.   He was a *Sacramentarian*, and, when Wriothesley and Gardiner, in 1546, commenced their persecution on the statute of the Six Articles, Blagge was clapt up in Newgate, and, after a hurried trial, condemned to be burnt.   But, the moment the King heard of it, he rated the Chancellor for coming so near him, even to his Privy Chamber, and commanded him instantly to draw out a pardon.   On his release, Blagge flew to thank his master ; who, seeing him, cried out, " Ah! my *Pig!* are you here safe again ?" " Yes, sire," said he; " and, if your Majesty had not been better than your bishops, your *Pig* had been *roasted* ere this time.*

GEORGE BLAGGE.

Orig.   ST. P. OFF.   *Domestic.*

" The Lord Admiral, talking of sundry matters

---

* Ridley's Life of Bishop Ridley, p. 176-178.

which now I remember not, among other things
said unto me, Here is *gear* shall come amongst
you, my masters of the nether House, shortly;
wagging a paper which he held in his hand.—
What is that, my Lord ? said I.—Marry, said he,
requests to have the King better ordered, and not
kept close that no man may see him: and so entered with sundry mislikings of my Lord Protector's proceedings touching the bringing up of the
King's Majesty, liker that way to grow a *Fool* than
otherwise ; whereby I perceived him not brotherly
affected towards my Lord Protector's Grace : and I
said, Who shall put this into the house ?—Myself,
said he.—Why then, said I, you make no longer
reckoning of your brother's friendship if you purpose to go this way to work.—Well, said he, for
that I care not ; I will do nothing but that I may
abide by.

"I then, in as much as was in me, dissuaded him
from attempting any such matter ; objecting, as I
then thought, the dangers which might ensue ; and
seeing my words like to take small effect, said,
What an my Lord Protector, understanding your
mind, commit you to ward ?—No ; by G—d's
precious soul ! said he, he will not commit me to
ward.   No, no, I warrant you.—But if he do, said
I, how will you come out ?—Well, as for that, said
he, I care not ; but who shall have me to prison ?—
Your brother, said I.—Which way, said he?—Marry,
well enow, said I ; even send for you, and commit

you ; and I pray you, who shall let him ?—If the *Council* send for me, said he, I will go ; *he* will not be so hasty to send me to prison.—No ; but when you are there, said I, how will you come out ?   I asked him that question so often that he seemed not contented, and always answered me, Care not for that.   This was the sum of our communication ; which I so misliked, as since that time I never talked with him.

" GEORGE BLAGGE."

The following Declaration is entirely in LORD CLYNTON's hand-writing. This nobleman had distinguished himself highly in the Scottish war. We shall afterwards meet with him as Ambassador to the French King, when he was sent to represent the person of his sovereign at the christening of one of the sons of Henry the Second.

LORD CLYNTON'S DECLARATION.

Orig. ST. P. OFF. *Domestic.* 1548.

" THESE words following were spoken by my Lord Admiral to me, the Lord Clynton, in the hearing of my Lord Marquis Dorset, whom I did ride behind from the Parliament House at that present time.   The said Lord Admiral, talking to my said Lord Marquis and me of an Act which passed the same day, for repealing another act for speaking of words wherein my said Lord Admiral would a had a

promise that men should not have had liberty to a
spoken any thing against the Queen, said, I do perceive what is meant by this matter; I have heard
speaking of a *Black Parliament;* an they use me as
they do begin, by G—d's precious soul I will make
the *Blackest Parliament* that ever was in England!
Whereunto I answered, that I was sorry to hear
such words pass him, and that such words would do
him much hurt; and that, if it should come to the
knowledge of my Lord Protector's Grace, it should
be an occasion to lose his favour utterly.

"My said Lord Admiral answered me, that he
would I should know it that he had no need of his
favour, and that he might better live without my said
Lord's Grace than he might do without him.   And
after my Lord Admiral had spoken to me, the Lord
Clinton of the black Parliament, he talked with my
Lord Marquis; in which talk I remember he said to
my Lord Marquis, he would take his [* * *]† from
the best of their ears from the highest to the lowest:
saying, that he would not spare my Lord Protector's
Grace.   My Lord Marquis answered, that these
words should not need; he trusted that all should be
well, and that my Lord's Grace and he should be
friends, and persuaded him to pacify himself; for my
Lord showed himself to be much moved against my
Lord's Grace, as my Lord Marquis can declare: in
the which talk my said Lord Admiral said, Why

† The word is illegible; but from an abstract in Haynes,
p. 76, it appears to have been "Fist."

was he made Protector ? there is no need of a Protector.

" F. CLYNTON."

It is singular that Dr. Lingard,* after giving a clear and impartial summary of the story of the Admiral, and stating facts which amount to evident treason, concludes his account by throwing a doubt upon his guilt, or rather with an assertion that the Depositions prove his innocence. That the Admiral had no designs against the King's *life* is perfectly manifest; but to coin money, to take measures for the levying of ten thousand men, and to lay a plot to carry off the King and depose the Protector, was just as much *treason* as to slay the King. An intention to change the form of Government by forcible means seems to me to be clearly proved by the depositions in Haynes, and those now before the reader : but Dr. Lingard not only exculpates the Admiral; he condemns the Protector for having attended (and this must mean voted) at each reading of the bill against his brother; and the same assertion has been made still more recently by Sir J. Mackintosh.† It is expressly stated, however, in the MS. Privy Council Books of Edward, in which by far the best account of the proceedings against the Admiral is to be found, that, when the Bill for the attainder of the Lord Admiral was brought in, *the Protector, for*

---

* History of England, vol. vii. p. 50.

† Mackintosh, vol. ii. p. 256.   Lingard, vol. vii. p. 48.

*natural pity's sake, desired leave to withdraw.** Mackintosh and Lingard were misled by the Lords' Jour-
nals, which no doubt show that the Protector was
present in the house on the 25th and 26th of February; other bills probably required his presence and
consent; but, when his brother's bill came on, he
withdrew. It is worthy of remark also, in considerar-
ing the charge of a want of natural affection made
by our historians against Somerset, that the Privy
Council, who at this moment were incensed against
him, describe the necessity by which he was compelled to consent to the attainder of his brother, as
felt by him to be *"heavy, lamentable, and sorrowful."*†
I may lastly cite a *royal witness* in favour of the brotherly feelings of the Protector upon this occasion,
from whose evidence it appears that Somerset was
anxious to have had a personal interview with the
Admiral; that, after the Admiral's death, the Protector declared that, had they been allowed to meet,
Lord Seymour would never have suffered; and that
this meeting was prevented from taking place by
the Council. The witness is no less a personage
than Queen Elizabeth herself; who, when Princess,
in a letter, already alluded to, and addressed to her
sister, Queen Mary, in which she disclaims having
any connection with the conspiracy of Wyatt, uses
these remarkable words: " I have heard in my time of

---

* The fact has been stated on the authority of the Privy
Council Books by Burnet, vol. iii. p. 205, Oxford edition.

† Burnet, vol. iii. p. 205.

many *cast away* for want of coming to the presence of their prince ; and, in late days, I heard my Lord Somerset say that, if his brother had been *suffered to speak with him,* he had never *suffered;* but the persuasions were made to him so great, that he was brought in belief that he could not live safely if the Admiral lived, and that made him give his consent to his death."*

Dr. Lingard has also animadverted in strong terms upon LATIMER for having not only arraigned the life, but the death of the Lord Admiral; and yet no one who has read the depositions in Haynes, or who has even examined the same evidence as it is abridged in the general historians of the times, will deny that the life of Lord Seymour of Sudley, was that of a fierce, ambitious, proud, and revengeful man : and if the story told by Latimer be true,—that his last hours were employed in a device to sow jealousies between the Princesses Mary and Elizabeth and the Protector, that he wrote letters for that purpose, which letters Latimer saw, —it proves that he laid his head upon the block in the same violent, unforgiving, and vindictive spirit in which he had lived. Was it too much to call such a death dangerous, irksome, horrible ? I think not.

The woe pronounced in Scripture upon the country whose King is a child, is nowhere more strikingly exemplified than in the history of the minority of the sixth Edward. Somerset the Protector,

* Ellis, vol. ii. Second Series, p. 256.

not long after his election to that dignity—we might almost say his usurpation of it—procured a *Stamp* of the King's signature, which placed in his hands a power that might too easily have been abused. This is a fact which I do not remember to have seen elsewhere noticed, but which is proved by several papers I have found during the early part of this reign, to which the royal signature is thus affixed.   But if the young King was liable to be abused in this way by one uncle, he was exposed to the artful solicitations of another ; as the following Declaration of Sir John Cheke, his domestic Tutor, clearly shows.   Nor can we wonder that Somerset should have been deeply incensed by such secret practices to procure the interest and goodwill of his royal ward.   There is a Confession by the King himself, printed in Haynes,* which betrays to us the feelings with which Edward regarded the two brothers.   " At another time," says the young King, " within this two year at least, he (the Admiral) said, ye must take upon yourself to rule, for ye shall be able enough, as well as other Kings, and then ye may give your men somewhat ; for your uncle is old, and I trust will not live long.   I answered, it were *better that he should die !*"

* Haynes, p. 74.

SIR JOHN CHEKE'S CONFESSION.

Orig. St. P. Off. *Domestic.* 1548.

" In the first session of the Parliament, the King's Majesty lying then at Westminster, the Lord Admiral came unto me with a piece of paper in his hand, declaring unto me that he had a suit to the Lords of the Parliament House, and that the King's Majesty was well contented to write unto them for him; wherefore he gave me the piece of paper in his hand, and desired me to get it written of the King, as he had promised him to do. The contents of the bill, as far as I remember, written with the Lord Admiral's hand, was this : ' My Lords. I pray you favour my Lord Admiral mine uncle's suit, which he will make unto you.' I answered, My Lord Paget had given me commandment that the King's Majesty should sign no bill without his hand were at the same before; and therefore I durst not be so bold to deliver it, nor to cause the King's Majesty either to write it, or else to set his hand unto it. He said, I might do it well enough, seeing the King's Majesty had promised him : and although he was an ill speaker himself, yet, if he had that bill, he was sure the best speakers in that house would help him to prefer it. But I earnestly denied the receiving of the bill, and so departed from him. The King's Majesty knoweth what I afterwards said unto him in private exhortation; whereupon the King's Majesty said, that the

Lord Admiral should have no such bill signed nor written of him : and, neither afore nor after, I heard, of the Lord Admiral's part, any more of this bill.

" JOAN. CHEKE."

Endorsed.   " *Mr. Cheek*, 20th February."

Our next letter carries us to the Continent. " The fair boy," of whom Wotton states that the French Queen was delivered, died in his cradle.

The Sieur D'Essé, who is reported by the Dean of Canterbury to be coming home from Scotland, was Andrew Montalembert Sieur D'Essé. He was one of the favourite officers of Francis the First, and in 1543, acquired extraordinary credit by his protracted defence of Landrecy against the united troops of Spain, Germany, Italy, and England, commanded by Charles the Fifth ; thus giving time for the French King to come up and raise the siege. Francis the First made him a gentleman of his bedchamber, observing, with a smile, that he was afraid he knew better how to give the Enemy than the King *a dressing ;* at least, so we may be allowed to paraphrase his Majesty's pun : " Qu'il étoit plus propre à donner une *camisade* à l'ennemi, qu'une *chemise* au Roi."

Montalembert was so enthusiastic a soldier, that, soon after peace was concluded in 1550, he began to droop ; and retiring to Epanvilliers, his estate in Poitou, was seized with a severe and obstinate jaundice, which for three years resisted every remedy. As he lay one day languidly on his couch, a messenger arrived with an order from the King that he should undertake the defence of Terouenne against the Emperor : the old warrior sprung up in a transport of joy, " Thank God," cried he; " after all, I am not to die in my bed! If Teronenne is carried, it shall be over the dead body of D'Essé; and thus, at all events, we'll cheat the jaundice!" And he kept his word. Terouenne thrice repulsed its assailants ; but, in the fourth assault, D'Essé was slain on the breach, and the Emperor gained the town. He was killed in his seventieth year. His name is well known in Scottish history as commander of the French auxiliaries who were sent to support the Queen Dowager, Mary of Guise, against the reformers.

N. WOTTON TO THE PROTECTOR.

Orig. St. P. Off. *France.* Feb. 23rd, 1548-9. *Paris.*

" It may please your Grace to be advertised that the first day of this month the French Queen was brought a-bed of a fair boy,—cause of much joy in this court. I hear that the King of Portugal, the Duke of Ferrara, and the Queen Dowager of Scotland, shall be Godfathers. I hear that the French King hath sent gentlemen expressly to the Emperor and Bishop of Rome, to signify unto them the birth of his said son.

" Monluc is not yet departed.* I hear that he

---

* *Monluc.*—John de Monluc, Bishop of Valence. He had gained great reputation as ambassador to the Sultan.

shall be President of the Council in Scotland. Monsieur de Termes * is yet here too ; but, by the common voice, shall go shortly into Scotland. And it is thought that Monsieur D'Essé [cometh] home. I hear that divers captains of gens-d'[armes come] out of Provence, that shall go into Scotland. And where I was informed that Petro Strozzi was gone into Piedmont, I [hear not] now of it, for he is now in the Court again.

" I hear that the French King hath news that the Provenceaulx that were sent into Scotland are arrived there safe already ; and that, in the beginning of March next, two thousand men of war more shall be sent thither. At what time Monsieur de Vendosme was at Venice, the French King being in Piedmont, he found there certain Captains, Corvates, or Stradiotes, and retained them, with certain number of men, that they should bring hither. The Captains are now here; their men, as they say, are coming.

" Some bear me in hand that the first thing that these men will do this year in Scotland shall be that they will besiege, not Haddington, but Berwick; the which is reckoned easy to be won : and that won, all the rest, they say, that we hold in Scotland, is all lost. The second part seemeth not unlikely; but the first part I wonder if they mean, or believe.

* *De Thermes.*—Paul de la Barthe, Seigneur de Thermes, an experienced military commander; afterwards Maréchal de France, and placed at the head of the French army in Italy. He died in 1562, aged eighty.

" The Emperor's ambassador saith that the Constable, talking with one of my Lord Admiral's *matter*,* said that he lacked wit, for if he went about any such matter, he must have made them privy to it. These men here talk full merrily of the arrests of ships made in Eng[land] and Flanders, trusting that that matter will breed a scab, [which] if it once begin to itch they will help to [open it till it] bleed. I hear that the French King hath renewed a league with the Switzers, by the which, among other things, they are bound to serve the French King for the defence of Savoy and Piedmont, and also in Scotland, whensoever he shall require it of them; the which being true, is not best for the poor Duke of Savoy.

" Here was of late a *Fray* made in this court, which is esteemed to be a matter of importance; the occasion whereof began thus. The late Seigneur de Rieux left no issue of his body, but three sisters; whereof the eldest, being married to the Marquis de Neuilly, but divorced from him, succeeded her brother, almost in all his lands; and, not long before, she was also inheritor to the Compte de la Val. She hath no children by her husband; and, being divorced, is like to have none. Her second sister is married to Monsieur D'Andelot, Chastillon's brother; and there hath been

---

* The plot of the Lord Admiral, Lord Seymour of Sudley, against his brother the Protector, for which he was attainted of treason and beheaded, March 20th, 1549. See supra.

labour made to marry the said third and youngest
of all to René, Monsieur the Duke of Guise's
youngest son.*   And, to the intent that marriage
might be [had], the said René, Monsieur the
Prince de la Roche sur Yonne, younger brother to
the Duke of Montpensier, and both of the house of
Vendosme, laboured to the said Lady Marquise of
Neuilly, now called Madame de la Val, to agree
by covenant, that if she died without issue, that
then a certain good portion of her lands should
descend to her said youngest sister.   But Andelot,
perceiving this, was not contented with it; taking
it to be much to his prejudice who had married
the other sister,—eldest, save one; and hereupon
spake with the said Prince of it, and said he did
him wrong: and, what answer soever the said Prince
made him at that time, it seemeth that afterwards
Andelot made his boast among others, that he had
well spoken his mind to the Prince, using certain
high words in his tale.

This communication was reported to the Prince;
and one day, the King being at hunting, the
Prince called Andelot, and told him that he had
spoken certain words of him that did not become him; and Andelot made such froward an-
swers (as it is spoken), that the Prince said he
would break his head; and therewith they drew

---

* *René, Marquis d'Elbœuf,* youngest son of Claude de Lorraine and Antoinette de Bourbon, brother of the great Duke of
Guise and the Cardinal Lorraine.

their swords, and with the Prince took part Monsieur D'Enghien, Louis, Monsieur, brethren to the Duke of Vendosme, and the young Duke of Nemours, and, as I hear, one other gentleman took Andelot's part : finally, the Prince was hurt in the hand ; but Andelot is sore hurt in the head or forehead, in the arm and the hand, and had his hat cut in divers places, and the head therewith not touched. It is thought that the young Prince had not strength enough to strike through ; but everybody saith that, unless they had been parted, Andelot had been undoubtedly slain, for Monsieur D'Enghien had his sword at his throat to have killed him. At the last the King came thither, and chafed with the Princes ; and used certain threatening words to Monsieur D'Enghien. Andelot being the Constable's nephew, and one of the King's *minions*, it is thought that factions and [broils] are like to be engendered hereof; the more for that it seemeth that they of Guise must take part with the princes, seeing the matter began for the preferment of their youngest brother ; and also because that commonly in France Princes hold with Princes, and will not be made fellows or suffer injury of mere gentlemen, but will be known and taken for Princes.

" The eleventh of this present I received your Grace's letter of the third of the same. *   *   * Undoubtedly the French King sendeth another aid into Scotland this next month ; and they that should go are hasted to go down into Britain, and yet more shall be sent thither afterwards. And thus, having no other news to give advertisement of, I beseech Jesus long to preserve your Grace in health, honour, and prosperity! Written at Paris, the 23d of February 1548.

"N. WOTTON."

The following letter, from John Dymock to the Protector, is valuable from the particulars it contains regarding the practice of employing mercenary forces in England, and the terms upon which they consented to serve. One of the accusations brought against the Protector by his brother the Admiral, was a design to enslave the country by introducing mercenaries whom he had employed in his Scottish wars.

JOHN DYMOCK TO THE PROTECTOR.

Orig. ST. P. OFF. *Germany.* 24th March 1548-9.
Hamburgh.

"PLEASETH your Grace to be advertised, that since the last letter that I sent unto your Grace from the city of Bremen, concerning the Earl Christopher of Oldenburgh's answer made unto me at that time, I thought I should have had him to have served the King's Majesty for twelve hundred crowns; but at such time as we should conclude, and the writings to be made of the same, then the said Duke answered and said, that there was no prince living which he had rather serve than the King's

Majesty, howbeit, for so small pension as that was, he was not able to serve: so that I declared unto him then, how that the King's Majesty was contented to give him the full of fifteen hundred crowns, desiring him to be contented therewith; whose answer was, that he never had less of the French King than two thousand crowns for himself, and two thousand crowns for the entertainment of twelve captains, which thing he would have in like manner, or else he would not serve.

" This done, I thanked him, promising to write in his favour unto the King's Majesty and his Council; and so remained there for the space of six days ere I could make a final conclusion with the said Earl of Oldenburgh.

" I judge no less but the Earl of Mansfield and his son are they who have persuaded the said Earl of Oldenburgh that he should not serve the King's Majesty, because his son was in England and had no entertainment: also I do know that the Ringrave did both dine and sup with the old Earl of Mansfield when he was at Breme, being very merry together; and what as was betwixt them I cannot say.

" Thus [I] departed thence, and came unto the castle of Harborough the 18th of this present; there the Duke Otho of Brunswick and Lunenburgh doth lie: and there [I] delivered the King's Majesty's letter according unto my duty; being compelled to tarry till nine of the clock the next day after to have his answer, which is as follows :—

First, the foresaid Duke of Brunswick and Lunen-
bourgh giveth thanks unto the King's Majesty,
with the rest of the Lords of his Majesty's Council,
for the annuity of fifteen hundred crowns given
unto him, and the five hundred crowns given unto
his son, but for such a small pension as that was he
was not able to serve ; and, as for the service that he
had already done, he was very well contented therewith, albeit it hath been to his great hurt and
damage ; yet, notwithstanding, seeing he had done
pleasure unto a King who favoureth the word of God,
he esteemed the damage much less.   This done, the
said Duke showed me two letters sent unto him from
the Ringrave, the one written at Elshowe in Denmark, the other written at Breme the whiles the
Ringrave was there, the effect whereof was this :
that Duke Otho should send or come unto him, and
he would assure him to have two thousand crowns
a year for himself, and to maintain certain captains
one thousand crowns a year, and to have his son
entertained in the French King's court, over and
besides this ; with the condition that he should send
for his son out of England." * * * *

The Duke of Lunenbourg, we find, after much
persuasion, was content to serve in England for
fifteen hundred crowns a year.   In the same letter
the dislike of the *Interim* is strongly marked.

" Here be many subtle practices put in use : divers
men are taken up here, both horsemen and footmen, for the use of the Duke of Pruesse [Prussia],

the two Dukes of Pomery [Pomerania] ; and every
town hereabouts doth take in certain men of war
to defend themselves against the Emperor, for
they will in nowise receive his ' *Interim.*'   Also
Duke Maurice and the Margrave of Brandenberg
do take up divers men : howbeit all the best horsemen which do favour God's word might yet be
gotten for the King's Majesty, to the number of two
thousand five hundred, in the space of twenty-four
days, and four thousand good footmen, if that your
Grace's pleasure was known. * *

           " Your Grace's for evermore,

                      " J. DYMOCK."

The English reader need scarcely be informed
that REGINALD POLE, the eminent prelate who writes
the following letter to the Earl of Warwick, was
the younger son of Sir Richard Pole, Knight of the
Garter, and Margaret, daughter of George Duke of
Clarence, younger brother to Edward the Fourth.

He was born in March 1500, sent when seven years
of age to be instructed in the Carthusian monastery
of Shene, and from thence removed at twelve to
Magdalen College, Oxford, where he had the good
fortune to have Linacre and Latimer for his masters.
At nineteen he travelled into Italy, and took up his
residence at Padua, where he pursued his studies
with much enthusiasm, living in the literary society
of Bembo, Sadolet, Longolius, and other eminent
scholars.   After five years he returned to England,

where he was received with great distinction by Henry the Eighth; and where he would have risen high in the church, had not this monarch quarrelled with Rome and asserted his own supremacy. Pole was too sincere a Romanist to accommodate himself to Henry's theological and matrimonial vagaries; and, after many struggles and occasional flights to the Continent, he retired finally to Italy, where he resumed his favorite studies in divinity and general literature, and wrote his work " Pro Unitate Ecclesiasticâ," to which Henry replied by withdrawing his pension, stripping him of his ecclesiastical dignities, and attainting him of high treason. This may be regarded as the usual rejoinder of this monarch; but, if thus punished in England, he was rewarded in Italy by the bounty of the Emperor and the red hat from the Pope; not to mention his alleged refusal of the Papacy in 1548, which, although much dwelt upon by his encomiasts, seems a doubtful point.

CARDINAL POLE TO THE EARL OF WARWICK.

Orig. St. P. Off. *Domestic.* 6th April 1549. *Rome.*

" My own good Lord and Cousin. With that heart and spirit that most fervently can desire your most prosperous and honourable state both afore God and man, I commend me unto you. And whereas, at this time, I do write and send two messengers unto my Lord Protector to give information to his Grace in this present state of the realm of all that which my love to God and [*torn*] country

hath long stirred my mind to communicate to the
* * * † if there had been given any opportunity; for
the same cause I am moved to write this unto your
Lordship for the confidence that I have that, by
your authority in the Council, such advices might
take the sooner and better effect; which hath no
particular designment, but only the wealth universal, and specially of them that do now rule, to whom
this advisement is given.

" And in this behalf I will extend myself no further
by letters to disclose the particularity of my information, having comprised the same in such instructions as I have sent to * * * * † the whole with your
Lordship; and what lacketh to be plainly expressed
by writing, the messengers shall supply by mouth.

" Only this : I shall pray Almighty God that the
fruit of this offer that I make at this time of a paci-
fical and serviceable mind to the honour of God and
the wealth of the realm, and specially of the King's
Majesty, and you my Lords of the Council, do not,
by your refusing, turn wholly unto me; but by
accepting it, to the rejoice of both parties, as my
greatest and most entire desire is, as knoweth
Almighty God, the true searcher of man's heart and
judge of all, who preserve you long, my good [lord]
and cousin, in all prosperous estate to his honour.

" Written at Rome, the 6th of April 1549,

" By your loving cousin and servant in Christ,

" R. POLE, Car ."

† Illegible.

What were the precise instructions communicated by Pole to the two messengers whom he sent at this time to the Protector does not clearly appear ; but it seems probable that his object was to persuade Somerset and Warwick to co-operate with him in mediating a peace, or, to speak more definitely, in arranging the differences between the French King and the Emperor. It is evident, from one of the "*Articles*" presented some time after this by the rebels in Devonshire, that the Cardinal had many friends in England :—" We think it very meet," say they, " because the Lord Cardinal Pole is of the King's blood, that he should not only have his pardon, but also be sent for to Rome, and promoted to be of the King's Council."*

WILLIAM WIGHTMAN, who addresses the following eloquent letter to Cecil, was a servant of the Lord Admiral, in whose troubles he seems to have been involved. In Haynes,† we find a Confession of his, in which some interesting particulars are detailed which throw light on the violent, ambitious, and tyrannical courses of the Admiral ; and which proves that the jealousies and heartburnings for precedency between the proud Duchess of Somerset and the Queen Dowager, the Admiral's wife, were not mere court scandal. A new fact comes out of this letter from Wightman to Cecil : on the 30th of January, 1546-7, as we have seen in our first letter, the Earl

* Strype's Cranmer, vol. ii. p. 835.
† Haynes, p. 68.

of Hertford carried Edward from Hertford to Enfield, where the young King was first informed of
his father's death.* And here, Sir Anthony Browne,
Master of the Horse, *held a consultation " on the
State"* with Hertford in the garden, and gave his
consent that Hertford should be Protector; " thinking it the surest kind of government." The conversation reported to have been afterwards held between Wightman and the Admiral, throws more
light than any paper I have elsewhere met with, on
the hot and fiery character of Lord Seymour ; and
exposes, in strong colours, the scramble for ecclesiastical wealth, and the *"sore plucking* at the Bishopricks and Deaneries," which took place on the
promotion of Somerset.

WILLIAM WIGHTMAN TO MR. CECILL.

Orig. St. P. Off. *Domestic.* 10th May 1549.

" GENTLE MR. CECILL.—If I had as much art
to persuade the truth as I have truth to persuade
mine innocency, I should assuredly, with few words,
both satisfy you and quit myself from suspicion of
fraud towards my Lord's Grace ; but, lacking the
one, I must cleave to the other ; not doubting but,
with God's assistance, I shall vanquish and overcome those false accusations or declarations which
proceeded from the hand of him † who was as far
from the fear of God as he was from the observation

* Haynes, p. 16.   † The Lord Admiral.

of his bounden duty towards the King's Majesty
and his country. And specially to answer to the
points so cursedly invented and maliciously uttered,
I will use one simple answer to two of them.

" And that is, that, as he was of himself all untrue, so are his wicked allegations utterly false ; for,
as touching mine old master, the Master of Horses,*
albeit (as it is commonly known) he did much dissent
from the proceedings in matters of Religion, yet was
I long since by himself right well assured that he,
communing with my Lord's Grace in the garden at
Endfield, at the King's Majesty's coming from Hertford, gave his frank consent [in] communication in
discourse of the State, that his Grace should be *Protector,* thinking it (as indeed it was) both *the surest*
kind of government, and most fit for that Commonwealth ; and, as God shall save me, I never heard
him speak word contrary his first determination till
the day of his death.

" And wherefore should I then untruly report the
dead man, to whom in his life I was so much
bounden ; specially to him who, by certain knowledge, should at the first be able to have charged
me with untruth ?

" For my Lord's Grace's* lands, I never heard to
what sum it rose, nor to my knowledge ever inquired after it. And is it like that I should then
so impudently declare to him, being a nobleman,
and my master, an uncertainty, whereof I should

* Sir Anthony Browne.   † The Duke of Somerset.

not, nor could not, by any means be able to make proof?

" Marry, as concerning the matter of the *abatement* of the tenths, thus much have I heard himself say, upon occasion for the communication of the answer to my Lord's Grace's letter touching Mr. Bridggs matter; at the writing whereof he was in a great heat, and amongst many other things said,

" By God's precious soul! my Lord, my brother is wondrous hot in helping every man to his right, saving me. He maketh a great matter to let me have the Queen's jewels, which, you see by the whole opinion of all the lawyers, ought to belong unto me; and all under pretence that he would not the King should lose so much,—as who say it were a loss to the King to let me have mine own? But he maketh nothing of the loss that the King's Majesty hath by him in his Court of First-fruits and Tenths, where his revenue is abated, as I have heard say, almost ten thousand pounds a year. I told him that I thought it was not so much, for the whole land that had been surrendered since the King's death was, by all men's guesses, far under that sum.

" Well, well, said he, they are at this point now that there can neither Bishoprick, Deanery, nor Prebend fall void, but one or other of them will have a *fleece* of it. Indeed I did, in this point, both grant his saying to be true, and aggravate the matter, to confirm his opinion, with naming the Deanery of Wells, the Bishoprick of Lincoln, and others, which I told him had been *sore plucked at.*—It maketh no matter, said he; it will come in again when the King cometh to his years, as he beginneth to grow lustily.   By God's precious soul! said he, I would not be in *some of their coats* for five marks when he shall hear of these matters. For mine own part, I will not have a penny after that rate, nor they shall not all be able to charge me with the value of a farthing.—Sir, said I, there is nothing shall discommend you more than your evil waiting and slackness in service in this time of the King's Majesty's tender years, when one day's service is worth a whole year's.   To the which he answered, and I replied, as in my first Confession is mentioned.

" And for that I did not, according to my bounden duty, make declaration hereof before, I do most humbly upon my knees ask mercy and pardon of my Lord's Grace.   Beseeching the same that, like as he hath used pity towards the poor penitent and sorrowful persons by all the time of his authority, so that I, most miserable man, may taste of his sweetness thereof; and that my continual service to be done during my life to his Grace may be a ransom to pay some part of the debt of this my fault.

" And thus much, good Mr. Cecill, if you think it convenient, say on my behalf to his Grace; and of your wonted goodness help further, that the hand of him* who hated to serve his country do not heap the

* The Lord Admiral.

heavy and intolerable burden of displeasure upon
my weak back ; that the mind of him that meant
nothing but mischief may not move his Grace's
mercy from me, that never thought him ill; that the
practice of him who would have made his brother's
blood a prey to his purpose, pluck not pity from so
penitent a person as I am ; that the heart of him
that was so horribly hardened with hatred towards
them to whom he was so manifoldly bounden, harm
not the party that never thought his Grace's hurt ;
and, finally, that the head of him whose brain was
busied in matters to break down the quiet state of
this Commonwealth bring not me, a poor member
of the same, to misery and extreme mischief, wherein
I have so lamentably remained since the time of this
overture, as, for lack of coming to declare, I must
pass over with silence.

"Helas! Mr. Cecill, if it so were that I were
culpable in all the things proposed, (as, God to
record, more than before confessed I am not,) yet
consider with yourself whether so pestilent and
perverse a person might not easily have plucked
to his purpose so poor a man, and his servant, as
I was, when, under pretence of zeal to the common
tranquillity, he had nearhand won to his part men
both honourable and honest, and, in my conscience,
as far now different from his desires as the lamb is
different from the devouring wolf. Water quenches
hot burning fire, and mercy reconcileth sinners. I
protest unto the living God, who hath to judge all

right and redress all wrong, that if my labour and service, even to the shedding of my heart's blood, might stand his Grace to stead, I am as well bent to employ the same to the uttermost drop, as ever man was inclined to advance his own most commodity. I can no more say ; but as one opprest with dolour and deep sighs, lamenting this mine unhappy hap, I do commit the report of this my cause unto your indifferent hands.

" From London, the 10th of May 1549.
" By him that beareth you his hearty
" good-will, and wisheth your wealth,
" W. WIGHTMAN."
" To the Right Worshipful Mr. Cecill, Mr. of
the Requests to my Lord Protector's Grace."

One of the remarks of the Lord Admiral, as to the shameless manner in which the royal demesnes had been fleeced and plundered during the King's minority, came from him with peculiar ill grace, whose castle and estate of Sudley was itself royal property. It appears, however, by a passage in Tyrwhit's confession,* that Seymour had informed the Queen, his wife, of an intention he had to restore Sudley to the King.

" One day," says this witness, " walking in the park, among many communications. the Queen's Grace said thus : Master Tyrwhitt, you shall see the King when he cometh to his full age ; he will call his lands again as fast as they be now given

* Haynes, p. 104.

from him.—Marry, said I, then is Sudley Castle gone from my Admiral.—Marry, said the Queen, I do assure you he intends to offer them to the King, and give them freely to him at that time."

This confession of Wightman is dated 10th of May 1549. Two days before this Paget had addressed a remarkable letter to the Protector, which has been printed by Strype,* in which, with the frankness, honesty, and boldness of true friendship, he warns him of his growing unpopularity with the Council, and implores him to give up that violent and despotic mode of conducting himself,—"*those great cholerick fashions,*" which had already begun to threaten the worst consequences. He reminds Somerset of his own sensitiveness; observing that, if King or Cardinal had formerly spoken to him as he spake to them, "it would have scarcely been tolerated." " Poor Sir Richard a Lee" (says he), "this afternoon, after your Grace had very sore, and much more than needed, rebuked him, came to my chamber *weeping,* and there complaining, as far as became him, of your handling of him, seemed almost out of his wits, and out of heart; your Grace, to be sure, had put him clean out of countenance." Paget, after a few more remarks, has this striking sentence, so completely prophetic of the Protector's fast approaching ruin. " A *King* who shall give men discouragement to say their opinions frankly, receiveth thereby great hurt and

* Strype's Memor. vol. ii. part ii. p. 427.

peril to his realm; but a *Subject* in great authority, as your Grace is, using such fashion, is like to fall into great danger and peril of his own person, beside that to the Commonwealth, which for the very love I bear to your Grace, I beseech you, and for God's sake, consider and weigh well."

Happy had it been for Somerset had he listened to such advice, urged as it was with so much solemnity. At this moment Paget was probably no stranger to the intrigues of the EARL OF WARWICK for the overthrow of the Protector; and the circumstances of the country, both in its foreign relations and its internal state, gave his enemies an advantage which they were eager to employ against him.

He was already greatly embarrassed by the expense of keeping up a war at once with France and Scotland. The finances of the country were embarrassed; Boulogne and its adjacent forts cost him a large sum; and he had become convinced that, unless he could prevail upon the Emperor to undertake its defence, it would be impossible to retain it much longer. Paget and Hoby were for this purpose despatched on an embassy to the Emperor, but Charles's hands were full, and the demands upon his exchequer as heavy as the calls upon the Protector's purse; so he paid the ambassadors in kind words, but absolutely refused to entangle himself with Boulogne.

Nor were embarrassments arising from foreign wars the only difficulties with which Somerset had to struggle; a more dreadful enemy was at hand in the shape of a Rebellion at home, which, from a small beginning, soon swelled into alarming strength, and threatened to embroil the whole kingdom. It had its origin in the hatred of the commons against *Enclosures.* "Many lords and gentlemen," says Carte, * " possessed of abbey lands, had enclosed abundance of waste grounds in their manors, which deprived poor people of the advantages they used to receive from the *commoning* (the right of common pasturage) they enjoyed before; and wool, by increase of trade, turning to more profit than any thing produced by tillage, the humour of enclosing grew general. Whole villages were demolished, and the houses pulled down to get rid of the inhabitants; rents of farms were raised to three or four times their usual value; thousands of farmers were turned out of their way of livelihood; and this raising of rents enhanced excessively the price of provisions. * * * Hence arose a general spirit of discontent and mutiny among the yeomanry and lower sort of people all over the nation."

Hales, one of the commissioners for inquiring into enclosures, whose letter we have lately given, had endeavoured in the last parliament to afford them some relief by introducing three bills, which met with great opposition, and were thrown out by the enclosers. The Protector, in May, issued a

* Carte's Hist. of England, vol. iii. p. 233.

Royal Proclamation, by which all who had enclosed lands were, under certain penalties, commanded to throw them open again; and he openly espoused the cause of the Commons, giving great offence by such conduct to the higher nobility and many of the Council, who accused him of encouraging a spirit of revolt. This "epidemic distemper of disloyalty," to use Fuller's words, began in Wiltshire, from which it soon spread to Gloucester and Oxford; in these places, however, it was soon put down : but a more serious rising of the Commons took place, about the 10th of June, in Devonshire; and on the 20th of the same month in Norfolk, where they were led by one Ket, a tanner, who assumed the title of Master of Norfolk and Suffolk, and held his court under a large tree, which they termed the Oak of Reformation. It was soon perceived that Enclosures were not their only grievance : some clamoured against the Reformation; others declared for complete religious liberty; " some," says Strype, " were papists, and required the restoration of the old religion; others were anabaptists and libertines, and would have all things common." *

The Council at first made light of these disturbances; and the Protector, always inclined to mild methods, trusted they might be put down without severity. Paget, the Secretary of State, an austere man, and, as Strype suspects, an *Encloser* himself, reprobated such middle courses, and de-

* Strype's Memoir. vol. ii. part i. p. 260.

clared that this medicine of pardon and expostulation would rather irritate than cure the distemper. His prediction was accomplished. The rebel leaders were soon at the head of ten thousand men in Devonshire, and of twice that number in Norfolk; and it required all the efforts of Lord Russell and the Earl of Warwick to subdue them.

The following " *Answer*" to the "Articles" presented by the insurgents, has escaped the industry of Strype and Burnet. The Protector addresses them rather in the tone of paternal remonstrance than angry denunciation; and this, too, even after the rebellion had risen to an alarming height.

THE KING'S MAJESTY'S ANSWER TO THE SUPPLICATION MADE IN THE NAME OF HIS HIGHNESS' SUBJECTS OF DEVON AND CORNWALL.

Orig. St. P. Off. *Domestic.* 8th July 1549.

" If ye our subjects, who by God's ordinance and your own oath do owe to us obedience, would hear us as readily according to your duties, as we of our princely clemency have taken and perused your Supplication, we do not doubt but that ye would easily return to your old quiet and good order; and ye should plainly perceive what difference there were betwixt the heart and words of a King anointed, that ruleth by counsel, and keepeth his realm in defence and quietness, and such blind guides of sedition and uproar who now take upon them to rule you our subjects and people, to lead you against us your natural Lord and King, and to bring both you and themselves with all haste to destruction.

" Ye do require things of us by a bill of Supplication ; * * but after what sort do ye come to your King to demand ? With sword in hand, and in battle-array. What manner is that to come to your Prince ? What other order would ye keep if the French or Scots should invade you ? Content —content yourselves, Good People. See our shires of Devonshire and Cornwall well in order. See the corn and the fruits of the earth, which God hath sent of his most great clemency, gathered now in time, whereby ye should be sustained in winter. Do not with this rage and fury drive yourselves to the sword, your wives and children to famine and hunger. If any thing be to be reformed in our laws, the Parliament is near at hand,—a place and time where men ought, and ever hitherto have been wont to commune on such matters; where the wise heads and the Three Estates of the realm be congregated together for that purpose, deliberately to consider and wisely to debate what laws or statutes are to be made or revoked. * * *

" First, of Baptism: ye are put in fear that your children should not be christened but upon the holy day. There is no day, time, nor hour, but by our order the priest may christen the child if it be brought unto him, even as he might before this time.

"The order of Confirmation ye seem not to mislike; but you think your children shall not learn it except they go to school. The men are appointed to teach it them without going to school; and it is not so long, and again it is so godly, that one child once having learnt it will soon teach it twenty. How did ye all learn before the Paternoster, Ave, and Credo, in Latin, which was a strange language, and which ye did not understand? And cannot your children learn so much in English, which is no more but the Belief in effect, and the Ten Commandments?   *   *   *

"The 'Six Articles,'† and the statutes that made words treason, and other such severe laws, ye seem to require again; the which all our whole Parliament, almost on their knees, required us to abolish and put away; and, when we condescended thereto, with a whole voice gave us most humble thanks, for they thought before that no man was sure of his life, lands, or goods * * * And would you have these laws again? Will you that we shall resume the *scourge* again, and *hard snaffle* for your mouths? If all the realm consent, and ye require to have our sword again awake, and more nearer your heads, ye`may soon have it by us and by Parliament restored to his old power. But, we fear us, they that most desire it will soonest and sorest repent it. When we are

---

† A bill passed by Henry the Eighth in 1539, making it capital to deny transubstantiation, or question the efficacy of private masses and auricular confession.

content to rule like a Father with all mercy and clemency, ye do call for the bridle and whip. Ah! our loving subjects, who be they that put this into your heads? Do ye know what ye demand, and what the end will be of that request?

"Where ye complain of the blindness and unwillingness of your *Curates* to the setting forth of our proceedings, we do not think your complaints much untrue in that behalf, and do fear that a great part of the dangerous stir cometh of them. But what blind heads they be, how ungodly and untoward, your own supplication doth declare. * * * And where ye say certain Cornish men be offended because they have not their service in Cornish, for so much as they understand no English, why should they now be offended more, when they understand it not in English, than when they had it in Latin and understood it not? And why should you not, all the rest, then, be glad and well pleased, that have it in English that ye do understand?

"Ye object unto us as tho' these things were done, us not knowing. But we do declare unto you that there was nothing but at our consent and knowledge, nor nothing passes in Parliament but our consent is at it. And for that, our Book of Orders of the Church, we know nothing is in it but according to the Scriptures and the word of God; and that we ourselves *in person*, altho' as yet young in age, are able to justify and prove, we trust, by Scriptures and good learning, against whosoever will defend the contrary.

" Last of all, ye require to have the relief granted unto us by the Parliament, of cloth and shorn
sheep, to be remitted unto you, affirming that we
have no need thereof. *   *   * And ye do not consider what infinite charge it is to keep such wars as
hath been both towards France and Scotland, now
continued almost these eight years.   *   *   * Ye
do not reckon how many thousand pounds Boulogne doth stand us in monthly, besides the other
pieces which be there.   *   * And we do know our
father was at no less charge, whom ye do account
to have left us so rich.   We do marvel what occasion ye have to think so; seeing he was constrained
to take so many loans, subsidies, and benevolences,
and also sell his land, which were no tokens of
abundant riches.   And how rich soever you think
he left us, we know he left us above three hundred
thousand pounds in debt.   Now guess you whether
we have need of relief or no ?"   *   *   *

There are in the State Paper Office three contemporary *Drafts* of this answer, none of them
signed by Edward or Somerset.

It is singular to mark how very soon the mutinous state of the commons in England was known
on the Continent.   In a letter from Sir William
Paget to Secretary Petre, written from Brussels,
July 8th, 1549, *(Orig. St. P. Off. Germany,)* he
observes,   *   * " It is a wonderful matter to hear
what bruits come abroad here of your things at

home, which killeth my heart to hear ; and I wot
not what to say to them, because I know they be
true, and they be as well known here in every
man's mouth as you know them at the Court, and
I fear me better ; and that not by Frenchmen, but
by these countrymen, and our own good nation."

It appears that Paget and the Council were not
singular in their opinion of the imprudent lenity
exercised by the Protector towards the rebels.
Granvelle, Charles' prime minister, in a conversation with the English ambassadors, recommended
that Somerset should imitate his master the Emperor, who had experienced from his subjects in the
Low Countries some resistance of the same kind,—
that he should draw his sword and show his authority.

Paget to Petre, in a letter dated July 13th, 1549,
(*Orig. St. P. Off.*) says, * * * " I long to hear
whether all things be appeased well, which would
be much to my comfort, and those men here ; I
mean the greatest seem to desire it much ; for
Granvela, at our being with him, did somewhat
touch it, upon th' occasion of th' excuse for our delay, in that the Emperor for the establishing of his
son had somewhat to do among these people, which
be somewhat *rude* (quoth he) ; and if the Emperor
had not at the beginning drawn his sword and
showed authority, the things he doth with them
now would not have been brought to pass ; and
now, thanks be to God! he hath as obedient sub-

jects of them as ever prince had. Marry, we here say that your commons at home *font grand bar-bularye;* but it is nothing (saith he), if Monsieur Protector step to it betimes, and travail in person as the Emperor himself did, with the Sword of Justice in his hand. We told him the matter was at a point, and made little of it, how heavy soever our hearts took it."

This avowal, by Granvelle himself, of the difficulty experienced by Charles the Fifth in procuring his son Philip to be acknowledged Sovereign of the Netherlands, is important, as we do not find in De Thou, Sleidan, Robertson, or the most popular general historians of the times, any allusion to the incipient feelings of revolt which, according to Granvelle, so strongly manifested themselves; and yet we see, had not the Emperor drawn his sword, and bestirred himself vigorously, the people of the Low Countries were so violent that they would have refused to acknowledge Philip as their sovereign.

The following letter of Sir Thomas Smith shows how deep was the impression made by the rebellion in England, upon one of her most upright and able statesmen. It relates chiefly to the disturbances raised by a sort of men thus graphically described by Strype.* "There was now [in England] a sort of lewd idle fellows, the most part whereof had neither place to inhabit, nor sought any stay to

* Strype's Memor. vol. ii. part i. p. 363.

live by; persons, many of them condemned for felony, or prison-breakers, run from the wars, or sea-
rovers, departed from the King's garrisons, and loi-
terers. These persons ran from place to place, from
county to county, from town to town, to stir up rumours, raise up tales, imagine news, whereby to stir
and gather together the King's subjects. * * And
by that means such lewd ruffians and unruly vaga-
bonds became ringleaders and masters of the King's
people, seeking to spoil, rob, and ravin whom they
listed or might; and so lived, waxed rich, and fell
on other men's labour, money, and food. And when
the poor of one part of the country, raised up by
these felons, repented, and saw their folly, * *
and received the King's pardon, the said runagates
escaped from the places of their first attempts, and
daily resorted to new places; and so from place to
place, shire to shire, never quieting themselves, but
devising slanderous tales, and divulging to the people such kind of news as they thought might most
readily move them to uproars and tumults."

SIR THOMAS SMITH TO SIR WILLIAM CECIL.

Orig. St. P. Off. *Domestic.* July 19th, 1549. *Eaton.*

" Sir, I most heartily thank you for your letters,
howbeit I could never be quiet since I read them. I
have for long time—as methinketh, marvellous long
time,—lamented [this miserable estate of our commonwealth.] And surely the grief and care that I do
take for it almost every day, as well troubled here

as you be there, is all the sickness that I have, as methinks. This day I thought to have been at the Court, but I could not all this night sleep one wink, and I think this seven-night I have not much slept; so that this morning, when I would have taken horse, I could not well stand, not for sickness, but for weakness of so much sweating and lack of sleep; for I never sleep but I sweat so, that, as much as the one comforteth, the other weakeneth. Yet this should not let me ; but that I fear me I do as much good here in keeping this part quiet, as I should do there, or rather more.

" But, Sir, on my life, if my Lord's Grace would give authority to any one man or two to execute this now last Proclamation against these mutinies, all this part, yea and the whole Shire, shall be not only quiet, but ready to serve the King's Majesty where they shall be commanded. I do not only hear, but I see by the countenances when they be afore[me], by the murmurs when I have spoken to them, that all that ever hath aught, be as weary of this tumultuous world as may be, and would be ready to help to the redress. Marry, now when the Proclamations be directed so generally, every man looketh upon another. I do not mean that the Proclamations should be otherwise directed; but I would wish letters directed to one or more special men of trust in every shire to be attendant upon the execution thereof, and to call to them upon occasion the gentlemen and other head and grave yeomen householders, as need or occasion shall be, so that they might give the King's Majesty good accounts of the order and quiet of that shire, as men in whom the King putteth a special trust.

" These men should consult with the gentlemen their neighbours, being already in a readiness, as be ye sure they be, every man for his own fear; and where they hear tell of any evil rule, or beginning of stir to be, there suddenly in the night to come with a sixty or a hundred horse, and take and lead away the *stirrers* before any more company be come unto them. And after they have once begun, they must follow still, and be attendant thereon till they have searched up the greater number, or all those *Runabouts*. Marry, there is one thing I have to you to inform my Lord's Grace, that as in times past the *Watchmen* were well ordered and for a good purpose, so now they be those that doth all the mischief, themselves being for the most part of that number that hath nothing, and in the night then do they consult how they may invent some mischief; and by reason of them, from town to town, they spread their news faster than any post can. If any gentleman come thro', he is straight stayed, if they think themselves strong. Let one of those *Runabouts* come, or *Camp-man*, to tell them news, straight they call up their neighbours, and make exclamations out of all truth and reason. So that all things would be quieter, yea, and these *Runabouts* more quiet, if there were no

watchmen. And the gentlemen might do the feat
I write unto you of so well; where else the watchmen shall descrive [discover] them, and post afore
them, do what they can. I know that the uproar
at Walden rose by the Watchmen; and, I ween,
thro' Essex; and well I wot here, where the watch
is, there watches more than are commanded; and,
where it is laid down, there all is quieter. Marry,
some doubteth whether they may lay down the
watch, or no; but I am in this mind, that I had
rather the Justice should command, on pain of
death, that no man should watch, except they had
a special commandment from the Justices.

" *Illud de Mario, vel Marianis, me valde angit,
immo prope exanimat.—Faxit Deus Opt. Max. pro
sua clementia malum id avertat.** And if that be
not, I have no fear but this fatal mischief shall be
well overpast.

" Here we can learn no certainty of my Lord
Grey's doing; but if it had been *for* the camp-men,
as I perceive it was *against* them, we should have
heard enough of it. Ye must call upon my Lord's
Grace to give him thanks, and to animate him to
use severity against all those specially as came out
of other shires thither; and if a great number of the
boisterous were despatched, the realm had no loss.

* A reply, perhaps, to some allusion of Cecil to a suspicion
then entertained that the Princess Mary and her adherents
were secret abettors of this rebellion. The masculine termination is probably used to avoid any *direct* implication of the
Princess. Strype's Memor. vol. ii. part i. p. 276.

His doings is better than ten thousand Proclamations and pardons for the quieting of the people.

"I pray you steal a little time, and let me know some news from you; or if you have no leisure, yet tell them, that I may hear, to Will my man, who is witty and secret, and he shall write them me. I trust I shall [be] (yea, and am, as I think now, if I once can sleep well but half a night,) able to serve again there, and to ease you of some of your pains, except it be my Lord's Grace's pleasure I shall still tarry here. I had been with you before this, but only for these commissions, and that I still looked for the King's Majesty here. Thus I most heartily commit you to God! From Eaton, the 19th July.

"Your most assured, T. SMITH.

"Sir, I heartily thank you for your gentleness towards Mr. Gascoigne; and if you can do him any pleasure in his matter, I pray you do it."

Endorsed.

" *To my most loving and assured friend, Mr. Cicill,*
Master of Requests to my Lord Protector's Grace."

Paget, when on the point of returning from his unsuccessful embassy to the Emperor, who refused to embarrass himself with the defence of Boulogne, addressed the following letter to Petre, the Secretary of State. He mentions the " melancholy matters at home," meaning the civil commotions in England; and in a passage, which is worthy of note, seems to allude to some design on the part of the Council to introduce " *innovations*," and alter the state of the realm. It would appear from this, that Paget already suspected the existence of some *Conspiracy* against the government of the Protector, and hoped they might appease things at home, without adopting any " new fantasies or dangerous schemes, which might bring far more evil than good."

SIR W. PAGET TO PETRE.

Orig. St. P. Off. *Flanders.* July 22nd, 1549. *Bruges.*

" Mr. Secretary,—I thank you with all my heart for your letters sent unto me by my servant Fletcher ; and also for your gentleness showed to him in a suit wherein Mr. Thynne hath showed him [self] much to his dishonesty, and to the disclosing of greedy covetousness, as shall appear to my Lord's Grace at my return. I beseech God that the covetous disposition of that man do my Lord's Grace no hurt. There is no one thing whereof his Grace hath need to take such heed as of that man's proceedings, for his Grace may be assured the world noteth them much. Well, let that matter go among the rest of your *melancholy matters* at home.

" As touching my proceedings here, you may perceive the whole by our common letter, which indeed is nothing. They have always answered here that they would depesche me away, whereby I conceive they mind not any great matter with us at this time; and I trust in God, by the next time they shall have need to require a depesche at our hands at home, which cannot fail the next year, by the judgment of all men that knoweth the state of the world in every corner.†

" With the Emperor himself I have not treated but at my first coming, which in all this time of delay I would not have missed if your first determination there contained in mine instructions had continued ; but all is for the best, and I trust for our benefit, if we may appease our things at home, and lean not too much to such *new fantasies as set forth innovations which be dangerous,* and little known to the setters forth what good or ill will come of them. To *alter the state of a realm would ask ten years' deliberation.* I trust we will beware, by things past, war abroad and war among ourselves. Marry, what prince that understands things would not gladly see one of them at an end ere he enter with us, and surely I know the state of our things at home in this present time to trouble these men here much ; for, howsoever he keepeth himself here aloof at this time, no doubt it stands him in hand that we do well, and it importeth us that he do well also, rather than our other neighbours. I will take such answer as they shall give me, * * * * and depart home. I intend by the long seas, * * for I will purge myself well, and not without need, being well *farsed* with Rhenish wine, which I assure

† He means that, by next year, there will be war between France and Charles the Fifth, and he hopes that Charles will then be asking aid of England, as England was now asking it as his hands.

you hath searched every joint in my body so certainly, that it hath made, many times, every vein in my heart oftentimes to shrink.

" The Emperor intends to depart from hence upon Friday, and I as soon as I am depesched. He cometh not to Gravelines, but turneth hence into Henault; and therefore I am glad to be rid of him, for that I am unfurnished of all things for the purpose, and specially of money; for at my coming forth I received two hundred pounds, which was worth to me scant one hundred and fifty, and that is all spent, and three hundred pounds more (so God judge me) at the least; but I trust my Lord will be good Lord to me. Thus, with most hearty commendations, I bid you as well to fare as your gentle heart can desire.

" From Bruges, the 22nd July 1549.

" Your own,　　　Paget."

In the following letter, the hardy, politic, and ambitious Warwick appears in a more amiable light than we could have anticipated from his general demeanour. The Marquis of Northampton had been sent against the rebels; but being, as Fuller says,* more acquainted with the *witty* than the *warlike* part of Pallas, he was defeated with severe loss, and compelled to fly to London.

Warwick, considered one of the best military leaders in England, was chosen to supersede him;

* Fuller's Church History, vol. ii. p. 322.

but he earnestly pleads that Northampton should be continued in the command, " lest he think himself *utterly discredited*," and generously offers to serve under him. Warwick's request was in part complied with; for, although Northampton did not command the second expedition against the rebels, he accompanied it.*

WARWICK TO CECIL.

Orig. St. P. Off. *Domestic.* 10th August 1549. *Warwick.*

" Gentle Master Cecill.—After my very hearty commendations for your friendly letter [and] occurrents. Perceiving how we stand now to the French, which in my opinion is better for us than under their coloured friendship, [which] used us as evil as now they can do, being open war, wishing, if it were the will of God, that we had no more to deal withal at once; but since it is thus, we must pull up our hearts and put our confidence in the Lord.

" And whereas with your letter I received a Commission, in the which it appeareth that I am appointed to have the leading of the Shires of Cambridge, Bedford, Huntingdon, Northampton, Norfolk, and Suffolk; for the which, like as I do think myself much bounden to my Lord's Grace and the Council for enabling me to receive so great a charge, so I cannot but wish that it might please the same to permit and suffer my Lord Marquis of Northampton to continue still in the force of his Commission,

* Fuller's Church History, vol. ii. p. 323.

or at the least renewed, forasmuch, the nobleman having lately by misfortune received discomfort enough, haply this might give him occasion to think himself utterly discredited, and so for ever discourage him ; which, in my opinion, were great pity. Wherefore, if it might please his Grace to use his services again, I shall be as glad for my part to join *with* him, yea, rather than fail, with all my heart to serve *under* him, for this journey, as I would be to have the whole authority myself ; and by this means his Grace shall preserve his heart, and hable [enable] him to serve hereafter, which, otherwise, he shall be utterly in himself discouraged [to do].

" I would wish that no man for *one* mischance or evil hap, to the which we be all subject that must serve, should be utterly abject; for, if it should be so, it were almost a present discomfort to all men before they go to it, since those things lie in God's hand. Therefore, good Mr. Cecill, use your accustomed wisdom, and good heart that you bear to my Lord's Grace, in declaring this matter with effect to the same, and with diligence let me hear from you again; and in the mean time I shall forslow no time to put these shires in a readiness to serve as appertaineth.   Fare you well.

" At Warwick, this Sunday, at four in the morning, the 10th of August.

" Your faithful friend,

" J. WARWICK."

Endorsed.—" *The Earl of Warwick to my Mr. the 10th of August* 1549."

It appears by a letter, or rather draft of a letter, from the Council to the Lord Privy Seal Russel, dated 21st August 1549, that on the 19th of that month he had completely defeated the rebels. Part of the letter is interesting, as it points out the chief leaders in the insurrection.

" Ye do well to make the most diligent search ye may for Thomas Pomerey. And we pray you send up hither, as ye can conveniently, Sir Humphrey Arundel, Maunder, the Mayor of Bodmyn, and two or three of the most rankest traitors and ringleaders of them, here to be examined, and after to be determined against as shall appertain."

The successful military exertions of Lord Russel and the Earl of Warwick had now succeeded in restoring the country to tranquillity, the rebels having been defeated at Exeter by Russel, with the loss of a thousand men, and in Dussindale in a still more sanguinary action by the Earl of Warwick. Ket was hanged on Norwich Castle, his brother William on Windham steeple, and nine others on the Oak of Reformation.* The following letter explains itself.

THOMAS WODHOUSE TO SIR WILLIAM WODHOUSE.

Orig. St. P. Off. *Domestic.* 3rd Sept. 1549.

" BROTHER.—You shall understand that my Lord of Warwick doth execution of many men at Nor-

---

* Fuller's Church History, vol. ii. p. 325.

wich ; and the gentlemen crave at his hands the gift of the Escheats, and do daily bring in men by accusation. But I have neither accused any man nor asked the gift of any, although I am spoiled of two thousand sheep, and all my bullocks and horses, with the most part of all my corn in the country. All the ordnance and spoil that was taken in the Camp is the King's; I moved my Lord for my two pieces of brass, but I cannot have them at his hand, yet he is very gentle to me. Ralf Symonds made a great complaint of Turcock to my Lord ; and yet he was in the camp but two days in the beginning, and then went to Newcastle, and came not home again till the battle was done. Notwithstanding, the Sheriff seized all his goods; and, if I had not made earnest suit to my Lord, he had lost his goods and been in danger of death.

" I pray you write unto me if you think it meet that I come up. There is a Commission come down of Oyer determiner. We have many prisoners at Yarmouth, which shall be ordered by Sir Thomas Clere and me. There is in the Commission my Lord Willoughby, my Lord Wentworth, Sir Edmund Windham, and Sir John Clere, with other gentlemen, and yet I am left out; yet there be in my charge at Yarmouth seven score or eight score prisoners, and they shall sit upon the delivery of them.

" You may tell my Lord Great Master that I think it not meet that others, which were not in service at the taking of them, should have the order of deli-

very, and I be left out. I am sure that Daniel declared to you the truth of all things in taking of the
prisoners, for if Gellat had not there been with those
men that came from London, there had but few prisoners been taken; and because I was so venturous
to go out when others kept within the gates, the ruffians of the town writ a letter to Sir Thomas Clere,
that if he kept my company he should be in danger
of his life, for they were determined to kill me with
*   *   *, and the bailiffs more.

"This was on the Monday, when they thought
my Lord of Warwick had been overthrown. I pray
you speak with Mr. Cecill, that when any Commission or letters be sent down for order of things here
that I be not forgotten, for then I shall lose my credit in the country. I did speak with Mistress Anne
Wotton; she is well; and little Henry is with me at
my house. Thus fare ye well!

"From Waxhen, the 3rd of September.

"Your loving brother,

"THOMAS WODHOUSE."

Endorsed.

"*To my loving Brother, Sir Wm. Wodhouse,
Knt. at Sir Anthony Archer's, beside the
Tower Hill in London.—Haste! haste!*"

Captain Thomas Drury, who is mentioned in the
following letter, had greatly distinguished himself
under Warwick by his gallant conduct against the
rebels; but I give it chiefly because it establishes
two facts which appear to me of some importance

in the early biography of Cecil: the first is, that
Warwick addresses him as having great influence
over the Protector,—as the *organ* through which
court patronage flows; the second, that Cecil is evi-
dently on the best terms with Warwick himself,
and yet Warwick was at this time the mortal enemy of Somerset, and must have been plotting his
destruction. In so singular a position stood this
extraordinary man.

WARWICK TO CECIL.

Orig. St. P. Off. *Domestic.* 14th Sept. 1549.

" THESE shall be to desire you to be an inter-
cessor to my Lord's Grace that this bearer, Thomas
Drury, Captain of ix [nine score] footmen, serv-
ing the King's Majesty against the rebels in Norfolk [should receive for them his pay,] for the
space of two months, that is to say, from the first
day that the Marquis of Northampton took his
journey into Norfolk until this present, except
three score which were killed at the battle and
other skirmishes there; for the which number of
three score he doth demand nothing since the 27th
of August hitherto: requiring you to help that this
said bearer may have brief despesche, and that his
band be speedily employed or cayssed [cassed, bro-
ken]. Thus most heartily fare you well!

" At Ely Place, this 14th of Sept. 1549.

" Your assured friend, J. WARWYK."

Endorsed.—" *To my very loving friend, Mr. Cecille,
these be delivered with speed at the Court.*"

The reader will be amused by the business-like manner in which, in the following letter, the Lord Chancellor Rich, *previous to the trial,* arranges not only the best evidence for the *conviction,* but the best place for *the execution* of his prisoners.   It is of this Rich that David Lloyd says, " Cromwell was the *mall,* and Rich the *hammer,* of abbeys;" adding, that the reformers took their *religion* from Cranmer and Ridley, and their *law* from Rich.*   One must not look for this man's real character in the encomiastic pages of Lloyd, or the Biographia Britannica.   Many facts could be brought to show that he was base, crafty, treacherous, and time-serving.

THE LORD CHANCELLOR RICH TO CECIL.

Orig.   St. P. Off.   *Domestic.*   18th Sept. 1549.

" Mr. Cissell.—With hearty commendations. These shall be to advertise the same, that the commissioners for the commission of Oyer determiner for this Shire of Essex are appointed to sit at Brentwood upon Saturday next for the arraignment of Essex and Nicholas More, now prisoners in the Tower ; wherefore, I pray you know my Lord's Grace's pleasure for the sending of them down by some of the guard, or by the Knight Marshal's servants, for that they may be at Brentwood on Friday at night next : and that ye will cause further to be sent down Essex's boy, for the giving of evidence

* Lloyd's England's Worthies, pp. 203, 205.

against his master; for it is very requisite for the
Jury to hear what the boy can say upon his oath.
And that my Lord's Grace's pleasure be further
known for the appointment of the places of *execution* for the said prisoners.   And if it stand with his
Grace's pleasure, Sir Thomas Darcy and the residue
of the commissioners think it best that Essex should
suffer at Malden, and More at Brayntrey; whereof
I heartily desire to be advertised of his Grace's
pleasure herein.   Thus most heartily fare ye well!

   " From my house of Lees, the 18th of September.

     " Your loving friend, R. RYCHE, Cancell^r."

Endorsed.—" *To my very loving friend,*
  Mr. Cyssell, be these delivered."

I believe it to be an error in the author of Lord
Burleigh's Life in the Biographia Britannica to ima-
gine that Cecil was made Secretary of State by
the Protector Somerset previous to 1550.   In the
Domestic Correspondence of the State Paper Office
I find an original letter from Sir Edward North,
Sir Walter Mildmay, and others, dated 13th July
1548, addressed to the Right Worshipful Master
Cecil, *Secretary to my Lord Protector's Grace;* but
this appellation, which confirms a conjecture of Dr.
Nares, in his Life of Burleigh,* proves that his office
was completely distinct from that of Secretary of
State.   At this time he was also Master of Requests;
and, in addition to those already given, I could quote
many letters which show that at this early period he

* Life of Lord Burleigh, vol. i. p. 307.

enjoyed the chief confidence of Somerset, and possessed a power equal to that of principal adviser or prime minister.

The following letter from Parry, the *Cofferer* or treasurer to the Princess Elizabeth,* afterwards Queen, shows that *she* then considered Cecil as the person in highest authority about the Protector. It demonstrates also the excessive caution and prudence which this great Princess was compelled to use during her early years. The short letter which succeeds it, from Sir Edward Wotton, proves also the great influence which his " cousin Cecil" possessed with the Protector.

THOMAS PARRY TO CECIL.

Orig. St. P. Off. *Domestic.* 25th Sept. 1549.

" Sir.—The Ambassador of Venice came yesterday with letters of commendation from the Duke, importing that he, being the Orator of the King's Majesty, should also on the Duke's behalf see her Grace, with general credit therein ; and perceiving that my Lord's Grace had spoken with him as he said, [he] was used thereafter : he talked with her Grace at sundry times yesterday, and hunted here; and at night took his leave, and is departed.

" Hereof her Grace hath with all haste commanded me to send unto you, and to advertise you, to the intent forthwith it may please you at her earnest request either to move my Lord's Grace, and

* Haynes, p. 95.

to declare this unto him yourself, or else forthwith to send word in writing, that her Grace may know thereby whether she shall herself write thereof; not for that the talk did import weight, but that her Grace will neither know nor do in matters that either may sound or seem to be of importance without doing of my Lord's Grace to understand thereof: and in case ye shall advise her Grace to write, then so forthwith to advertise her Grace. And in the mean season she enjoineth you to make his Grace privy to that which she hath enjoined you, with hearty commendations to give his Grace knowledge hereof; because, as I said, though there be no great thing yet appearing, or sounding or seeming to be of any importance, it shall no sooner be in her Grace's head than my Lord's Grace shall have intelligence thereof.

" Herein she desires you to use her trust as in the rest, using such speed as you shall think best to appertain.

" I deferred to write of matter of Surbery upon this occasion, being then at hand, and thought it sufficient that Outrede might declare unto you what seemed good to me if you shall like it; as presently to be certified of the next year's wood sale, for setting forwards thereof, and such like, whereof by the next I will write more.

" The 25th of Sept. 1549.

" All your own bounden, THOMAS PARRY."

" *To the Right Worshipful Mr. Cecil, Esquier.*
Endorsed 26th Sept.—" *Mr. Parry to my Mr.*"

SIR EDWARD WOTTON TO CECIL.

Orig. ST. P. OFF. *Domestic.*

" COUSIN CYCELL.—In my very hearty manner, I commend me unto you. These shall be to desire you, the rather at this my *contemplation,* to further this bearer, my kinsman, Hugh Darrell, in his suit to my Lord Protector's Grace for the obtaining the office of bailiwick of certain lands and revenues in Kent, that Sir Thomas W. * * *, deceased, late exchanged with the King's Majesty * * * * *, which office is now void by the death of ———— Deryng, late bailiff there; so as by y[our] furtherance and friendship he may the rath[er] obtain the same. Thus most heartily fare you well !

" From my house in Warwick Lane, this 18th of September, A.D. 1549.

" Your Cousin,

" E. WOTTON."

Endorsed.

" *Sir Edward Wotton to my Mr.*"

It is well known to the reader of English history, that the fall and disgrace of the Protector followed hard upon the suppression of the great rebellion in Devonshire and Norfolk ; and the rapid formation of the Conspiracy which hurled this great man from his almost regal elevation, and consigned him to the Tower, humbled and ruined, is one of the most obscure portions of the history of this time. On the 25th of Sept. we find him in full power; on the 10th of October he is in the hands of his mortal enemies ; and on the 13th a prisoner in the Tower.

" It would be unreasonable to expect a critical account of the revolution in our general historians ; but even Strype, usually so rich in his illustrations, is brief and somewhat careless in his treatment of the subject, being contented, seemingly, with the narrative of Burnet, which is more full.   The following letters throw new and more certain light on the progress of the struggle between the Protector and his enemies.

" The best account we have of the rise of the conspiracy is given by Holinshed.*   Alluding to the civil commotions which had been recently put down, he says :—

" Now, after that these *hurly-burlies* were thoroughly quieted, many of the Lords of the realm, as well Councillors as others, misliking the government of the Protector, began to withdraw themselves from Court, and, resorting to London, fell to secret consultation for redress of things ; but, namely, for the displacing of the Lord Protector.   And suddenly, upon what occasion many marvelled, but few knew, every Lord and Councillor went thro' the City *weaponed*, and had their servants likewise weaponed, attending upon them in new liveries, to the great wondering of many ; and, at the last, a great assembly of the said Councillors was made at the Earl of Warwick's lodging, which was then at Elie Place in

* Hollinshed, vol. iii. p. 1014.

Holborn, whither all the confederates in this matter came privily armed, and finally concluded to possess the Tower of London."

It is evident from this passage, that the *first* hostile demonstrations were made by the Council, not by Somerset.   They withdrew their presence from the court; they suddenly armed themselves and their dependents; they held secret meetings for the displacing of the Protector.   On being informed of these alarming preparations against him, Somerset issued the following proclamation, which is signed by the young King and by himself.

Orig.   St. P. Off.   *Domestic.*   1st Oct. 1549.

" Edward.

" The King's Majesty straitly chargeth and commandeth all his loving subjects with all haste to repair to his Highness at his Majesty's manor of Hampton Court, in most defensible array, with harness and weapons, to defend his most royal person, and his most entirely beloved uncle, the Lord Protector, against whom certain hath attempted a most dangerous conspiracy.   And this to do in all possible haste.   Given at Hampton Court, the first day of October, in the third year of his most noble reign.

" E. Somerset."

There is added to the Proclamation this certificate, by an unknown hand.

" I received this letter the vi day of October, of George Tunstal, my Lord of Canterbury's servant, between the hours of one and two before noon on the same day."

The letter is endorsed,

> " *A letter, signed by the King and the Duke of Somerset, for the people's repairing to Hampton Court. Dated, primo Octobris* 1549."

At the moment the Conspiracy broke out, the young King and the Protector were at Hampton Court. Here also were Archbishop Cranmer, Sir William Paget, Sir William Petre, and Sir Thomas Smith, the two Secretaries of State, and Mr. William Cecil, Master of Requests and private Secretary to Somerset. These were the chief of the leading men with whom the Duke might advise in his distress; and it would appear that all of them recommended him to enter into an amicable compromise with the revolted Lords of the Council. But he had other friends with him, who assumed a bolder tone. They earnestly counselled him to collect an armed force, and, having summoned the Lords of Warwick's faction to repair instantly to Court, and proceed with the utmost rigour against all who dared to be refractory. From one of these, whose name does not appear, proceeded the following Directions.

Orig. St. P. Off. *Domestic.* 4th Oct. 1549.

" If it please the King to write a letter unto all the Lords generally, saying, forasmuch as it is known unto him what false and untrue doings, and most vilest reports [are] made of my Lord his uncle ; [and that he] is too sorry to see that all they should be led to believe and credit the same, which his Majesty is most able to answer, and will answer himself to be untrue and most detestable : wherefore he wills them to trust to his letter, written with his own hand; that all such of them as will be taken for his true and loving subjects, should repair to him from the rest that willeth the contrary,—not with their powers, but their own persons.

" Or else, not doing this, let them assure themselves he cannot nor will not take it that it was his *uncle* that they seek to defeat and put down, whom he does most entirely love, as he can well charge all them of his Council that they have said to him that he has had no less cause so to do, for his most true and painful service in his most tender youth ; but it is *himself* that they seek to put down, and not his uncle, and so he takes it; and no [otherwise will deem] * * * of it, except they follow his letter and commandment. And if it were not for the love he beareth to his Nobility and subjects, he would not write unto them, but he beareth with them because he does see that they are too much blinded; for he is assured that God will in this

thing, if he had no power at all, see the destruction
of them that seek to danger him, and all his realm
so ungodlily."

The next paper in illustration of this Conspiracy
is not a little curious. It is a Proclamation, or
hand-bill, written by a friend of the Protector, dropped in the streets of London, and having this in-
scription on the back : *Read it and give it furth !*
Its account of the causes and object of the plot will
of course be read with caution, as proceeding from
a quarter where we cannot look for impartiality.
Its indignation against the new nobility,—" men,"
as it terms them, " come but of late from the dunghill, more meet to keep swine" than to sit as councillors,—and its concluding allusion to Merlin's prophecy, mark strikingly the feelings and superstitions
of the time.

Orig. St. P. Off. *Domestic.*

" Most loving and true Englishmen, which love
God and your King, unto such do I write. Remember with yourselves your loyal obedience, and
be not carried away with the painted eloquence of
a sort of *crafty traitors*, which draw at one mark
and shoot at another. Weigh their devilish policy. First : whereas they have like bribers undone and murdered the King's true subjects; and
now fearing that the Lord Protector, according to
his promise, would have redressed things in the
Court of Parliament, which he shortly intended to

have set, to the intent that the poor Commons might be godly eased, and things well redressed; to defeat him of the said good purpose, they now of mere malice have conspired his death; which done, they will find the means shortly after, to dispatch your most noble liege Lord; partly for their insatiate covetise and ambition, and partly to plant again the doctrine of the Devil and Anti-Christ of Rome.

" Wherefore, let not their persuasions, nor their proud Proclamations, move your hearts any thing at all; but think and know this for a surety, that in case the Lord Protector hath done any thing contrary to truth and justice, without all doubt *they* were partakers and of counsel in the same, altho' now they would pluck their heads out of the collars, and put him headlong into the briers.

" But if ye will diligently ponder and weigh what they be, and what their accustomed conditions be also, ye shall easily perceive what they intend. And here also note, how they be come up but late *from the dunghill;* a sort of them more meet to keep *swine* than to occupy the offices which they do occupy; and now [conspire] to the utter impoverishing and undoing of all the Commons of this realm. Wherefore I desire you, for the tender mercy of God, give not hasty credit unto their doings and sayings, but stick fast unto your most godly and Christian Prince and King; for tho' they traitorously call them the body of the Council, yet they lack the head : then may ye call it a *monstrous* Council, for truly every body is nothing without the head. But the Lord shall destroy such a body at his pleasure! And as for London, called Troy untrue, Merlin sayeth that twenty-three aldermen of hers shall lose their heads on one day, which God grant to be shortly. Amen!

    " By the King's true and loving subject

               " To his power,

                     " HENRY A———."

At the same time that the Proclamation which we have just given was dropped in the streets of London, the Protector dispersed the following short *hand-bill* amongst the commons in the different counties.

                Orig. ST. P. OFF. *Domestic.*

" GOOD PEOPLE.

    " In the name of God and King Edward, let us rise with all our power to defend him and the Lord Protector against certain lords and gentlemen, and chief-masters, which would depose the Lord Protector, and so endanger the King's royal person; because we, the poor Commons, being injured by the extortions of gentlemen, had our pardon this year by the mercy of the King and the goodness of the Lord Protector; for whom let us fight, for he loveth all just and true gentlemen

which do no extortion, and also the poor commonalty of Englonde.*

> " God save the King and my Lord Pro-
>   tector, and all true lords and gentlemen,
>   and us the poor Commonalty."

Endorsed.   " *The copy of the bill sowed
    amongst the commons.*"

Somerset, although surrounded by difficulties,
did not forget his public duties in the midst of
his individual danger.   Boulogne was threatened
by the French at the same moment that he was
himself proscribed as a traitor by Warwick and
the Lords conspirators at Ely House.   The following letter is probably amongst the last *foreign*
orders sent in his character of Protector.   It
proves also, that the Councillors, Sir William Petre
and St. John, who deserted him afterwards on the
5th, continued still faithful on the 4th of October.

THE PROTECTOR AND THE COUNCIL TO LORD
COBHAM.

Orig.   HARLEIAN. 284. fol. 46.   4th October 1549.

" AFTER our right hearty commendations to your
    good Lordship.

" We desire the same to chuse out of the gunners
that were at Newhaven, and now remain at Calais,

---

* This hand-bill of the Protector supplies a hiatus in the
MS. Privy Council Books of Edward the Sixth, where an
allusion is made to it, but the words " Good people" are all
that are given.

twenty of the best and most expert, whom we pray
you to send out of hand to Buloign, by sea, to the
Lord Clinton.   We pray your Lordship to see this
done both diligently and speedily.   And so we bid
you heartily well to fare.   From Hampton Court,
the 4th of October 1549.

" Your loving friend,

" E. SOMERSET."

" TH. CANT.   WM. ST. JOHN.

" WM. PETRE.   WM. PAGET."

Letters were now hurried off by both factions to
such of the nobility as they judged would be
soonest ready to assemble their powers.   The Lords
at London, controlled and led by Warwick, Somerset's mortal enemy, asserted that the King's person
was in imminent danger from the falsehood and
treasons of the Protector.   The Duke, on his side,
speaking in the name of the young King, upbraided the Lords as the authors of a grievous
conspiracy against his royal person, and that of his
beloved uncle; whilst both factions seemed determined to appeal to the sword.   This appears to
have been the state of things on the 6th of October;* but the following letter, written on the suc-

* SOMERSET TO GOLDING.

Orig.   ST. P. OFF.   *Domestic.*   5th Oct. 1549.

" WE commend us unto you.   And for the confidence we
have in you, being our servant, we will and require you to soli-
cit and give order for our very good Lord the Earl of Oxford's

ceeding day, indicates a wavering in Somerset's resolution, and a recurrence to a more pacific tone. This change was probably occasioned by the fate

things, servants, and ordinary power, that he himself, and the same also, be in good readiness, whatsoever shall chance to require his service for the King's Majesty; whereof, if any occasion shall chance, we will signify by our letters. Thus we commit the order of the whole unto your good discretion, and will you to use herein convenient secrecy. From Hampton Court, the 5th October 1549.

" Your loving Lord and Master,

" E. Somerset."

" To our loving servant,

　" —— Golding, Esquire."

On the same day the Protector, in the King's name, writes thus to Sir Harry Seymour, as if still uncertain of the precise bearing of the conspiracy.

TO SIR HARRY SEYMOUR.

Orig.　St. P. Off.　*Domestic.*

" EDWARD.　　　　" *By the King.*

" We greet you well. For as much as we be given to understand by insinuations of rumours, that a *certain Conspiracy* is achieving against us and our royal person, which, we trust in God, shall never prevail, but come to that confusion that thereto belongeth." The remaining part of this letter, which is tedious, need not be given. It states that, " to the intent we would not be without the assistance and supportation of our trusty servants and subjects against all attempts," Sir Harry shall levy horse and foot, and come hither with all expedition.—" Hampton Court, 5th October, in the third year of our reign.

" E. Somerset."

On the 6th, however, it appears he had acquired more certain information, and had determined on resorting to more

of Secretary Petre, who, on being sent to the Lords
at Ely House, had been prevented from returning to
Windsor, probably without much compulsion being
used, and by the persuasions of Paget and Cranmer.

THE PROTECTOR TO THE LORDS AT LONDON.

Orig. St. P. Off. *Domestic.* 7th Oct. 1549.

" My Lords, we commend us most heartily
unto you. And whereas the King's Majesty, being
informed that you were assembled in such sort as
you do now remain there, was advised by us, and
such others of his Council as were then here about
his person, to send Mr. Secretary Petre unto you

decided measures. This is shown by the following proclamation.

Orig. Draft. St. P. Off. *Domestic.* 6th Oct. 1549.

"EDWARD.   " *By the King.*

" Right trusty and right well beloved, we greet you well.
Letting you understand that such a heinous and grievous *Conspiracy* as never was seen, is attempted against us and our entirely beloved uncle, the Lord Protector, the which they are
constrained to maintain with the most untrue and false surmises.
For they pretend and bruit abroad that our said uncle hath sold
Buloign, and detaineth wages, and such untrue tales, the which
we know of certainty to be merely false; and that, by the rest of
the Council's confession, nothing to have been done by our said
uncle but the rest of our Council did agree unto; as we do not
doubt ye shall firmly and truly perceive at your repair to us,
—the which we pray you to make with all speed for our defence in this our necessity, whatsoever letters, and from whom-
soever ye shall receive, to the contrary. And we shall take
the same most thankfully. Praying you in anywise not to fail
as ye tender our surety. Given at our honour of Hampton
Court, the 6th of October, in the third year of our reign.

" E. Somerset."

with such a message as whereby might have ensued
the surety of his Majesty's person, the preservation
of his realm and subjects, and the quiet both of us
and yourselves, as Mr. Secretary can well declare
unto you; his Majesty, and we of his Council here,
do not a little marvel that you stay still with you
the said Mr. Secretary, and have not as it were
vouchsafed to send an answer to his Majesty, neither
by him nor yet any other.

"And, for ourselves, we do much more marvel
and are right sorry, as both we and you have
good cause to be, to see this manner of your
doings, bent with force and violence to bring
the King's Majesty and us to these extremities.
Which as we do intend, if you will take no other
way but violence, to defend, as nature and our allegiance doth bind us, to th' extremity of death,
and put all into God's hands, who giveth the victory
as it pleaseth him : so, if any reasonable conditions
and offers will take place, (as hitherto none have
been signified unto us from you, nor we do not understand what you do require or seek, nor what you
do·intend,) and that ye do seek no hurt to the King's
Majesty's person, as touching all other private
matters, to avoid the effusion of Christian blood, and
to preserve the King's Majesty's person, his realm
and subjects, ye shall find us agreeable to any reasonable conditions that you will require ; for we
do esteem the King, and the wealth and tranquillity
of this realm, more than all other worldly things,

yea, than our own life. And, thus praying you to
send us your determinate answer herein by Mr. Secretary Petre, or, if you will not let him come, by
this bearer, we beseech God to give both you and us
grace so to determine this matter as may be to God's
honour, the King's Majesty, and the quiet of us all;
which may be, if the fault be not in you. And so
we bid you right heartily well to fare.

" From the King's Majestys' Castle of Windsor,
the 7th of Oct. 1549.

" Your Lordship's loving friend,

" E. SOMERSET."

The above letter, which is subscribed by the Protector alone, is in the hand-writing of Sir Thomas
Smith, who remained faithful to the last, and shared
in his imprisonment in the Tower. This last communication convinced the Earl of Warwick and his
faction that the spirit of Somerset was broken,
and they prepared to follow up the advantage which
they had gained. They addressed letters to the sheriffs and justices throughout England, commanding
them on their peril to prevent the raising of any force
within their bounds; and they sent a messenger to
Lord Russel and Sir William Herbert, who easily
persuaded these barons to adopt their quarrel and
take part against the Duke.

This defection of Russel and Herbert seems
to me to have been the circumstance which sealed
the fate of Somerset. These Barons were two

of the best officers in England; they were still at the head of a portion of the army which had been engaged with the rebels in Devonshire; the Protector relied upon their aid, and had written to them to come instantly forward for defence of the King.   If they had pushed on to London, Warwick and his friends were scarcely in a condition to make any head against them : but their answer must have been a knell to the Duke; it was as follows.   Its right feeling and good sense, with the pure and vigorous style of its composition, render it a remarkable document.

LORD RUSSEL AND SIR WILLIAM HERBERT TO THE PROTECTOR SOMERSET.

Orig. Copy.   St. P. Off.   *Domestic.*   8th Oct. 1549.

" Pleaseth your Grace.—We have received your letters, not without our great lamentation and sorrow to perceive the civil dissension which has happened between your Grace and the nobility.   A greater plague could not be sent unto this realm from God ; being the next way to make us, of conquerors, slaves, and to induce upon us an universal calamity and thraldom, which we pray God so to hold His holy hand over us as we may never see it.

" And for answer, this is to signify, that so long as we thought that the nobility presently assembled had conspired against the King's Majesty's person, so long we came forward with such company as we have for the surety of his Highness, as appertaineth.

And now, having this day received advertisement from the Lords, whereby it is given us to understand that no hurt nor displeasure is meant towards the King's Majesty, and that it doth plainly appear unto us that they are his Highness' most true and loving subjects, meaning no otherwise than as to their duties of allegiance may appertain; so, as in conclusion, it doth also appear unto us, that this great extremity proceedeth only upon *private causes* between your Grace and them; we have, therefore, thought most convenient in the heat of this broil to levy as great a power as we may, as well for the surety of the King's Majesty's person, as also for the preservation of the State of the Realm, which, whilst this contention endureth, by factions between your Grace and them may be in much peril and danger.

" We are out of doubt the Devil hath not so enchanted nor abused their wits as they would consent to any thing prejudicial and hurtful to the King's most noble person, upon whose surety and preservation, as they well know, the state of the realm doth only depend; and having consideration of their honors' discretions, and their continual truth unto the crown, we believe the same so assuredly as no other argument may dissuade us for the contrary. And for our own parts, we trust your Grace doubteth not, but that as we have, and will and must have, a special regard and consideration of our duties of allegiance unto the King's Majesty,

so shall we not be negligent to do our parts like
faithful subjects for the surety of his Highness accordingly.   Beseeching your Grace that his Majesty
in anywise be put in no fear, and that your Grace
would so conform yourself as these private causes
redound not to an universal displeasure of the whole
realm.

"Would God all means were used rather than
any blood be shed; which if [it] be once attempted,
and the case brought to that misery that the hands
of the nobility be once polluted each with other's
blood, the quarrel once begun will never have end
till the realm be descended to that woful calamity
that all our posterity shall lament the chance.
Your Grace's proclamations and billets sent abroad
for the raising of the Commons we *mislike* very
much.   The wicked and evil-disposed persons shall
stir as well as the faithful subjects ; and we, and
these other gentlemen who have served, and others
of worship in these countries where the same
have been published, do incur by these means much
infamy, slander, and discredit.

"Thus we end.   Beseeching Almighty God the
matter be so used as no effusion of blood may follow, and therewithal a surety of the King's Majesty
and of the state of the realm.

"From Andover, the 8th of October 1549.

"Your Grace's loving friends,

"JOHN RUSSEL.

"WM. HERBERT."

"*To my Lord Protector's Grace.*"

It is probable that the following letter from the young King to the Council at London, was dictated by Cranmer and Paget, who still remained with Somerset.   Their arguments had convinced this once powerful, but now fallen man, that he must leave the high ground he had at first attempted to occupy.   Resistance was hopeless ; it was evident he must resign the Protectorate, and all that remained was to capitulate on such reasonable terms as might secure his life and property.   It was with this object that Somerset sent those " Articles " which have been printed by Burnet, in his Appendix to the History of the Reformation,* from a copy in the Cotton collections.   The *original* Articles are to be found in the State Paper Office, enclosed in this letter of the young King.

EDWARD TO THE LORDS OF THE COUNCIL.

Orig.   St. P. Off.   *Domestic.*   8th Oct. 1549.

" RIGHT trusty and right well beloved Cousins, and right trusty and well beloved, we greet you well ; and have by your letters, which our trusty servant William Honnings presented to us yester-night, perceived the causes which you allege for your abode and assemblies there, with your excuse for the staying there of Sir William Petre, one of our Secretaries, and finally what opinion you have conceived of our dearest uncle the Lord Protector.

* Burnet, vol. ii. p. 184.

" For answer whereunto we let you wit, that, as far as our age can understand, the rather moved by the visage that we see of our said uncle and Council, and others our servants presently with us, we do lament our present estate being in such an imminent danger; and unless God do put it into the hearts of you there to be as careful to bring these uproars unto a quiet, as we see our said uncle and Council to be here, we shall have cause to think you forget your duties towards us, and the great benefits which the King our lord, and father, of most noble memory, hath employed upon every one of you.   For, howsoever you charge our said uncle with wilfulness in your letter, we and our Council here have found him so tractable, as, if you fall not into the same fault wherewith you burden him, we trust that both you and he may continue in such sort and surety without suspicion, by a friendly determination and agreement among yourselves, as may be to our safety and the quiet of you and the rest of our good subjects.

" Wherefore we pray you, good cousins and councillors, to consider, as in times past you have every [one] in his degree served us honestly at sundry times, so hath our said uncle, as you all know, and by God's grace may, by your good advices, serve us full well hereafter.   Each man hath his faults; he *his*, and you *yours;* and if we shall hereafter as rigorously weigh yours, as we hear that you intend with *cruelty to purge his,* which of you all shall be able to stand before us ?

"To our person, we verily believe, and so do you, we dare say, he myndeth no hurt. If in government he hath not so discreetly used himself as in your opinions he might have done, we think the extremity in such a case is not to be required at his hand : yet lyeth it in us to remit it, for he is our uncle, whom you know we love ; and therefore somewhat the more to be considered at your hands. And if he were another person, yet though he had offended us, if the offence tended not directly to our person, as we be credibly informed it doth not, ye would, we think, in nowise counsel us to proceed to extremities against him, for fear of any respect that might particularly seem hereafter to touch any of you ; which fear may be by wisdom on both parts provided for, and we the better preserved. Like as partly by CERTAIN ARTICLES exhibited unto us by our said uncle, which herewith we send unto you, signed by our hand, and partly by our trusty and well beloved Councillor, Sir Philip Hobbye, Knight, may appear to you ; unto whom we require you to give credit, and to return him again with your answer accordingly, without failing hereof, as ye tender our preservation and the weal of our realm.

"Given under our signet, at our Castle of Windsor, the 8th day of Oct. in the third year of our reign."

This letter from the King, written, as may be supposed, under the dictation of his uncle, produced no effect. The Lords at London were led by Warwick, who saw his advantage. They listened also, as was believed, to the violent counsel of Southampton; and had already determined, first to get Somerset into their hands, and then to debate what should be done with him. In this spirit, on the day preceding the last communication, (namely, 7th Oct.) they had addressed a letter to the Lords at Windsor, declaring their resolution to remove Somerset from the office of Protector, and insisting upon his leaving the King, dispersing his force, and submitting himself to be ordered " *according to justice and reason;*" a phrase which, Turner justly remarks, was " full of indefinite and fearful meaning." This letter has been printed by Sir Henry Ellis;* it drew forth the following excellent reply from Cranmer, Paget, and Smith.

PAGET, CRANMER, AND SMITH, TO THE COUNCIL AT LONDON.

Orig. St. P. Off. *Domestic.* 8th Oct. 1549.

" AFTER our right hearty commendations unto your good Lordships. We have received from the same a letter by Mr. Honnings, dated at London yesterday, whereby ye do us to understand the causes of your assembly there; and, charging the Lord Protector with the manner of

* Ellis, vol. i. p. 166.

his government, require that he withdraw himself from the King's Majesty, disperse the force
which he hath levied, and be content to be ordered
according *to justice and reason:* and so you will
gladly commune with us touching the surety of
the King's Majesty's person, and the order of all
other things, with such conformity on your behalf as
appertaineth ; and otherwise you must (you write)
make other account of us than you trust to have
cause, and burden us if things come to extremities.

" To the first part: we verily believe that, as bruits,
rumours, and reports, that your Lordships intended
the destruction of the Lord Protector, induced his
Grace to fly to the defence which he hath assembled; even so your Lordships, hearing that his
Grace intended the like destruction towards you,
have been moved to do as you have done ; so as, for
want of good understanding one of another's right
meaning, things be grown to such extremities as, if
the saving of the King's Majesty's person and the
Commonweal take not more place both in his
Grace and your Lordships than any private respect
or affection, you see, we doubt not, (as we do,) that
both our King and country and also ourselves shall
(as verily as God is God) be utterly destroyed and
cast away. Wherefore, good my Lords, for the
tender passion of Jesus Christ, use your wisdoms,
and temporize your determinations, in such sort as
no blood be shed nor cruelty used neither of his
Grace's part nor of your Lordships' ; for, if it come

to that point, both you and we are like to see presently with our eyes that which every vein of all
our hearts will bleed to behold.   Wherefore, as true
subjects to the King, as faithful councillors, though
unworthy councillors, to his Majesty and this realm,
and as lamentable petitioners, we beseech your Lordships most humbly and from the bottom of our
hearts to take pity on the King and the realm,
whereof you are principal members, and to set apart
summum jus, and to use *bonum et æquum*.

"And think not that this is written for any private
fear or other respect of ourselves, but for that undoubtedly *we* hear and know more of this point (with
your favours) than *you* there do know yet.   And,
howsoever it shall please you to account of us, we
are true men to God, to the King, and the Realm,
and so will we live and die wheresoever we be; and,
in respect of them three, esteem little any other person or thing,—no, not our own lives,—and, having
clear consciences, are sure, whatsoever evil may follow upon the use of extremity, there neither now is,
nor ever shall be found, fault in us; and, so quieting
ourselves, we rest.

"Now to that which you would have the Lord
Protector to do for his part: his Grace and we have
communed therein, and much to our comforts and
yours also, if it shall like you to weigh the case well.
He is contented (if ye will again for your parts use
equity) to put that now in execution by his *deeds*,
which many times he hath declared by his *words;*

that is to say, that so as the King and the realm
may be otherwise well served, he *passeth* little * for
the place he now hath.   Marry he doth consider,
that by the King's Majesty, with all *your* advices
and the consent of the nobles of the realm, he was
called to the place, as appeareth in writing under
his Majesty's great seal and sign, whereunto your
hands and ours, with all other the Lords in the
upper house of Parliament, are subscribed ; and
therefore, in violent sort to be thrust out against his
will, he thinketh it not reasonable.

"He is here with the King's person where is
his place to be, and we be here with him, we trust
in God, for the good service of the King, the
weal of the realm, and the good acquieting both
of his Grace and your Lordships ; which we
most heartily desire, and see such hope here thereof, as, if you be not so sore bent upon extremity as is reported, and as equity can take no
place, my Lord's Grace may live in quiet, and the
King's Majesty's affairs [be] managed in such order as by his Majesty's councillors shall be thought
convenient.

"Marry, to put himself *simply* into your hands,
having heard as he and we have, without knowing
upon what conditions, is not reasonable.   Life is
sweet, my Lords, and they say you seek his blood
and his death ; which if you do, and may have him

---

* To pass; to heed, or regard.
"As for these silken-coated slaves, I pass not :
    It is to you, good people, that I speak."—SHAKSPEARE.

otherwise conformable to reason, and by extremity
drive him to seek extremity again, the blood of him
and others that shall die on both sides innocently
shall be by God justly required at your hands;
and when, peradventure, you would have him again
upon occasion of service, you shall forthink to have
lost him.

" Wherefore, good my Lords, we beseech you
again and again, if you have conceived any such determination, to put it out of your heads, and incline
your hearts to kindness and humanity, remembering
that *he* hath never been cruel to any of *you ;* and
why should you be cruelly minded to him?   As we
trust ye be not, whatsoever hath been said; but you
will show yourselves as conformable for your parts
as his Grace is contented, for the zeal he beareth to
the King and the realm, to be for his part, as this
bearer, Sir Philip Hoby, will declare unto you, to
whom we desire you to give credit, and to return
him hither again with answer hereof.

" And thus, beseeching the living God to direct
your hearts to the making of a quiet end of these terrible tumults, we bid your Lordships most heartily
well to fare.

" From the King's Majesty's Castle of Windsor,
the 8th of Oct. 1549.

   " Your Lordships' assured loving friends,
        " T. CANT.   WM. PAGET.   T. SMITH."

Endorsed.—" *To our very good Lords, and others of
the King's Majesty's Council, at London.*"

Q 2

This communication was sent by the hand of Hoby to Warwick* on the 8th of October; and on the same day Sir Thomas Smith addressed the following pathetic letter to Sir William Petre. It is evident from its contents that Somerset was completely humbled; he had agreed to the sacrifice of "office and dignity." He only stipulated *for his life,* and was ready to agree to any *reasonable* conditions. Are we to wonder that Smith, in such a case, should remonstrate against all violent courses, and beseech the councillors at London "not to require that *with blood,* which might be had with persuasion and honour?"

SMITH TO PETRE.

Orig. St. P. Off. *Domestic.* 8th October 1549.

"Sir, after my most hearty commendations.

"Having by reason of vicinity and office with you most acquaintance, I am boldest to write unto you. Now is the time when ye may show yourself to be of that nature whereof I have heard you, and, as I think, worthily, glory; that is, no seeker of extremity nor blood, but of moderation in all things.

"These things have gone already too much that way, if it had pleased God otherwise. And it is

---

* This letter, although printed by Stowe in his Chronicle, p. 598, I have given as necessary for the clear understanding of the rest.

now brought to that pass, by our persuasions at the last, that my Lord Protector is content to refuse no *reasonable* conditions. Office, dignity, or whatsoever else it be, he will leave, rather than it should come to extreme points. I trust no man seeketh his *blood*, who hath, as ye know, rather been too easy than too cruel to others.

" Then, to require with blood that which may be had with persuasion and honour, I cannot think it should be in any of my Lords there, and as little in you. I pray you join you with us on that side, that things may be brought to moderation; and rest not to labour herein. You shall do the best deed, I think, that ever any gentleman did, tho' ye be but an earnest motioner herein. I need not dilate the goodness of the success, if it might follow, to you, who conjectureth it as well, and better than I can declare it.

" For my part, I am in a most miserable case. I cannot leave the King's Majesty, and him who was my master, of whom I have had all ; and I cannot deny but I have misliked also some things that you and the rest of my Lords there did mislike,—as ye know, no man better, yourself. But now let Christian charity work with you, Sir, for God's love, the King's, and the realm's ; refuse not the offer which is so good, so godly, and so honourable unto you, that this realm be not made in one year a double tragedy and a lamentable spoil, and scorning-stock of all the world. God keep you, and convert yours and all my Lords' hearts there to this most reasonable and moderate way, as we trust He shall! From Windsor Castle, the 8th of October.

"Yours always assured, T. SMITH.

"And, if ye may, I pray you write to me, though it be but *two* words of comfort."

When Sir Philip Hoby arrived with these letters from Windsor, which was on the 8th of October, the same day they were written, Warwick and his faction were anxiously looking for a reply from Lord Russel and Sir William Herbert to the message which they had sent them. These last-mentioned leaders had already decided against Somerset;* but of this important fact the conspirators at London were still ignorant. Russel's answer was hourly expected; but it was necessary to gain time till it came, and to mature their measures. Had Hoby been a firm man and true to Somerset, any delay would have been difficult; he might have insisted on carrying back a definite and instant reply, and the Protector would have been thrown upon his defence. But the open and unsuspicious temper of the Duke was little able to comprehend or oppose the refined craft of his adversaries. He had first sent Secretary Petre, and he remained with Warwick; he had now despatched Sir Philip Hoby, and he acted with still greater treachery, as we learn from this passage of a narrative by Sir

* Supra, p. 216.

Thomas Smith, an eye-witness, and, which was a rare commodity in those times, an honest man.

" Sir Philip Hobby," says Smith, " received an answer of the Lords in London by letter, came out of London, and by the way *feigning* he had lost the letter out of his packet, said to his man he would return for a new, and willed him to go to the court and tell the Council all should be well. This excuse was of purpose before devised by the Lords, to the end they might win time the better that they might do their *feats."*

Hoby accordingly remained with Warwick till the next day, being the 9th of October, and at this critical moment the following letter from Lord Russel and Sir William Herbert arrived. It showed Warwick that all fears as to any protracted struggle might be dismissed; that neither from these leaders, nor from the people, was any resistance to be apprehended.

LORD RUSSEL AND SIR WILLIAM HERBERT TO THE LORDS OF THE COUNCIL AT LONDON.

Orig. St. P. Off. *Domestic.* 9th October 1549.

" Right Honourable. After our most hearty commendations unto your good Lordships. Incontinently upon our arrival here at Wilton, we received divers letters from the King's Majesty and the Protector, to come forth to the Court with all diligence; and especially one that he sent by his son, the Lord Edward : the copies of which letters we send unto you herewith, to the intent your Lordships may the more fully understand * * * * * *. † Upon the receipt whereof, we prepared ourselves to come up; and with such gentlemen as were then in our company, and with our own servants, came as far as Andover, where we understood many things, for the countreys every way *were in a roar* that no man wist what to do.

" The gentlemen had received like letters from the King's Majesty as we had done ; and the commons had found bills that were *sown abroad,* to raise them in the King's name and the Protector's quarrel ; as by a copy of one of the same bills, which ye shall also receive herewith, your Lordships may more plainly perceive : so that undoubtedly God was the guide of our journey; for, if we had not been here at this time, there had been raised five or six thousand men at the least, to have gone to Windsor ; besides the uncertain rage that the commons might have taken upon this occasion ; but, as God would, the gentlemen of these parts, hearing of our being here, have stayed upon our setting forwards, and divers of them have sent unto us for our opinions, wherein we have satisfied [them].

* * * *

" Thus being at Andover, and weighing as well the state of the things above, as also the tickleness ‡ of the country, which hitherto understandeth not what the matter may mean, we despatched the

† Illegible.
‡ Tickleness ; tottering, uncertain state.

Lord Edward to the Protector with such answer
as by the copy thereof, which we also send herewith, it may appear; and thereupon thought it
very requisite to return to Wilton, there to abide
the assembly of the gentlemen of all these parts,
and to gather such power as may serve us to come
thro' withal to do good, if need should so require;
and [we] have sent to Bristol for some light ordnance, and for money, with such other things as
may be necessary.

"Nevertheless, by that we have learned   *   *
especially by Mr. Stanhope's man, who hath been
here this morning, it seemeth to us that, if ye send
thither, there shall not need any great business,
and the less if it be well followed;† for we cannot
believe that the Protector will stand to violence, his
quarrel being private; and, tho' he would, he is not
able, considering that we have stayed all these parts,
Hampshire, Wiltshire, Gloucestershire, Somerset,
Wales, and the west parts, so that these ways he
can draw nothing unto him to do any hurt withal.
And having with him so few as we know he hath,.
we marvel that your Lordships have not seen the
passage kept free between you and us, and that we
have not had better advertisements of your Lordships' proceedings than hitherto we have had.

"All this notwithstanding, to be sure ‡ for the
worst, we endeavour ourselves to be strong, and
shall be shortly in that point that we shall be able

---

† Speedily followed up.   ‡ Secure against the worst.

to keep the highway unto you, though resistance
were made.   Heartily beseeching your Lordships
to signify your minds unto us, what ye would have
us to do [not putting you to] charges in bringing
more or less number of men than needeth, nor yet
to be weaker than your Lordships may think the
case doth require.

"And as we are glad that our chance was to be
here now, where undoubtedly the place and the
time both have served us to stand in better stead,
and to do better service, than if we had been there
with you; so, if we had known what Proclamations your Lordships would have set forth touching this matter, they had been published here ere
this: and being a thing necessary to be opened in
time, we beseech your Lordships to let us know
your pleasure immediately, as well in that behalf
as in all other things; and to give credit to this
Bearer, whom we have [fully] instructed in our
minds in every part, and whom we know to be a
faithful man towards the King's Majesty, and the
Commonwealth of the realm, and therefore worthy
of credit, as the everlasting God knoweth, who
preserve the King's Majesty and your good Lordships in good life and health, with increase of
honour!   From Wilton, the 9th of Oct. 1549.

"I, Sir William Herbert, received also a letter
from Sir Michael Stanhope, which I also send to
your Lordships herewith.

   "Your good Lordships' assured friends,
          "J. RUSSEL.   W. HERBERT."

" Since writing of this letter, we have received your Lordships' letters by our servants; before the which we received none but from my Lord Great Master,* and yet we know he wrote it not without making your Lordships privy thereunto. For the stay of the countrys, we have done that substantially already, as we have written before;† so that there resteth no more but that we may know your Lordships' pleasure touching the number ye would have us bring up, and what proclamations we shall set forth. We have stayed to send your commission to the sheriffs and justices of the peace, because our order is past to them already, which we trust you will not mislike; so that, till our number that your Lordships shall appoint us be assembled, we think we may not well alter it ; and, as for the number, we trust to satisfy your pleasures, [with] as many or as few as shall like you."

" *To the Lords of His Majesty's most*
Honourable Privy Council."

Although assured by this letter that the Protector could no longer stand against them, Warwick and his confederates did not even yet abandon the craft and caution with which they acted. Their object was to secure his person; and as he still had the King in his power, and was surrounded by his own armed servants and those of the royal household,

* Warwick.

† See Orig. St. P. Off. Oct. 9th, 1549. Lord Russel and Sir William Herbert to the Sheriff of Gloucestershire.

this required great management. To effect it, it was necessary to deceive Somerset, to seduce Cranmer, Paget, and Smith, who hitherto had stood by him, to desert and betray him, and to enlist the feelings of the young King upon their side by a false statement of their motives and proceedings.

Hoby was accordingly again despatched to Windsor. He bore letters and messages of very different complexions; the first *open,* the second *secret :* the open letters appear to have been addressed to the Duke, the King, and the Lords ; the secret to Edward, and to Cranmer, Smith, and Paget. The secret letter to the King contained a laboured defence of their conduct, and a severe exposition of the tyranny and violence of his uncle the Protector.* It has been given by Burnet from the original in the Privy Council Books, and its effect was fatal to the little remaining cordiality between the youthful prince and his uncle.

The secret letter to Cranmer, Paget, and Smith was couched in severe and threatening terms. † It accused them of having permitted the person of the King to be removed from those servants to whom this high charge had been intrusted, and guarded by strangers " armed with his Majesty's own armour :" it warned them that, if any evil happened, they must answer for it at *their uttermost peril;* and it desired them to weigh well the *verbal*

---

* Burnet, vol. ii. Appendix, p. 185.
† Ibid. ii. p. 187.

message which was brought by Hoby.* This *secret*
message was none other than they must either forsake the Duke, lend themselves to the deceit about
to be practised on him, and concur in measures for
securing his person, or continue true to him, and
share his fate.†

At this moment, Cranmer, Paget, Smith, and
Cecil were the only friends left around the unfortunate Protector. The three first had, as we have
seen, taken an active, and hitherto a sincere part in
attempting to bring about a reconciliation between
Warwick and the Duke. Cecil's name, and it is
an extraordinary circumstance, does not once appear in these negotiations : although, up to the
moment of the conspiracy, he was undoubtedly the
most confidential and the most powerful person
about Somerset, and although he was certainly
still at Windsor, this most wary of statesmen seems
to have carefully disentangled himself from the
dangerous meshes which he saw gradually being
drawn around the Duke. But, although cautious,
Cecil's conduct was upright, whilst that of Smith,
who clung to his master, was generous and brave.
The same cannot be said for either Cranmer or
Paget. Terrified by the last threats, they not only
agreed to join the faction of Warwick ; but Paget
sent a secret message by his servant, in which he

* Burnet, vol. ii. Appendix, p. 187.
† This appears evident from a letter printed by Ellis, vol. ii.
p. 175, Lords of the Council to Sir William Paget.

directed the Lords of his faction in what manner the person of the Duke might be apprehended.*

Having thus secretly concerted all things with the Archbishop and Paget, Hoby was ready to proceed with the second and more public part of his commission. How villanously well this part of the drama was acted appears from the following paper.

" SIR P. HOBBY'S SAYING OR MESSAGE DECLARED TO THE DUKE OF SOMERSET, THE ARCHBISHOP OF CANTERBURY, SIR WILLIAM PAGETT, MR. COMPTROLLER, SIR THOMAS SMITH, SECRETARY, IN THE PRESENCE OF MR. CECIL, SIR JOHN THYNEE, SIR RICHARD COTTON, AND DIVERS OTHERS, REPORTED BY SIR THOMAS SMITH."

HARLEIAN. 353. *Fol.* 77.

" MY LORD, AND MY LORDS AND MASTERS OF THE COUNCIL.—My Lords of the Council yonder have perused your letters and perceived the King's Majesty's requests and yours, and have willed me to declare unto you again, that they do marvel much why you do so write unto them as tho' they were the most cruel men in the world, and as tho' they sought nothing but blood and extremity.   They say, of *their honours* they do mean nothing less ; and they bade me declare unto you, from them, that of their faiths and honours they do not intend, nor will hurt, in any case, the person of my Lord

* Ellis' Letters, vol. ii. p. 175.

the Duke, nor of none of you all, nor take away *any of his lands or goods*, whom they do esteem and tender as well as any of you, as they ought, and as one whom they are not ignorant, no more than you, that he is the King's uncle.

" They do intend to preserve *his honour* as much as any of you would; nor meaneth not, nor purposeth not, *no manner hurt to him*, but only *to give order for the Protectorship*, which hath not been so well ordered as they think it should have been; and to see that the King be better answered of his things, and the realm better governed for the King's Majesty. And for you, my Lords and Masters of the Council, they will have you to keep your rooms and places as you did before, and they will counsel with you for the better government of things.

" My Lord, then saith he to the Duke, be you not afraid. I will lose this, my neck, (and so pointed to his neck,) if you have any hurt. There is no such thing meant, and so they would have me tell you; and mark you well what I say. Then he willed the letters directed to the King to be read openly before all the gentlemen of the Privy Chamber and others, and other letters according to the direction.

" Upon this, all the aforenamed there present wept for joy, and thanked God, and prayed for the Lords. Mr. Comptroller [Sir William Paget] fell down on his knees, and clasped the Duke about the knees, and weeping said, Oh! my Lord, ye see now what my Lords be."*

Deceived in this base manner, the Protector appears to have been thrown completely off his guard. He had already made up his mind to retire from the Protectorate : he had stipulated only for life and liberty, and not these only, but his honour and estates were now solemnly promised to be secured to him. Relying on the honour which had been pledged, and the tears which had been shed by Mr. Comptroller, he entertained no suspicion, but permitted his guards to be removed, his servants disarmed, and the young Monarch to be once more attended by those officers of the household who had been suspected of a leaning to Warwick and the conspirators.

Intelligence of all this was immediately sent to London; and it appears, by the undoubted evidence of the Privy Council Books, that the Lords there ascribed the success which had attended their schemes to the " diligent travail" of the Archbishop of Canterbury and Sir William Paget.† Nothing remained now but to obey the directions which had been sent as to the manner in which their victim might be secured : nor was this difficult.

* To this paper, which I have found in the Harleian MSS. is added a note, informing us that it was copied from " that which Sir Thomas Smith *wrote with his own hand."*

† MS. Privy Council Books, 10th Oct. 1549.

Availing themselves of the secret message of Paget, they sent Sir Anthony Wingfield, Vice-chamberlain, on the 11th of October, to Windsor, with orders to communicate with the Archbishop and Paget; and not only to seize the Duke of Somerset, but to secure Mr. Smith, Mr. Cecil, Mr. Thynne, and Mr. Whalley. This arrest was accordingly made; and the following letter to Warwick and the Lords of the Council, informs us of the circumstances under which it took place.

CRANMER, PAGET, AND WINGFIELD TO THE COUNCIL.

Orig. St. P. Off. *Domestic.* 11th Oct. 1549.

" AFTER our most hearty commendations to your good Lordships. These may be to signify unto you, that I, the Vice-chamberlain, arrived here this morning, and, according to your instructions, have the person of the Duke in my keeping : and, for because his chamber was hard adjoining to the King's bedchamber, he is removed to the tower which is called the Lieutenant's, which is the high tower next adjoining to the gate of the middle ward—a very high tower; and a strong and good watch shall be had about the same. The rest also be forthcoming, contained in your billet to me, saving Whalley; who yesterday, upon the hope conceived by the Duke of Mr. Hobbie's report, was sent by him to the Duchess, his wife, to re-comfort her. She is at Bedington.

" Here was with the Duke, his son, the Earl, and his young brother. We have appointed them to be conveyed to the Duke's house, to remain there with the other children till your further pleasures known. The King's Majesty is much troubled with a great rheum, taken partly with riding hither in the night, and partly increased by the subtlety of this air, as the gentlemen of his chamber say; and much desireth to be hence, saying that Methinks I am in prison; here be no galleries nor no gardens to walk in. Your Lordships may consider of it, and give order as you shall think convenient.

" I, the Comptroller, have spoken for provision to be made at Richmond, where there is already five tonnes of beer and five tonnes of wine. But the physician dispraiseth the house, and wisheth us rather to Hampton or London. The King's Majesty, thanks be to the living God ! is in good health and merry; and this day after breakfast came forth to Mr. Vice-chamberlain and all the rest of the gentlemen, whom, I promise your Lordships, he bade wellcome with a merry countenance and a loud voice; asking how your Lordships did, when he should see you, and that you should be wellcome whensoever you come : the gentlemen kissed his Highness' hands every one, much to their comfort.   And thus we bid your good Lordships most heartily well to fare. From Windsor, the 11th of October 1549.

"Your Lordships' assured loving friends,

"T. CANT. WM. PAGET. A. WINGFIELD."

" To the Right Honourable and our very good Lords and others of the King's Majesty's Council, presently at London."

Having once determined to act against him, Cranmer and Paget appear to have taken their measures so effectually, that the arrest of the Protector was effected without any resistance upon his part. He had trusted to Sir Philip Hoby's report, his hopes had been revived, he had sent his servant with the good news to his wife, he suspected no evil; and, when Wingfield arrived, he pounced upon his victim, who instantly saw that he was lost, and silently resigned himself into the hands of his enemies.

At the same time that Somerset was secured and shut up in Beauchamp's tower, Smith, Cecil, Thynne, Stanhope, and some others of his servants, were confined in their own apartments;* and Warwick, with his adherents, having received Wingfield's letters on Saturday the 12th of October, repaired to Windsor, " presented themselves to the young King most humbly on their knees, and declared the occasion and order of their

* MS. Privy Council Books, 10th Oct. 1549.

R 2

doings."* It is stated in the record of the Privy
Council, that Edward accepted their explanation in
the most gracious manner, and gave them hearty
thanks; but they are here their own historians,
and the King was in their power, yet it may be
suspected, from what we have already seen, that the
young Prince dreaded his uncle and did not lament
his fall.

Their next step was to call before them Sir
Thomas Smith, Sir John Thynne, Sir Michael
Stanhope, Edward Wolf, one of the Privy Chamber, and Mr. Grey. These knights and gentlemen
are denominated, in the Privy Council Books, the
principal instruments and councillors of the Duke
in his ill government. Smith seems to have been
particularly obnoxious to them: the reason is probably to be found in his devoted attachment to the
Protector, and that unblemished and upright mind
which would not suffer him to imitate Paget, and
save himself by the sacrifice of his master. He
was deprived of his office of Secretary, declared
unworthy of being any longer a privy councillor,
and sent with the Duke, Thynne, Stanhope, Wolf,
and Grey, to the Tower, on the 13th of October.

And here it is remarkable that CECIL again disappears from view. When the Duke, Smith, and
the rest were called before the Council and upbraided with their offences, Cecil was permitted to
continue in the privacy of his chamber. Although

* MS. Privy Council Books, 12th Oct. 1549.

he was undoubtedly the principal instrument through whose hands all the power and patronage of the Protector's government had passed,—a fact proved by innumerable letters in the State Paper Office,—still it was his good fortune to escape censure, whilst his master and his other adherents were called up to receive their sentence; and it seems certain, from the silence of the Privy Council Books, that he was not sent at this time,* with Somerset and Smith, to the Tower.

In what way are we to account for this fact, the explanation, or, indeed, the bare notice of which we in vain look for in any of his numerous biographers? I ascribe it to the caution which prompted him to preserve a strict neutrality in the Duke's troubles; to his former habits of friendship and intimacy with Warwick, who now ruled all; and to the high character he had gained with both parties, as a man of indefatigable application and great ability. Yet, although he escaped at this time, it appears by an entry in his Journal,† that some time in the month of November he had been sent to the Tower: " *Mense Novembris, A° 3° E. 6, fui in Turre.*" At what precise time he was imprisoned, and how it happened that, having escaped in October, he was shut up in November, are difficult points in this obscure, and, as he himself

---

* MS. Privy Council Books, Monday, 13th Oct.

† Nares' Life of Burleigh, vol. i. p. 60 Facsimile of Lord Burleigh's Private Journal.

tells us, most unhappy period of his life : nor have I hitherto found any letters which solve the problem.

We are now arrived at the concluding scene of this remarkable revolution. I may give it in the words of Sir John Hayward. " On Monday, the 13th of October, the Duke was brought to London as if he had been a *captive* carried in triumph. He rode through Holborn between the Earls of Southampton and Huntingdon, and was followed with lords and gentlemen to the number of three hundred, mounted on horseback.   *   *   At Soper Lane he was received by the mayor, sheriffs, and recorder, and divers knights of especial note, who, with a great train of officers and attendance bearing halberts, conducted him to the Tower."†

Warwick was now all-powerful ; and a great majority of the councillors being at his devotion, he proceeded vigorously against the Protector. Having already broken one solemn promise made to Somerset, in sending him to the Tower, he felt little scruple in trampling upon the remaining conditions. Articles were drawn up, accusing him of high crimes and misdemeanours; and he was given to understand that, if he hoped to escape, it must be by an unqualified acknowledgment of his guilt. To this he consented, knowing well that his life would be the penalty if he refused. He signed the Articles, acknowledged his presumption, and asked pardon

† Hayward's Life of Edward VI.   Kennet, vol. ii. p. 307.

on his knees : this was granted him; but on condition that he should be deprived of all his offices, forfeit his goods and chattels, pay a fine of two thousand pounds, and remain in prison. Such was the manner in which the conspirators fulfilled Hoby's solemn assurance, that his lands and goods should be saved, his honour preserved, and no manner of hurt inflicted on him. " This revolution," says Dr. Lingard, " was concluded, as usual, by rewards to the principal actors in it. The Earl of Warwick obtained the offices of Great Master and Lord High Admiral ; the Marquis of Northampton, that of Great Chamberlain ; and the Lords Russel and St. John, created Earls of Bedford and Wiltshire, were appointed Lord Privy Seal and Lord Treasurer."*

In the MS. Privy Council Books of Edward the Sixth, under the date of the 9th of October, is this passage. " The Lords, (meaning the faction of Warwick,) thinking it to be expedient to communicate their proceedings with the Lady Mary's and the Lady Elizabeth's Graces, wrote to the same, letters of the whole discourse, as aforesaid."

These letters do not appear in the MS. Books of Privy Council, but I have found them in the State Paper Office ; and they will form an interesting conclusion to the original documents, in which we have traced the history of this remarkable conspiracy from its origin to its consummation.

* Lingard's History of England, vol. vii. p. 64.

"TO MY LADY MARIE'S GRACE, AND MY LADY
ELIZABETH'S GRACE."

Orig. St. P. Off. *Domestic.* 9th October 1549.

" It may please your Grace, with our most
hearty and humble commendations, to understand,
that where some trouble hath chanced between us
of the King's Majesty's Council and the Duke of
Somerset, because the same may be diversely reported, we have thought it our parts to signify to
your Grace briefly how the matter hath grown,
and by what means it is now come to some extremity.

" We have long since, and daily more and more,
perceived his pride and ambition, aspiring further
than became a good governor, or a true subject. We
have travailed with him, the number of us together,
and in manner every [one] of us apart, to stay himself within reasonable limits, ever hoping to do good ;
but all hath not prevailed : for, as we have devised
with him for the preservation of the King's Majesty's person and honour, so hath he (from time to
time, as he durst,) covertly laboured to bring his
Majesty, who God long preserve ! and his whole
estate, to such confusion as he might of both dispose at his pleasure ; declaring in his continual proceedings, that he meant never to account with any
superior.

" When we saw that no counsel could prevail,
and that his pride grew so fast as to do what he

listed, [that] he would hear nothing spoken by
the Council for his Majesty's affairs, but either he
would contemptuously reject it, or, doing nothing,
pass it over in silence,—we thought we could suffer
no longer, well weighing with ourselves the state,
and remembering therewith our duties, unless we
would in effect be parties with him; and so resolved friendly and quietly to have treated the matter with him, and, if we might by any means have
brought him to reason, to have avoided all trouble
and slander, and to have appeased all things without extremity.

"But we had not a few of us *dined* above twice
together, but immediately he took the Tower,
and raised all the country about Hampton Court,
bruiting and crying out that certain Lords had
determined to repair to the Court to destroy the
King's Majesty, whom we pray to God on our
knees to keep and make as old a King as ever was
any of his progenitors. And, when he had thus
gathered the people and commons together at
Hampton Court, then he brought his Majesty into
the base-court there, and so after to the gate to
them that were without; and after he had caused his
Highness, good Prince, to say, 'I pray you be good
to us and our uncle,' then began he his Oration ;
and, among many his untrue and idle sayings, declared that one special cause of our displeasure to
him was that we would have him removed from
his office, and that we minded to have your Grace

to be Regent of the realm, and also to have the rule and government of the King's Majesty's person : dilating what danger it should be to his Majesty to have your Grace, next in succession and title to the crown, to be in that place ; and that therein was meant a great treason, which, as God knoweth, we never intended, considering all laws touching government to provide to the contrary ; neither any of us all at any time, by word or writing, hath opened any such matter to your Grace, as your honour knoweth; [and] concluded, like a most irreverent and unkind subject, that if we should attempt any thing against him the said Duke, ' Here he is,' quoth he, pointing to the King's Majesty, ' that shall die before me !' which was the most abominable saying that ever passed the mouth of a subject towards his Prince and Sovereign Lord.*

" When we understood this his manner of proceeding, we thought it neither meet to go to the Court, as we had determined, neither to rest so unfurnished as he might use his will first upon us, and after the more easily proceed in his purpose ; and so have in quiet sort both gotten the Tower for the King's Majesty from him, and furnished ourselves with the help of the good City of London, who have showed themselves most loving and faithful subjects in this

---

* This sentence is first written thus in the draft: " Concluding in the end, like an irreverent and unkind subject, that, or he would be destroyed, his Majesty should die before him. Oh, what abomination !"

great matter, content to serve his Highness, even when the Tower was not in our order for his Majesty, as it now is, as we should command and appoint them, in such sort as we trust in God to deliver our Sovereign Lord from his danger, and to establish a better order for his Grace's surety than he hath used. Beseeching your Grace not to conceive any lack to be [in] us that we have not advertised the same hitherto of our doings, for the matter was so much to us unlooked for, and so quick, that we were fain to travail almost night and day since the *ruffle* to keep him from advantage and put ourselves in order for him.

" He hath now carried his Majesty to Windsor late in the night, in such sort as may declare that he maketh no great store of him; but God, we trust, will help us to deliver his Majesty out of his cruel and greedy hands; wherein, if it should come to an extremity, as we trust it shall not,—and for our parts we shall do what we can to manage it so, if it can be possible, as no blood be shed on the occasion of it,— we trust your Grace, in our just and faithful quarrel, will stand with us; and thus we shall pray to Almighty God for the preservation of your Grace's health. From, &c."

It will be scarcely necessary to observe that we must receive with much caution this account of the revolution, written under the dictation, if not by the hand of Warwick, and with the express object of enlisting the feelings of Mary and Elizabeth upon his side. The original papers and letters which have been given above, will enable any reader to correct its partial statements, and to detect the craft and hypocrisy of Warwick, the treachery of Hoby, the duplicity and desertion of Paget and Cranmer. I may add that the detailed account now given of the progress and termination of this remarkable conspiracy, is new to English History. Nothing of it is to be found in our most popular general historians, or even in the pages of Burnet, Strype, or Fuller; another proof that historical truth is progressive, of slow attainment, and to be found, if anywhere, in the original letters of the times.

And now let me say a few words on the character of Somerset, the victim of this singular revolution. He had risen to power partly by legal, partly by illegal methods. The will of Henry the Eighth had made him a Councillor; so far all seems to have been fair and honest. The consent of all his brethren in Council, except Wriothesley, the Chancellor, Earl of Southampton, had made him Protector; this was certainly a departure from the *letter* of the King's will: but by the spirit of it there was an evident necessity that some one should have the highest place and should take a lead in the Council; and, if such a one was to be chosen, Somerset's near relationship to the King, and the declaration of Paget that the late monarch had intended to honour him above the rest, pointed him out as the fittest person to be Protector.

His next step was far more objectionable. Without consulting Parliament, he procured his Office to be re-granted and confirmed to him by the King's letters patent; and he introduced into these letters, which were signed not only by Edward, but by all the Privy Councillors, some clauses which made his power almost despotic. By this new commission, which has been printed by Burnet, from the Privy Council Book,* the King, being a minor, was made to ratify not only all the public measures which had been already adopted by the Protector, but this high functionary was empowered to choose his own Privy Council, to add to its number such persons as he thought fit, and by their advice to administer the affairs of the kingdom. It is no doubt true that the old Councillors named in the King's will were also named in this new commission ; but it was not stated in it that the Protector must be regulated by their opinion, or that even in all cases he must consult them. These letters patent were undoubtedly illegal, and a usurpation upon the part of the Protector. But then we are to remember that the instrument was signed by the whole of the Councillors and Executors named in the King's will ; and that if the Duke of Somerset assumed, as they contended, an almost regal power, it was they themselves who had conferred it upon him. To the old nobility, who regarded him as a new man lately ennobled, he was

* Burnet's History of the Reformation, vol. ii. p. 98. Appendix.

impatient and arrogant; and being quick in his temper, and open and bold in expressing his opinion, he often gave deep offence where little was intended. But to the commons he was a mild and paternal governor; he saw them oppressed by the great barons, whose power under the feudal law was so crushing that it needed such an arm as Somerset's to interpose in their defence; and they, in return, named him the " *Good Duke*," an epithet which seems by no means to have been unmerited.

We found him, in kingly power and state—we leave him stript of all—expelled from the Council —glad to escape with his life. The final catastrophe yet remains.

INTRODUCTION TO PERIOD SECOND.

1549—1553.

THE second period into which I have divided these Letters, embraces the interval between the deposition of the Duke of Somerset and the death of Edward the Sixth.

The fall of the Protector was beheld with great exultation by the Popish party in England: it had been the work of the Earl of Warwick; but, in the intrigues by which it was brought about, the Earl of Southampton, a principal leader of the Roman Catholics, had so cordially co-operated, that both he and his friends conceived the highest expectations of the influence which they would acquire under the new state of things;—but here they were grievously disappointed. Warwick had, indeed, been willing to use Southampton and the rest of his faction as his tools; but, having accomplished his purpose, he cast them aside, and both King and Council soon discovered that this ambitious, bold, and crafty leader meant to reign, with-

out the name indeed, but with as absolute a sway
as the Protector.   The Romish party were discouraged.   Gardiner and Bonner, who expected their
freedom, remained prisoners in the Tower; and
Warwick, perceiving that the feelings of the young
King were, owing to his education, decidedly anti-
Romanist, thought it prudent to conciliate his royal
pupil by a series of enactments which confirmed the
Reformation, and for a season crushed the hopes of
all who were attached to the ancient faith. *

On turning to France, Warwick found himself
much embarrassed.   It was easy, when he acted in
opposition to Somerset, to arraign this nobleman
for his pusillanimous project of restoring Boulogne,
which Henry the Second was evidently resolved to
recover either by force or treaty; but he himself
now found the difficulty of retaining it, trammelled
as he was by the war in Scotland, where the united
forces of the French and the Scots were carrying
every thing before them.

To propose its restoration in Parliament would
have been highly unpopular; to wait till it was
wrested from his hands, still greater folly.   Warwick, a master in political intrigue, did neither : after
a second unsuccessful attempt to induce the Emperor Charles the Fifth to receive it under his protection, he employed a secret agent, one GUIDOTTI, an
Italian merchant settled in England, to negotiate
the matter.   Guidotti repaired to Paris, insinuated

* Carte, vol. iii. pp. 243, 244.

himself into the household of the Constable, and hinted that, if the proposal came from France, he believed the English Council would willingly restore Boulogne upon payment of an adequate equivalent in money.   Montmorency understood the suggestion; negotiations were opened; the French and English commissioners met first at Boulogne, afterwards in London, and peace was signed on the 24th March 1549-50.   Henry the Second agreed to pay to England, as the price of Boulogne and its fortifications, the sum of four hundred thousand crowns; and the town was delivered into the hands of the French King on the 15th May 1550.*   Calais was now the only possession which the English held in France.

Meanwhile, the great struggle between Charles the Fifth and the Protestant faith continued on the Continent, in the history of which the Siege of Magdeburgh formed a leading event.   The enterprise was committed by the Emperor to MAURICE the Elector of Saxony, in whom he seems to have had perfect confidence; and whose high military talents he believed would soon reduce this city, a principal hold of the Protestants, to submission. But here, for once, the Emperor's noted astuteness deserted him, and he found himself a dupe to dissimulation still deeper than his own: Maurice, incensed by the cruelty and injustice with which Charles

* Sismondi, Hist. des Français, vol. xvii. p. 390.   Flassan, Hist. de la Diplomatie Française, vol. ii. p. 27.

had treated his near relative, the Landgrave of Hesse had long and secretly cherished the thoughts of revenge. Already, when all Europe considered him the most potent ally of the Emperor, he had secretly deserted him, and was busily engaged in organising that formidable coalition with the Protestant princes, the King of France, and the Pope, which broke at last like a thunder-cloud upon the proud projects of Charles the Fifth, and threatened both himself and them with total destruction.

As a cloak for these grand designs, the Elector of Saxony had willingly accepted the charge of the siege of Magdeburgh. It afforded him a pretext for keeping up and even increasing his army; he artfully prolonged the war whilst he carried on his counterplot; and so skilfully did he manage his leaguer, that, when the city capitulated after a siege of more than twelve months, his plan was matured, and the Magdeburghers themselves ready to espouse his quarrel against the Emperor.

These secret projects of Maurice were privately communicated to Henry the Second of France, who eagerly embraced them. Jean de Fresse, Bishop of Bayonne, was sent into Germany to open a negotiation with the Elector and his associates; and a treaty was concluded, in Oct. 1551, at Fredwald in Hesse. By this league, the French monarch, the Elector of Saxony, and the Protestant princes engaged to resist, with their utmost power, the total destruction of the Constitution of the Germanic Empire, which appeared to be meditated by the Emperor; and to restore liberty to the Landgrave of Hesse, the brother-in-law of Maurice, who had been so shamefully imprisoned by Charles.* The parties to the treaty were Henry the Second on the one side; on the other, Maurice Elector of Saxony, George Frederick Marquis of Brandenbourg, John Albert Duke of Mecklenbourg, and William Landgrave of Hesse. It was ratified by the French monarch at Chambord on the 15th of January 1552; and having previously secured Boulogne, and concluded a peace with England, Henry found himself at full leisure to concentrate his efforts against the formidable encroachments of the House of Austria.

During the secret and unsuspected preparation of this powerful alliance against him, Charles' mind was completely occupied with the affairs of religion. A Diet had assembled at Augsbourg, (July 1550,) professedly for the termination of the differences between the Protestants and the Romanists; but it was conducted under the dictation of the Emperor, surrounded by an army, and it was vain to look for fair discussion. Charles insisted that the Protestants should accept the INTERIM, and he proposed to assemble a new General Council. The Protestants strongly argued against both the one and the other, as long as the Pope claimed the right of being considered supreme regulator in all matters of faith. Their opposition,

* Schoell, Hist. des Traités de Paix, vol. i. p. 40.

at this moment, was strengthened by the death of Paul the Third, and the election of the Cardinal di Monte to the triple crown, under the title of Julius the Third ;* a pontiff who signalised the commencement of his spiritual government by convoking anew the Council of Trent, and this by a Bull whose tenour clearly informed the Protestants that he considered himself rather as a judge by whom they were to be condemned, than as a potentate with whom they were to negotiate. They declared, at the same time, that it was their most anxious desire to behold a *free* General Council, in which their clergy should be allowed a voice, and whose decrees should bind the Pope himself; but against this the Emperor raised the most determined opposition, and the second Diet of Augsbourg concluded as fruitlessly as the first.

These religious feuds on the Continent had the effect of inundating England with Protestant dissenters, German, French, Italian, Polish, and Dutch, who, under the belief that this country was the only happy and favoured spot where complete religious toleration was permitted, flocked hither in great multitudes : amongst them came some distinguished and learned men,—Bucer, Peter Martyr, Paul Fagius, and John à Lasco; but others were Anabaptists, who gave great trouble, and occasioned, in the end, much scandal by their wild heretical opinions.

* He was elected on the 8th February 1549-50.

Amidst these events, Warwick's power continued to increase. He had negotiated a successful marriage treaty with France; Edward the Sixth being engaged to espouse Elizabeth, the daughter of Henry the Second. He was at peace with Scotland; and the Queen Dowager, Mary of Guise, on her return from France to assume the Scottish regency in the room of the Earl of Arran, had visited the English court, and departed with feelings which promised a continuance of the most friendly relations. He had strengthened his own hands, and his party, by ample rewards and dignities; procuring himself to be created Duke of Northumberland; raising his creatures, Paulet Earl of Wiltshire and Herbert Baron Cardiff, to the dignities of Marquis of Winchester and Earl of Pembroke: and having married his son, Lord Guilford Dudley, to the Lady Jane Grey, whose pretensions upon the crown were well known, it became apparent to many who knew his character, that his ambition might have a farther and more dangerous reach than was at first believed. All this was rendered more suspicious by that determined purpose which he manifested to remove the late Protector, the Duke of Somerset, out of the way of his ambition. This great nobleman, who had been restored to freedom, and to some little portion of the power which he had lost, was by the predominating influence of Warwick unjustly accused, condemned, and executed.—1551.

Meanwhile, the Emperor was much disconcerted

by the projected matrimonial alliance between France and England, the restoration of Boulogne, and the successes of the French arms in Scotland; whilst to these causes of annoyance were added the hostility of Solyman, whom Henry the Second had prevailed upon to declare war against him. A fleet of a hundred and fifty Turkish galleys was despatched to attack Sicily and Malta; Octavio Farnese, from whom Charles the Fifth had wrested his dominions of Parma and Piacenza, claimed the protection of France; and war, the seeds of which had been long fostering in secret, broke out at length in earnest between Henry and the Emperor.

The Marshal Brissac invaded Piedmont; the Dukes of Nesmours and Vendosme led an army against Flanders; whilst Leo Strozzi, the Prior of Capua, with a French fleet menaced the Spanish squadron in which Charles' nephew and son-in-law, Prince Maximilian, had embarked with his wife, Donna Maria, to return from Italy into Spain.

It is to be regretted that the foreign correspondence in the State Paper Office does not present us with many interesting letters in 1552,—a remarkable year, distinguished by the war of Maurice, the Elector of Saxony, with the Emperor, his former friend and patron; and by the coalition which we have already noticed between the Protestant princes of Germany and Henry the Second, a monarch whose policy at this time presented the singular and disgraceful anomaly of a furious persecution of the Protestants in his own dominions, and the strictest league with them in Germany.

The military talents of the Elector Maurice were conspicuously shown in his campaign against Charles the Fifth. Having assembled his army, he traversed Franconia, formed a junction with Margrave Albert near Donawerth, made himself master of Augsbourg, and pushed forward by forced marches against the Emperor, who was then at Inspruck in the Tyrol, superintending the deliberations of the Council of Trent. With such secrecy and rapidity was all this performed, that before Charles had time to retire, Maurice forced the famous passes of Ehrenberg;* made prisoners a division of three thousand Imperialists who defended them; and had nearly taken Cesar himself, who was just sitting down to supper. He escaped, however; but fled by torch-light from Inspruck with such precipitation, that Maurice, when he arrived, found the imperial banquet still smoking on the table. Nor did the Emperor think himself in safety till he had reached Villach in Carinthia. (May 1552.)

In his alarm, Charles restored to freedom John Frederick, the captive Elector of Saxony, and re-invested him with all his estates and dignities; but the magnanimous old man, although the personal enemy of Maurice, who had despoiled him of his kingdom, was the warm friend of the Protestant

* De Thou, book x. 1552.

faith, of which Maurice was now the champion; and he peremptorily refused to take any part against him.

This defeat led to important consequences. The Emperor was embarrassed with his war in France —he could not afford to divide his strength. He was thus driven to seek an accommodation with Maurice; and having committed the arrangement of it to Ferdinand, his brother, the celebrated peace of Passau was concluded on terms which were highly favourable to the Protestant princes.* The provisional formulary or directory of the faith, named the INTERIM, was declared no longer compulsory; the Emperor agreed to assemble a Diet for the adjustment of religious differences, in which the Protestants were to have a voice; and in the mean time full liberty of conscience was permitted. Lastly, the Landgrave of Hesse, father-in-law of Maurice, who had been so long and so perfidiously imprisoned by the Emperor, was restored to his freedom.

Nor were the affairs of Charles in a less calamitous state on the side of France. Henry the Second, on his progress to unite his forces with those of the Protestant Confederacy, made himself master of Metz, Toulon, and Verdun: the Queen of Hungary, however, then Regent of the Netherlands, invaded Picardy, and her successes arrested the French King in his career of victory.

* 31st July 1552.

The correspondence of our foreign ambassadors, in her Majesty's Collection, is, as I have said, defective during this year, and does not throw much light on its important events; a circumstance to be ascribed to the troubled state of England, the execution of the Protector Somerset, and the factions into which the country was divided. But there are to be found in the British Museum various letters, or rather fragments of letters, from Sir Richard Morysine, the English ambassador at the court of the Emperor, and from his secretary, the noted Roger Ascham, which afford us some interesting information regarding the proceedings of the Emperor. Of these, the reader will not be displeased to see a few extracts; and, when we come to the year 1553, there are valuable materials to be again found in the State Paper Office.

In this year, 1553, whether we look to Germany, France, or England, we find it marked by events of importance. In Germany, the most conspicuous parts were acted by Albert, Margrave of Brandenbourg, and Maurice, the Elector of Saxony. The former, Albert, actuated by the most rancorous animosity against the Elector and the Protestant princes of Germany, attacked them with his characteristic impetuosity, and, ravaging Franconia with fire and sword, was proclaimed a public enemy, and placed under the ban of the empire.

In these hostilities Albert was secretly supported by Charles the Fifth, who was pleased to see Maurice, at whose hands he had experienced so many indignities, reduced to the same distress he had himself felt, by the rapid successes of his rival. But Albert was too notorious and unprincipled an adventurer to be openly encouraged by the Emperor. His character seems to have presented a strange mixture of talent, ferocity, and profligacy. Most commonly intoxicated, brave or rather desperate in action, fierce and unforgiving in his resentments, lavish to profusion, and even capable at times of generosity, he resembled more a buccaneer than a grave and experienced commander : and yet his successes rendered him formidable to the best military leaders of his time ; nor did his constant dissipation impair his skill in war, which was of a high order.   He was beaten, indeed, by Maurice, in the famous battle of Siverhausen, fought near Peine, in the duchy of Lunenbourg ;* yet his enmity proved fatal to this great man, who was struck with a musket-shot in the very moment of victory, and survived only a few days.   The Margrave, who, as usual, had commenced the battle when drunk, was sobered by the defeat, and escaped to Hanover.

In France, Henry the Second, whose hopes in the preceding year had been raised to the highest pitch by the defeat of the Emperor before Metz, and the acquisition of Sienna, which was of extreme importance in his designs upon Italy, ex-

* July 9th, 1553.

perienced a severe reverse.   Therouenne, a city which he expected was to hold out as obstinately and successfully as Metz, was stormed and razed to the foundation by the Imperialists.   They were equally successful against Hesdin, a town of great strength and importance; and the campaign in Piedmont, in which the French army was commanded by Brissac, was languid, and could claim no victories to repay or even to balance such calamitous defeats.

Turning our eyes to England, we find the year 1553, the last year of this period, marked by great changes.   The death of Edward the Sixth; the extraordinary plot of the Duke of Northumberland to place the Lady Jane Grey on the throne, which ended so miserably for himself and this unfortunate and accomplished princess; the quiet accession of Mary, the restoration of the ancient faith, and the projected marriage of Mary to Philip the Second, all combined to throw the greatest historical interest over the year 1553; to strengthen the hands of the Emperor, to depress proportionably the Protestant party in Europe, and to rouse the suspicion and animosity of France.

PERIOD THE SECOND.

1549—1553.

WHEN Warwick and his faction sent the Protector and his supporters to the Tower, they deemed it proper to examine the state of that half-palace half-prisonhouse, the number and names of its captives, their offences, and the best mode to be pursued regarding them. This inquiry gave rise to a Report, from which I have made a few extracts; chiefly such as throw light on the injustice and oppression of these dark times : it is entitled,

" A REPORT *of the Prisoners being in the Tower, the 22nd of October* (1549), *made by Serjeant Mullinax and the King's Attorney.*"

Orig. ST. P. OFF. *Domestic.*

" THOMAS, late Duke of Norfolk, attainted of high treason.

" Edward Courtney, which, by procurement of others, brake the prison there.

" Robert Lord Maxfyld, [Maxwell,] a Scot, and hath his liberty in the Tower.

" Anthony Foster, late Marshal of Ireland, committed to the Tower because he was minded to sell

his said office, and to have gone with Geoffrey
Poole, being his father-in-law, as it is supposed.

" To be examined touching the King's supremacy. Mr.
Wotton, Mr. Gage, and the Lieutenant.

" The Bishop of Winchester, committed by the
Council for a contempt and preaching.

" Julius de Carcano, Italian, committed to the
Tower for bringing of counterfeit testoons; which
matter hath been divers times examined, and he
denieth it, and no witnesses to prove the offence.

" By Mr. Wotton. To be convened, and upon submission to
be pardoned.

" Robert Maule, Lord of Pammure, Scot, taken
out of his house in Scotland by the King's warriors.

" To be released for redemption of Mr. Dudley.

" David Douglas, son to Sir G. Douglas, Scot,
taken in the wars.

" James Douglas, his elder brother, taken also in
the wars in Scotland. I need scarcely remark that
this was he who afterwards became the celebrated
Regent Morton.

" William West, cousin to the Lord Delaware,
which intended to have poisoned the said Lord.

" James Noble, a Scot, brake Colchester Castle,
and was taken on the seas; and hath lands and
goods.

" Northampton.

" Patrick Baron, merchant and Scot, taken in

the wars, and brake the said prison of Colchester; and hath goods, but to what value is not known.

"Lambert.

" Sir John Rybald, of London, Knight, Frenchman, hath served in the King's wars about seven years past at divers and sundry places, and hath by the King's patent five hundred crowns for term of life; and he was committed to the Tower because he was going to Rye, to pass into France to see his children, as he saith; and was examined by Mr. Comptroller at two several times, and hath continued in prison two years; and, by the report of Mr. Lieutenant, he is an apt man for the wars.

" John Harrington, late servant to the late Lord High Admiral, was committed to the Tower at the apprehension of the said Lord Admiral, and hath been examined before the Lord Grand Master and before the Earl of Southampton, and at other times before Mr. Smyth.

"To be discharged.

"William Hychecocks, late of _____, in the county of Bucks, carpenter, committed to the Tower for conspiracies and seditious words, as appeareth by his examination taken by Mr. Comptroller.

"To justice.

" Richard Coole, of Mynnyt, in the county of Somerset, mariner, was a pirate by the space of one year, and took divers prizes; and at last he sued to

the Lord Deputy of Ireland, Mr. Bellingham, by
five supplications, to come in and submit himself to
the King's mercy; which Lord Deputy commanded
him to go to a castle in Straugham, in Ireland,
which the Scots had taken; and so he did, and took
the castle from them, and restored the owner to the
castle; and, after this, examinate did help the said
Lord Deputy's servants against one Savage, a rebel
in Ireland, and the said Lord Deputy promised to
sue for his pardon; and, after this, examinate went
to the Isle of Man, and there sent to land his mate,
in pledge to submit himself; and shortly after he
was taken by Cornelius and other, of his own good
will, and hath been in prison since May last.

" To be examined, and ordered by the Admiral's officers.

" Robert Bell, of Easeley, in Suffolk, labourer,
was committed to the Tower on Whitsun-even, by
the Lord Wentworth's commandment, because this
examinate and John Fuller were together, and sued
a supplication against Mr. Rouse for certain wrongs;
and he hath been examined by the said Lord Wentworth.

" To justice.

" John Fuller, of Canon, in Suffolk, collar-
maker, was committed to the Tower on Whitsun-
even, by the commandment of the Lord Wentworth, because this examinate and Robert Capp
procured a supplication against Mr. Syder and Mr.

Rouse for certain wrongs and destruction of their corn, as he saith.

" To justice.

" Robert Capp, of Canon, in Suffolk, labourer, was committed to the Tower on Wednesday in Whitsun-week, by the commandment of the said Lord Wentworth, because this examinate, John Fuller, King, Stephenson, and Bell made a supplication to the King against Robert Syder and William Rouse for the destroying their corn, and being every-years' land ; and all these persons were examinate by the Lord Wentworth, as he saith." * *

" Justice. †

PRISONERS LATELY COMMITTED TO THE TOWER.

" The Duke of Somerset.

" Sir Ralph Phane, Knight.

"   Fysher, Secretary to the Duke of Somerset.

" John Bowes, Treasurer of the Mint at Durham Place.

" Richard Palydye, Clerk of the Works to the said Duke.

" Sir Michael Stanhope, Knight.

" Sir Thomas Smith, Knight.

" Sir John Thynne, Knight.

† To justice—to immediate execution. The order seems to be given without any trial having been thought necessary; at least we have no proof that anything had taken place except an examination of the prisoners.

"   Wolfe, of the Privy Chamber.
" William Grey, of Redyng.
"   Hales."

On the deposition and imprisonment of the Protector, Sir Philip Hoby and Sir Thomas Cheney were despatched on an embassy to the court of the Emperor, to inform him " of the alteration of the state," whilst they were instructed at the same time to require aid of men, carriages, and victual out of the Low Countries for the defence of Boulogne." * Warwick, the Lord Great Chamberlain, was promoted to the important trust of Lord High Admiral, for which his experience in naval affairs eminently fitted him; and the Privy Council, by the following paper, made a division amongst themselves of the several departments of the state. This allotment is not alluded to in the MS. Books of Privy Council, and I find it nowhere mentioned in any of our chroniclers or historians.

" MINUTE OF THE LETTERS,

DECLARING THE ORDER FOR DIVISION OF SEVERAL MATTERS
TO SEVERAL OF THE COUNCILLORS."

Orig.   St. P. Off.   Oct. 31st, 1549.

" Boulogne,	My Lord of Arundel.
" Calais, with the Marches,	{ Sir Edward Wotton, Sir John Gage.
" Ireland,	{ My Lord Great Master, The Master of the Horse.

* MS. Privy Council Books of Edward VI.

" The North, with the victualling of the same,	My Lord of Shrewsbury, Mr. Comptroller, Sir Richard Cotton, Mr. Cofferer.
" Alderney, Scilly,	Sir R. Southwell, Sir Edward North.
" The Isle of Wight, Portsmouth,	The Earl of Southampton.
" The charge of victualling of the sea,	Men at the Lord Admiral's appointment.
" The foresight for money,	By report of the Treasurers every week to the Lords.
" The order of the Mint,	The Earl of Southampton."

I have already adverted to the obscurity which involves the fate and conduct of Cecil when his first master and patron, the Protector, was deposed and sent to the Tower. How he escaped immediate imprisonment when Sir Thomas Smith, Sir John Thynne, Sir Michael Stanhope, and other adherents, shared the fate of Somerset; at what precise time it was that he was confined in the Tower, and in what manner he procured his deliverance, are problems for the solution of which the critical inquirer into the life of this great man will look in vain in the accounts hitherto given of his early career. I have lately, however, found an entry in the MS. Privy Council Books of Edward the Sixth, which, although garbled in the transcription, resolves one of these doubts, and proves that Cecil, on the 25th January 1549-50, obtained his liberty; at the same time he appears to have become bound, under a penalty of one thousand marks, to present himself, on due warning, before the Privy Council to reply to any accusation which might be brought against him.* It is worthy of remark also, that, in obtaining his freedom, we find him associated with Edward Wolf, a gentleman of the Privy Chamber, Richard Paladye, Clerk of the Works to the Protector, and Richard Whalley, all three principal servants and adherents to the Duke of Somerset, who were released at the same time, upon payment of a like fine.

I once entertained a suspicion that Cecil had joined Cranmer and Paget in playing a double part to Somerset. The high situation which he held under the Protector, the singular and ambiguous manner in which he vanishes from our view during the busy week at Windsor, the skill with which he seems to have retained the friendship of the all-powerful Warwick, the tardiness of his imprisonment, and his sudden re-emerging into consideration, if not to power,—all seemed to me to throw a doubt upon the upright-

---

* The passage in the Privy Council Books is as follows:
    " In the Old Palace of Westminster,
            " 25th Jany. 1549-50.

" Willm. Cycill, Richard Whalley, Edward Woolf, and Richard Pallady, do recognise to owe to our Sovereign Lord the King, four thousand marks. That is to say, each of them M marks to be levyed, &c. upon condicion that they and every of them personally shall be forthcoming at all times, to appear before the Lords of his Majesty's Privy Council upon reasonable warning to answer such things as shall be objected to them."

ness and consistency of his conduct. The following letter of Whalley, however, goes a great way to remove every doubt. Cecil, it appears, was far from rich, and wished to have a grant of Wimbledon. This could not be effected; but in its place the park and lodge of Morthlak was to be given him,* at the request of Somerset, whose reason for applying to the proprietor, Mr. Tyrwhit, was his anxiety to have Cecil near him. It seems impossible that Somerset, had he entertained the slightest suspicion of Cecil's sincerity, would have desired to have him beside him, and, as before, would have committed to him the principal management of his affairs.

R. WHALLEY TO CECIL.

Orig. St. P. Off. *Domestic.* March 1549-50.

" Sir.—To be plain, as I see no likelihood at all to obtain Wimbledon, as ye desire, (altho', for my part, I can't do more for my father, yet I have no doubt but the park, with the tithe of Morthlak, one Ambrose Whalley's house, with such other parcels as may well serve your necessity, will be obtained upon your next *witty talk* with Mr. Chancellor therein. I am greatly deceived but he is now fully persuaded we are to use you friendly in the said park and lodge, I think for his whole interest therein ; in effect, even as he hath the same at Mr.

---

* Now Mortlake, near Wimbledon, where Tyrwhit held the office of Keeper of the Deer.—Bray's Surrey, vol. iii. p. 306.

Tyrwhit's hands, and so for the rest to serve your turn friendly. He hath promised me to speak with you himself this day in the premises, and so to conclude with you in all things right friendly ; which I pray the Lord may as duly take effect, as I desire to be at Welbeck with my poor nurse. Thus, thinking good to advertise you of the premises, I rest, at Darby Place, this present Thursday morning, at six the clock, 1549,　　Your own, as you know,

"　R. WHALLEY."

Addressed.
" *To the Right Worshipful Mr. Cycle,*
with my Lord's Grace at the Court."

Now the following passage in a letter addressed by Tyrwhit to Cecil, dated 12th April 1550, alluding to the same subject, proves that Somerset retained his friendship for Cecil. "I have received my Lord's Grace's letter and yours for the lodge and park of Morthlak for your commodity to have it, *because his Grace would have you nigh unto him.*"

The Protector, after having been deposed and sent to the Tower, remained for some months uncertain of his fate : anxiety to obtain his freedom, and perhaps some fears that an obstinate denial of guilt might endanger his life, induced him to sign the " Articles" which had been prepared against him and which the critical reader will find in Carte. *
This was on the 23rd of December ; and on the 6th of February, twelve days after Cecil had been set

* Vol. iii. p. 242.

free, the Protector, upon payment of a fine of ten thousand pounds, was released from the Tower, and permitted to reside either at the King's manor of Shene, or at Sion House, his own palace, according to his pleasure. He was not allowed, however, to travel beyond four miles from either; and it was stipulated that, if the young King should at any time come to Shene or Sion, the Duke should not attempt to have access to the royal presence, to the Court or the Council, unless expressly sent for.* In the same month, the late Secretary of State, Sir Thomas Smith, Sir Michael Stanhope, Sir John Thynne, and Mr. Thomas Fisher, who had been treated with severity during their imprisonment, and who are described in the Privy Council Books as principal instruments and councillors of the Duke in his ill government, were restored to liberty upon payment of a heavy fine; Smith, Stanhope, and Fisher being mulcted in three thousand, and Sir John Thynne in six thousand pounds.

After a while, a reconciliation took place between the potent Earl of Warwick and the late Protector, which seemed to be complete: Dudley's eldest son, Lord L'Isle, married Somerset's daughter; and, on the 10th of April 1550,† the Duke was once more admitted a member of the Privy Council. His son, the Earl of Hertford, had shortly before this been sent, in company with the Duke of Suffolk; the Lord Lisle, son of the Earl of Warwick; Lord

* MS. Book of Privy Council of Edward VI.   † Ibid.

Talbot, son of the Earl of Shrewsbury ; Lord Russel, son and heir of the Earl of Bedford; and
other noble youths, to the French court as hostages
for the performance of the late treaty with Henry
the Second.*   The following letter from Somerset
to the Lord Cobham is the first of any importance
which I have met with since his deposition : it
shows that Hertford, the young hostage, had been
gaining golden opinions when in France; and
alludes modestly to his own return to public life.

THE DUKE OF SOMERSET TO THE LORD COBHAM.

Orig.   HARLEIAN.   Fol. 86.   15th April 1550.

" AFTER our very hearty commendations to your
good Lordship.—By your letters of the 13th hereof,
we be advertised of the good health of our son, the
Earl of Hertford, and also of his behaviour towards
the company where he cometh, gaining thereby
much commendation, whereof we be right glad ;
and altho' we think him not able to deserve such
commendation, yet have we this opinion of you,
that as you make it by report, so both you would
have it, and, by advertisements of good counsel towards him, will help it.   Touching the latter part
of your letter, mentioning the revocation of us to
the Council, we perceive thereby your good affection; and, altho' this same cannot be so beneficial to
the commonwealth as you remember, yet in good-

* MS. Book of Privy Council of Edward VI.

will it shall not fail, but answer the expectation of the best. And, for that you number yourself amongst our friends, think you so assuredly; and, wherein we may by any deed confirm your opinion, ye shall not fail. So right heartily fare you well, with like thanks. From Shene, this 15th April.

> " Your Lordship's very loving friend,
>
> " E. Somerset."

Catherine Willoughby, Duchess of Suffolk, second wife of the gallant and accomplished Charles Brandon, the favourite and the brother-in-law of Henry the Eighth, married, after his death, Mr. Bertie, with whom, in Mary's time, she became a refugee. She seems to have consulted Cecil upon every matter of importance concerning the management of her family and estates, and her correspondence with this great man might of itself form a small volume. Her letters are lively, and often humorous; full of domestic details, for she appears to have been a notable *housewife;* but occasionally throwing glimpses of light upon the history of the times. The two epistles which follow exhibit Cecil in a favourable, and the Privy Council in a questionable predicament : Cecil, acting as an arbiter or judge who would look solely to the equity of the case, and scorn *" to break justice's head for friendship;"* the Council, as a venal tribunal, whose favourable judgment could only be secured by bribery; or, to use the Duchess' expressive phrase, when the suitors " *brought their letters in the battle, and their money in the rearward.*"

DUCHESS OF SUFFOLK TO CECIL.

Orig. St. P. Off. *Domestic.* 27th April 1550.

" Surely it is doubly worthy thanks that my Lord of Somerset hath of himself, unremembered, remembered and appointed the hearing of the matter between Mr. Fullington and Mr. Naunton. I do store up these thanks for him, but minding to bestow them sooner upon *him,* than *you* shall look for any for the pains you shall take in hearing the cause ; for such is my opinion of you, that *affection* shall so much turn you to either party for [from] the equity as if they *were Jews.* Therefore, when friendship prevaileth not, what availeth thanks ? If you will not *break justice's head for friendship,* look not for thanks at your friend's hand. But, indeed, you shall understand that the right is my friend ; and, being good to my friend in which side soever he be, my thanks are like ready: so fare ye heartily well.

" At Kingston, the 27th of April.

" Your assured,

" K. Suffolk."

THE DUCHESS OF SUFFOLK TO CECIL.

Orig. St. P. Off. *Domestic.* 18th May 1550.

" I have looked for letters from you. The season and want of counsel would have much com-

mended them.   Edmund Hall wrote to me that he
opened to you the answer of my Lord Paget unto
him as touching my desire to purchase Spil-
bye Chantry, and which way he adviseth me to
enter into the same.   He addeth in the same letter,
that you promised to write your advice to me in
that behalf; but I beshrew long the carrier that
bringeth them not.   I must therefore now proceed
like *blind Bayard.*   I have written a letter with an
ill-will to the whole body of the Council, according
to my Lord Paget's *device;* but so as I mind not
the delivery thereof, unless it like you the better.
Me seemeth it had been the readier way to have a
bill drawn of my suit, and the same to be presented
to the whole Council, and with my private letters
to labour my friends.   Devise what you think good ;
either that my letter be delivered, or a bill of supplication.

" I would have written to my Lord of Somerset
at this time, but my leisure serveth me not; and his
assuredness maketh me the bolder to wait upon
others.   I pray you declare to Edmund Hall which
way and how he shall give *this onset;* and afterwards, how I shall follow with my *letters* in the
battle, and my *money* in the rearward.   So with
you farewell.

" At Kingston, the 18th of May,

" Your assured friend,

" K. Suffolk."

The Embassy, of which our next letter contains a minute and interesting account, was that of Mons. de Chastillon, Mortier, and Bouchetel, to England in 1550. Chastillon and his colleagues were sent by Henry the Second to receive Edward's ratification of the treaty by which Boulogne had been ceded to France for the sum of four hundred thousand crowns. The letter is to be found in the original "*Letter Book*" of Sir John Masone, ambassador for England at the French Court, which is preserved in the State Paper Office, and in some places is corrected by his own hand.

Masone was a statesman who, like many of his brethren in those days of change and suspicion, must have had in him more of the willow than the oak, as he contrived to keep in constant favour during the reigns of Henry, Edward, Mary, and Elizabeth; and he has left us his own hints to all future trimmers in dangerous times. " Four things, he said, kept him *in* under all the revolutions during the four princes' reigns whom he served. 1. That he thought *few things* would save a man. 2. That he was always intimate with the exactest lawyer and ablest favourite. 3. That he spake little and writ less. 4. That he attained to something which each party esteemed serviceable to them, and was so moderate that all thought him their own." " His first undertaking," says Lloyd, " was in France, where his gravity was too severe, beyond the dalliances of that place ; his next was to Italy, where he showed as great a reach in countermining, as the inhabitants of that place do in managing their plots. His last voyage was to Spain, where he *outgrav'd* the Don himself; and then did he return with the Italian's quickness, the Spaniard's staidness, the Frenchman's air, the German's resolution, and the Dutchman's industry; qualities that demonstrated he understood other countries, and could serve his own." From the quaint and elaborate panegyric pronounced by the same author on this ancient and approved statesman, we may gather that Masone was a paragon of caution, coldness, and craft. His letters, however, present us with a spirited and graphic picture of the courts and countries which he visited.

LORDS OF THE COUNCIL TO SIR JOHN MASONE.

Copy in Sir J. Masone's Letter Book, from the Orig. 2d June 1550.

" AFTER our right hearty commendations.—To the intent whatever shall there occur for matter to be ministered touching the entertainment of Mons. De Chastillon and his colleagues during the time of their being here, we have thought good briefly to signify unto you the manner of their receiving entertainment, and what else hath passed during their abode here.

" First, therefore, ye shall understand that, on Friday was seven night, the galley *Subtle,* with two other of the King's pinnaces, under the charge of Sir William Woodhouse, Mr. Brook, and others, were sent to the Thames' mouth to meet with the French galleys, and to conduct them upwards.* And, at their first meeting, [having] received them with an honest banquet; so accompanied them along the Thames, where, passing by sundry of the King's ships, they were saluted with honest peals of ordnance; and, a little above Greenwich, I, the Lord Warden of the Cinque Ports, being accompanied with the Earl of Worcester, the Lord Gray of Wilton, the Lord William Howard, with divers other young lords and gentlemen to the number of sixty, in sundry barges, met with them upon the water, bade them welcome on the King's Majesty's behalf, with other good words to the purpose, and so received them into those barges.

" They were conveyed by water thro' the bridge to their lodging, being appointed at Durham Place, which was furnished with hangings of the King's for the *nonce;* where, against their coming, was ready laid in, a very large present of beer, wine, beeves, muttons, wild fowls, poultry, fish, and wax. By the way the King's ships at Deptford shot off; and at the Tower, as they passed, a great peal of

---

* In the MS. Privy Council Books of Edward the Sixth, under the date 18th May 1550, we find " a warrant to the M^r. of the Jewel House, to deliver to Benjamin Gonstone, Treasurer of the King's ships, one pair of pots, one pair of flaggons, three nest of bowls, two basins and ewers, a garnish and half of vessel, two dozen plates, and two salts of silver, for the furniture *of the galley* appointed for the Lord Warden to meet the French ambassador coming up by the Thames."

ordnance was discharged to welcome them. As soon
as they were landed and in their lodgings, a gentleman was sent from the King's Majesty, willing me,
the Lord Warden, in the King's Highness' behalf
to bid them welcome, and let them [know] that
if they wanted aught, being signified, it should be
provided; and so for that night left them.

" The next day being Saturday, early in the
forenoon we, the Lord Paget and Sir William
Petre, went to visit them from the King's Majesty,
to know as well what time they would gladliest
take for their access to his Highness, as also whether they wanted aught ; which if they did, order
should be given for the supply thereof.   They
thanked us, and required their time of access might
be appointed the self [same] afternoon, which was
done : and by water in barges, we, the Lord Viscount
Hereford, the Lord Admiral, the Lord Cobham,
and Sir William Petre, being sent to accompany the
four in commission, having also with us other lords
and gentlemen to entertain Mons. D'Andelot,* the
Rhinegrave, and others, brought them to the Court,
where, in the Chamber of Presence, the King's Majesty was ready to receive them ; and, at their coming, embraced them orderly, read their letters of
credence, and in the rest used them with so good
words and countenance as they rested very well
satisfied.

" The next day being Whit-Sunday, assigned for

* Andelot.—See Note, p. 36.

the taking of the oath and ratification, we, the Marquises of Dorset and Northampton, the Lord Privy Seal, and Lord Paget, went again with barges to conduct them to the court; which then, what with our own nation and theirs, was very much replenished. The King's Majesty, after the Communion and service in the chapel beneath, in presence of Mons. Chastillon and his colleagues, and us all of his Highness' Privy Council, besides divers others standers-by, did read the oath and subscribe the same, with the circumstances thereto belonging: and that day the French Commissioners, with their ambassador here resident, dined with the King, and were of his Majesty most friendly entertained.*

" Monday last, we, the Duke of Somerset and divers others of us, were invited by them to dinner, where they feasted us as the market would serve

---

* The peace has been, by most of the general historians of England, ascribed to the skilful advice and influence of Antonio Guidotti, a Florentine merchant. He had, undoubtedly, a great share in the negotiations, and was afterwards rewarded by knighthood and a pension.—Lingard, vol. vii. p. 65. There is a passage, however, in the Privy Council Books of Edward the Sixth, 20th April 1550, which ascribes the *first* motion of the peace, not to Guidotti, but to Mons. Gondi, Master of the French King's finances. In a letter addressed to Sir Morice Denys and Sir William Sherington, Knights, and Commissioners for the receipt of the first payment to be made by the French, they are directed to give Mons. Gondi, if he shall come with the French hostages, two thousand crowns in reward from the King's Majesty, " because he was the first motioner and procurer of this peace." I do not find this fact (which rests on the authority of the Privy Council Books) in any historian of the period.

very honourably; and that afternoon they saw the pastime of our bear-baiting and bull-baiting.

" Upon Tuesday, the King's Majesty had them on hunting in Hyde Park, and that night they supt with his Highness in the Privy Chamber. Wednesday, they were conveyed by me, the Marquis of Northampton, to Hampton Court, where they dined, hunted, and that night returned. Thursday, they sent word that they were desirous as well to have conference with us in Council, as also to know when they might wait upon the King's Majesty to take their leave. Word was sent them that, if it liked them that afternoon to repair to the Court to have conference with us, and so the next day morning to take their leave of the King, they should be welcome (which, nevertheless, was put to their own election how they would take their times) : so the same afternoon they were, according to their choice, conducted to the Court by us, the Lord Cobham, the Lord Paget, the Secretaries Petre and Wotton ;* and being set with us at the Council Board, Mons. de Chastillon said they had certain things to speak to us of, wherein albeit the ambassador resident should from time to time speak more as occasion should serve, yet for the present had they thought good to remember these few things unto us."

* Wotton had been recalled from his Embassy at the French court, where he was succeeded by Sir William Pickering. He was now joint Secretary with Sir William Petre.—Privy Council Books of Edward Sixth.

Some discussions follow upon subjects connected with the peace, which are not of general interest. They related to the liberation of prisoners, the restoration of ships taken in the war, and the demolition of the castles of Roxburgh and the fort at Aymouth.

These points being replied to by the English Commissioners, the French declared themselves satisfied, and having been "made to drink, with good words departed; that night they, with their whole trains, supt with the Duke of Somerset,† and after supper had sundry pastimes showed them upon the river.

" The next day," continues the letter, " being Friday, they spent the forenoon in riding about the town to see it; and in the afternoon were sent to them, we, the Lord Cobham, the Lord Paget, the Secretary Wotton, and Sir Anthony St. Leger, to commune with them on certain matters, and afterwards to bring them to the King. * * * To the chief of them the King's Highness caused rich and

† The Duke of Somerset, late Protector, had, as above noticed, p. 278, been pardoned, and he was now restored to a temporary possession of some of his former greatness. On the 27th April 1550, it was agreed by the whole Council, that the King's Majesty should be moved for the restitution of the Duke of Somerset unto all his goods, his debts, and his leases *yet ungiven;* and, on the 11th May 1550, the Council determined that, since it had pleased his Majesty to call the Duke again into his Privy Council, they would be suitors that he might be again admitted of the Privy Chamber.—MS. Privy Council Books of Edward the Sixth, sub anno 1550.

goodly presents and gifts to be sent ere they departed.† * * * And thus we bid you most heartily
farewell. From Westminster, the 2nd of June 1550.

" Your loving friends,

    " T. CANT. R. RYCHE, Cancellar.
    " W. WILTSHIRE, J. BEDFORD, E. CLINTON,
    " T. WENTWORTH, G. COBHAM,
    " A. WINGFIELD, T. DARCYE, N. WOTTON."

The reader, by turning to " Edward's Journal,"
which has been printed from the original by Burnet,
in the Appendix to his History of the Reformation,‡ will find a spirited abridgment of the proceedings of the French ambassadors, and the entertainment which they received, drawn up by the King
himself. I may here mention, by the way, that
a conjecture of Mr. Hallam's, § as to the non-origi-
nality of Edward's Journal, derives support from
some notes I have found in the State Paper Office,
which show, that the young Monarch was in the
habit of transcribing papers written for him by his
masters. In the present instance he specially
notices that, after the "fair supper" given them
by the Duke of Somerset, the ambassadors went
on the Thames, where they saw the "bear hunted
in the river, wildfire cast out of the boats, and
many pretty conceits."

† Privy Council Books of Edward the Sixth, MS. This
day (29th May 1550) Monsieur Chastillon, Mortier, and Bou-
chetell, Ambassadors from the French King, took their leave.
    ‡ Vol. ii. p. 14.
    § Constitutional History, vol. i. p. 116.

It is well known that, about this time, the condition of Ireland gave much uneasiness to the ministers of Edward. O'Neill, O'Docherty, O'Donnell, and other chiefs, weary of their dependence on England, proposed to Henry the Second of France to become his subjects, if he would procure the consent of the Pope, and send them assistance. This monarch entertained their offer, and in 1549 sent Monluc, Bishop of Valence, into Ireland, to inform himself more particularly regarding the real state of the country. Monluc was ambassador from France to the Scottish Court in 1549; and it was on his return from Scotland to France, that Henry commanded him to visit Ireland. ▪He took with him on this journey the well-known Sir James Melvil, then a youth of fourteen, whom Mary of Guise sent at this time to be educated at the French Court, as a page of honour to Mary Queen of Scots, then in France.*

It appears by the following letter from Sir John Masone to the Council, (of which I omit the first part, which possesses little interest,) that these secret practices between the Irish chiefs and the French Court had been renewed in 1550.

SIR JOHN MASONE TO THE COUNCIL.
Orig. Draft. St. P. Off.   June 14, 1550.

*   *   *   " It chanced me, three or four days past, to know by secret intelligence that there was

---

* Melvil's Memoirs, p. 9.   Bannatyne edition.

arrived at this Court one *George Paris*, sent from
M'William out of Ireland, with letters of credence.   This Paris was a gentleman of the English
Pale, whose father or brother was executed for treason, and therefore seemeth he to seek all the mean
he can to annoy the King and the realm ; and for
that purpose, this time of the wars, he hath been a
common post between the wild Irish and the French.

" I had intelligence further, that one Monsieur
De Botte, a Britain [Breton], should be sent from
hence into Ireland, disguised in merchant's apparel,
either since Easter, or not much before.

" I thought good somewhat to say hereof to the
French King ; and therefore, after I had received
his answer touching my first matter, Sir, quoth I,
I have another thing to say to you from my master,
rather to declare his frank mind to communicate to
you whatsoever he heareth, than that he hath any
great belief therein.   He is advertised, divers ways
out of Ireland, that there are yet *practices* continued between you and the Irish ; and that not long
since there was sent from hence a messenger
thither, and that very lately is come from them another, whom and whose name his Highness knoweth very well, who is thought to be at this time, or
will be within a day or two, in this court.   My
master's trust is, if any such messenger either come
or shall come unto you, you will consider the Irishmen to be his lawful subjects, and that therefore
you will not by any means animate them to forget

their duties of obedience, but rather declare unto
them the strait amity that is between you and
him, and to advise them to remember their allegiance, which if they should not do, you would not
fail, if need were, to assist your good brother
against them; and, this doing, you shall do the
part of a friend and of a prudent King; being an
ill example to your own subjects to see the subjects
of another prince maintained in rebellion; which if
the King my master had not considered, as it be-
hoved a prince of virtue, there was a time when he
lacked not succours to your disadvantage in the
like case; but he well weighed how unhonourable it
was—yea, and dangerous—to give courage to subjects against the prince, and therefore dismissed
he them in such a sort as small comfort had they
to return.

"Here he cut off my tale, and told me that,
indeed, in time of war he did the best he could by
all means to annoy his enemy, and for that purpose
had he entered a *practice* with the Irish, which,
immediately upon the peace concluded, he brake
off, and revoked from them such ministers as he
had sent thither for that effect, and since that time
he never would hearken to them. Truth it was,
he could not deny but messages hath he had
from them not long since, but to whom he had
given such answer as he thought they had small
cause to make any boast thereof; assuring the
King, his good brother, that he would neither in

that matter, neither in any other thing, otherwise use himself but as appertained to the straitness of the amity between them. I would no further wade with him, and yet am I well assured that the said Paris was on Monday last at the court, being appointed that day to have audience. Finally, I besought him to remember the Scots of St. Andrew's. He said, he thought the Constable had therein taken order, to whom he bade me go to know the certainty thereof.

" Thus, after many good and friendly words, I took my leave of him, and strait repaired unto the Constable, to whom I declared both my commission and the King's answer thereunto. He promised the despatch for the frontiers should be made out of hand, and willed me thereof to leave a memorial with him, which I did; as well touching Jones' Bullwark, as the grounds about Guisnes, Caphier, and Sandingfeld. I asked him what they meant to reinforce their garrisons at Arde, seeing they understood that we did all the contrary on our p[art]. I will tell you, quoth he: the King had in these forts about Boulogne a great many old soldiers, which being once dispersed cannot so soon be had again; and each of them, in time of need, is worth a thousand, and therefore he will in no case *casse* [disband] them. And knowing not how to bestow them better, he hath advised to place them in the garrisons of Flanders and Burgundy. And yet, quoth I, are we

informed otherwise; and that those of Arde, with
their aid, mean to lett us from the cutting of certain
grass, which hath always appertained to the King's
Highness. He sware that there was nothing meant
but friendship towards us, and that he had told the
very truth of the matter.

" Touching the Scots at St. Andrew's, he told
me that the Lord Grange and his brother are flown
he wist not whither, and two others were already
set at liberty; and that the rest, at the King my
master's contentation, should out of hand be put at
large.* Marry, out of the realm they should not
yet go. All other Scots that had served the King
in his wars, should also out of hand be set at liberty, the places being known where they do
remain. And for that purpose he sent for the
Prior of Capua,† and asked him whether all Englishmen that were prisoned in the galleys were not

* In another work, (History of Scotland, vol. vi. p. 88,) I
have said that none of his biographers had discovered in what
manner Knox, who was one of the prisoners made at St.
Andrew's, recovered his liberty in 1550. The fact is now
ascertained—he and his brother captives obtained their freedom
at the earnest and repeated application of Edward the Sixth.

† *Leo Strozzi*, Prior of Capua, brother of Peter Strozzi.
He commanded the armament which came to the assistance of
the Scots in 1547, and took the castle of St. Andrew's. De
Thou, book xiv, pronounces him one of the most consummate
generals of his time. He was killed at the attack of an insig-
nificant town in Piombino, in 1554. Although treated ungrate-
fully by France, no bribe could tempt him to enter the service
of the Emperor; the ruling passion of his life being to see his
native country liberated by the arms of Henry the Second.

at liberty.   He answered that he thought assuredly
they were all abroad, for he had long since taken
order therefore. I pray you, quoth I, yet write once
again therein, and require the certificate of the execution thereof to be sent to you, which I would be
glad to see.   He promised that he would not fail
so to do.   Yea, quoth the Constable; and let the
like order be taken with the Scots, if you have any
that have served the King of England in his wars.

*   *   *   *   *

"Here is divers talks of the occasion of the
Emperor going to Augsbourg to the Diet.†   Some
think it is to see what he may do to make his son
King of Romaynes, alleging that his brother hath
had it all this while but *in deposito;* and that he
promised, at the receiving thereof, to yield it up
again when the Prince of Spain should be of age.‡

† Sleidans' History of the Reformation, translated by Bohn,
p. 499.   The Diet was opened on the 26th July.

‡ Charles had long been intent upon the project of making
his son Philip King of the Romans, by inducing his brother
Ferdinand to renounce that dignity in his favour; but Ferdinand showed no inclination to abdicate.   His son Maximilian,
Archduke of Austria, was now twenty-two, and Ferdinand was
anxious to keep the dignity for himself, that he might afterwards secure it to this young prince, who was a favourite with
the Electors.   Charles prevailed on his sister, the Queen Dowager of Hungary, to use all her influence with her brother; but
without effect.   Ferdinand secretly imparted his griefs to Maurice of Saxony, and he, happy to widen the breach between
the two brothers, Charles and Ferdinand, declared that he
would perish sooner than see the King of the Romans despoiled
of his dignity.   It was accordingly resolved that neither Maurice nor Ferdinand should attend the Diet at Augsbourg.

The King of Romaynes seemeth not to mind to leave it; but the Archduke of Austria* most of all *kicketh* at the matter, and hath required, therefore, to be dismissed from his government in Spain, to the intent he may be present at the Diet. Others think the great matter is to confirm his authority in Almain, and to establish the *Interim.*

" The Bishop of Rome hath conditioned with the Emperor that, in case the General Council shall be kept, the Protestants shall not be admitted but as *Rei,* and in no case to be there as members otherwise. The French seem much to be against the General Council, and say plainly that there is therein meant nothing but the confirming the Emperor's greatness. The French King hath lately made an ordinance, that whosoever of his subjects buyeth any spicery in Flanders, shall custom there four for every hundred; but buying it of Flemings, or any other within any of his own ports, they shall pay but the ordinary. The substance of the Cardinal of Lorain's *punitions* is bestowed upon the Cardinal of Guise, which beareth no small swing in this court. The French King mindeth to continue in these quarters till the beginning of August.

Ferdinand upon this took a fit of the gout, which confined him to his bed; and Maurice discovered that Magdebourg could not be taken so soon as was expected.—Barré, Histoire D'Allemagne, vol. viii. part 2, p. 828.

* Maximilian, Archduke of Austria, son of Ferdinand King of the Romans, nephew of Charles the Fifth. He married, in 1549, the Infanta Mary, daughter of Charles, and his own cousin.

" It is a marvellous thing to see the dearth of this country. I assure your Lordships that all kinds of victuals bear double the price of that they do in England; whereof, and of the loss by exchange, which is every fourth penny, I trust your good Lordships will have consideration: otherwise, I wot not by what possibility I can wade through my charge.

" Sturton, who hangeth poorly upon this court, is much desirous to return into England; being able, as he saith, to show unto your Lordships such probable reasons of his doings as he doubteth not to satisfy your Lordships therewith. Marry, he standeth in such fear by ill reports as he dareth not to adventure to come home, unless it may like your good Lordships by your letter, or some other mean, to assure him that he shall be heard at length, and, upon his honest declaration, to be permitted to go at liberty. The poor man liveth here in much misery; and to what inconvenience lack and desperation may drive him to, a man cannot tell: and here is a good companion called Horsemonden, that ceaseth not to egg him to Italy; and so, as I am informed, to Rome. It may like your good Lordships at convenient leisure to signify unto me what I may say unto him in this matter. Your Lordships shall herewith receive a certain ordinance which the French King hath lately made touching apparel.

" And forasmuch as it may chance that it shall

be requisite, before my return home, to write such matter as should not behove by interception to come to the knowledge of others, I send to you herewith a *cipher*, which it may please you to command to be kept, or else to cause some other like to be devised, and to send the copy thereof unto me. And thus, &c. From Paris, the 14th June 1550."

The French intrigues with Ireland appear to have given great disquiet to Sir John Masone. It is reported of this crafty ambassador, that, " when in Italy, he showed as great a reach in countermining as the inhabitants did in managing their plots;"* but this habit, although it often led to the prevention of real danger, made him an alarmist, whose accounts were often over-suspicious and exaggerated. In the present instance, it may be suspected that he was needlessly sensitive regarding these French plots.

In the following letter we again meet with George Paris, the envoy from the discontented Irish. We learn something of this person from Sir James Melvil, who, in describing his voyage to Ireland with the Bishop of Valence, and their arrival at the mouth of Loch Feuill, says, " Before our landing we sent one George Paris, who had been sent into Scotland by the great O'Neill and his associates ; who landed at the house of a gen-

* Lloyd, p. 211.

tleman that had married O'Docherty's daughter, dwelling at the Loch edge; who came into our ship and welcomed us, and convoyed us to his house, which was a great dark tower, where we had cold cheer, as herring and biscuit, for it was *Lent-roun*." *

If we could forget its folly and cold-blooded cruelty, one might be apt to smile at the simplicity with which Masone, a statesman of the old English school, introduces his plan for the pacification, or, in his own words, the "hunting down and bearding these wild-beasts of Ireland."

His description of the "notable pensiveness" of the Emperor in his journey to Augsbourg, and the Spanish gravity and exclusiveness of Philip, is striking; but Charles' melancholy was to be ascribed more to his signal failure in the favourite scheme of making his son King of the Romans, and to a similar disappointment in another plan which he entertained of procuring Philip to be chosen Perpetual Vicar of the Empire in Italy, than to the causes mentioned by the ambassador. The Emperor had seen his projects detected, and for the time defeated, by Ferdinand his brother and the Electors. Hence the low spirits of Cæsar.

In this letter we meet for the first time with the Maréchal de Brissac, well known as one of the bravest and ablest captains and most accomplished gentlemen of the age. He had distinguished him-

---

* Melvil's Memoirs, p. 10. *Lentroun* the season of Lent.

self highly, in 1541, at the siege of Perpignan; and, when Charles the Fifth invested Landrecy in 1543, Brissac thrice threw reinforcements into the town, and afterwards formed a junction with Francis the First, who lay with his army at Vitry.

His future career under Henry the Second, when he commanded in Italy, and was opposed to Ferdinand Gonzaga and the Duke of Alva, was equally brilliant. Although bred from his boyhood in the camp, and equal to the most daring projects, Brissac shone equally as the ornament and idol of the court. He was a little man with a slight figure, but finely formed; and his countenance was so beautiful, that the ladies called him " *le beau Brissac.*"

SIR JOHN MASONE TO THE COUNCIL.

Orig. Draft. St. P. Off. 29th June 1550.

" It may like your good Lordships to be advertised. Since the despatch of Francisco, in conference had once or twice with the Constable, he hath with much earnestness declared to me what diligence he had used, by the King his master's commandment, touching the matters of the frontiers. * * *

" I have been again in hand with him touching Ireland; being moved thereunto by the bragging of the party who I wrote in my last letters was lately arrived from Ireland, with letters from M'William and sundry others; who letteth not to say to such as resort unto him, that the whole nobility of Ireland, from the highest to the lowest, had conspired to rid themselves from the yoke of England; and that it was time for them so to do, for otherwise, by little and little, they looked for none other but to be driven out of their ancient possessions, one after the other, in such sort as had lately been served to O'More and O'Connor; and, finally, he boasteth that he hath desired of the French King the castle of Trim, with the appurtenances, in recompense of his other lands and possessions taken from him by the English.

"His [the Constable's] answer touching this matter is still after one sort; which is, that indeed the Irishmen had sought succour at their hands, but have had a plain answer that none they get, but, contrarywise, were advised to keep themselves quiet and knowledge their obedience. And as for this last messenger, he told me he had been sick, otherwise he had before this time been sent away with such answer as he thought he would not gladly return with any such Commission. What trust may be given to these sayings, it will not be long but deeds will declare.

"Monluc was within these two days with the said messenger, named George Paris, and presented him fifty crowns, to help him in his sickness. Whether it be of himself, or from the King, I cannot yet learn. But once there is in this court much talk of Ireland, and there should seem some stir worthy to be looked unto. If it so be, I doubt

not but your Lordships will in time provide therefore, to the intent the world may perceive neither
foresight, courage, nor ability to lack. We have,
these many years past, wasted there great sums of
money by piecemeal, which, if it had been spent
together, might perhaps have bred more quietness than we have at this present. These *Wild-
beasts* would be hunted aforce, and at the beginning should so be bearded, before the whole herd run
together, as they might know with whom they had
to do; wherein the old and necessary policy hath
been to keep them by all means possible at [war]
between themselves.

" The saying is here, that the Emperor continueth still his journey towards Augsbourg, where he
mindeth utterly to be the 20th of this present; and
from Spires he departed thitherward the 13th hereof. He is grown into a notable pensiveness, and
seemeth to be troubled specially for two points.
The one, that this peace was concluded both without him, and contrary to his expectation,* whereby
he is in fantasy that his reputation is much blemished, as indeed it is, both in Almain and in
Italy. The other, for that he can by no means
frame his son to such a sort as he much desireth;
which is, by gentle mean and loving entertainment
to win the love of such as by whose service he may
hereafter the better preserve his estate. But he
continueth still in such a Spanish gravity, and de-

* The peace between England and France.

lighteth in no nation but his own, as all other nations make small account of him. So as whatsoever he shall do after his father's death, must be by force and fear, which are " *mali custodes diuturnitatis.*"

" These men here take all the ways they can in the world to enrich themselves, both by bringing in and sparing; and so narrowly look they unto their expences, as nothing escapeth their hands without great consideration. The Emperor, as they say, doth the like; appointing therein the whole hope of his son's keeping his things together. One day these riches, gathered together with so much diligence, will abroad; and by that time I trust others shall be able, with the like instrument, to look upon or to do as for the time shall be thought most expedient. For once [in a word], that is the thing that giveth reputation; and what prince hath that, may be doing, or sit still, as he shall think most commodious for himself and his dominions.

" There dwelleth in Champagne one Monsieur De Roynacq, who was with the King that dead is * in good reputation, and was Colonel of the Almains at Landerseye. This Roynac hath, nigh unto the Emperor's frontiers, a Castle of much strength, which Monsieur De Nevers, Lieutenant in those parts, hath been in hand with him in the King's behalf to have upon exchange; but, the gentleman refusing by any means to depart therewith, Mon-

* Francis the First.

sieur De Nevers hath assayed to take it by stealth.
In the which attemptate the said castle was so well
defended, that it remaineth still in the possession of
the owner, with the death of a great many of the
assailers ; wherewith Monsieur De Nevers being
much offended, hath *engrewed* the matter very sore
to the French King, who sendeth presently thither
all the old bands that served about Boulogne, with
many others of the garrisons about the frontiers.
What the end thereof shall be, time will declare.
The Prince of Melphi, † who hath a good time
served in Piedmont, is now revoked, being both by
years and sickness grown to such an impotency as
he is no longer able to serve in such a charge.   In
his place goeth Monsieur De Brisac.

" The Bishop of Rome hath made an old bawd
of his Cardinal, having neither learning, neither
any other virtue or good quality, wherewith the
holy College of the rest are much offended ; thinking thereby the estimation which that estate hath
in the world to be touched. ‡   *   *   *

† *John Caracciolo*, Prince of Melphi, Governor of Piedmont;
" a province," says De Thou, book vi, sub anno 1550, " over
which he had presided with the highest reputation, having restored military discipline, and restrained the petulant and quar-
relsome humour of the French."

‡ On the election of Julius the Third (the Cardinal di
Monte) to the Popedom, he presented his Cardinal's hat to In-
nocent, a young man in his household, whose business it was
to keep his ape ; " and who," says De Thou, " retained the
name of Ape even after his promotion." The story gave rise
to a pun of Roger Ascham's, who wrote to a friend, ' Par-

" Here hath been of long time very great lack of rain, whereby the people stood in great fear both of their corn and wines; and therefore have they, the space of eight or ten days last past, continually assembled themselves both in towns, cities, and villages, praying together as well in their superstitious processions, as otherwise in churches and fields, that God would vouchsafe to have pity upon them. Within these three days hath fallen much rain, to their great relief and comfort. The French King hath appointed two ambassadors to go to the Regent for the pacifying the matters of Scotland :* the one a Frenchman, brother to Aubespine, named Basse Fontaine; the other, a Scottish man, which either shall be Erskine or Livingston. † These men have ample commission to treat and conclude with the said Regent, at whose hands, if they find not the party that is desired, then have they commission to resort unto the Emperor's court; howbeit, it is thought surely that they shall not need to travel so far, for that the matter was in train before the Emperor's departing, and therefore it is likely that he hath left power with the

turiunt Montes, nascitur Simia turpis." It is but justice to the Cardinals to add, that they were scandalised at this unworthy promotion, and complained that one who had no good qualities should be preferred to such a place. " And pray, my friends," said the Pope, " what *good* qualities did you see in me to instal me in St. Peter's chair ?"

　* The Regent Mary, Dowager Queen of Hungary.

　† The Master of Erskine was the person sent, and the embassy was successful; peace being concluded between Scotland and the Emperor, January 1550-1.

said Regent, as much as may serve for this purpose. These men prepare a strength to the sea: marry, they say it is to defend the Scots, in case this communication take no place.

" The 27th day of this present, between three and five in the morning, the Queen was delivered of a man-child, whom they call Monsieur De Engoulesme. Here is divers talks who shall be godfathers. They that know much, say that the Queen is desirous to have the King our master to be one of them, and that for that purpose a gentleman shall be shortly sent from here to England. And thus, &c. From Poissy, the 29th day of June 1550."

In the following letter, Masone touches, shortly but ably, on the affairs of Europe at this period; describing the relative position of the empire and France, and the effect of the politics of their allies upon the great struggle about to commence between Charles the Fifth and the French King.

The voyage of Leo Strozzi to Scotland, the expected return of the Queen Dowager from that country to the French Court, the French intrigues to encourage the emulation between the Emperor and his brother and nephew, the opening of the Diet at Augsbourg, the intrigues of Charles and Henry at the Roman court, with the bribery of Pole and the Cardinals, are brought before the reader with a clear and rapid pencil.

SIR JOHN MASONE TO THE COUNCIL.

Orig. Draft.   St. P. Off.   3rd August 1550.

" It may please your good Lordships to understand that I have received your letters of the 17th of July, whereby I understand your Lordships' proceedings in sundry matters with the French ambassador, knowledge of which may upon divers occasions serve me to good purpose.

" The Prior of Capua,† who hath many times told me that he meant to take England in his way toward Scotland, hath now, I know not upon what occasion, altered that determination, (he saith it is for that the year is so much past,) and goeth by sea; for the which purpose he hath here taken his leave, and is gone to Roan, intending to depart from thence so soon as the six galleys, which are now a rigging, shall be ready to put to the seas, which is thought will be within three or four days. He hath promised the King to be at Roan again with his carriage within one month after his departing, unless either fault shall be in the Queen for lack of being in a readiness, or else that the weather shall be too ill.   *   *   *

" I was required to write to your Lordships for

---

† "Leo Strozzi, brother of Peter Strozzi.   He sailed to Scotland with a small squadron soon after this; and the Queen Mother, Mary of Guise, with her suite, having embarked on board his fleet, he brought them to Dieppe, on the 19th Sept. 1550."
—Tytler's History of Scotland, vol. vi. p. 50.

the good intreating of the Queen Dowager of Scotland, in case fortune of weather or any other occasion should drive her into any of our ports; and, besides that, in case she should desire passport for a
hackney or two, that your Lordships would show
unto her your gentle favour. Herein they have
themselves also written, as they told me, to the
King's Majesty. I promised that I would write
earnestly in this matter; not doubting but the amity
being such as it is, and she being so notable a personage, your Lordships would not fail to show unto
her as much gentleness as reasonably should be required.

"She shall marry, as I hear say, with the King
of Navarre, whom the Lady Margaret,* sister to the
King, hath refused, for that she thinketh it is a
great cumbrance for a woman of any understanding to be coupled with a foolish husband. Andelot
is not yet returned from Spain, upon whose return
this court is in much expectation.

"I doubt not but your Lordships can well consider the occasion of this so far seeking of this gossip.
These men have had their hands full with the Emperor, and have learned by experience that too
great a neighbour is not most for their profit, and

---

* This Princess inherited some of the best qualities of her
father, Francis the First. She not only became a patroness of
the most learned men of her time, but was eminently learned
herself. She married Emanuel Philibert, Duke of Savoy, in
1559, and died in 1574. As to Mary of Guise marrying the
King of Navarre, it turned out to be mere court gossip.

therefore be they very loath that the Emperor's son should succeed him in the empire; which the Emperor hath by all ways sought to bring to pass. And albeit, the King of Hungary* hath given him a resolute answer, that he will in no case give up his possibility to the same, yet giveth not the said Emperor up the matter so; but being content, seeing there is no other remedy, that his brother shall be Emperor if he overlive him, he seeketh yet, nevertheless, to have his said brother's and the Electors' consents that the Prince of Spain† may be in that case King of Romaynes after him, and so to defeat the Archduke; ‡ wherewith the said Archduke is so much offended, as he seeketh by all means to be rid of his charge in Spain,§ and to be near unto his father, whose tractable nature he much suspecteth in this matter. The French King,

---

* *Ferdinand*, brother of Charles the Fifth, sometimes called the King of Hungary, sometimes King of the Romans.

† *Philip*, afterwards Philip the Second.

‡ *Maximilian*, Archduke of Austria, eldest son to Ferdinand, who had married the Infanta Mary, his cousin, daughter of Charles the Fifth. He had been carefully educated by his father, Ferdinand, "but chiefly in variety of tongues; wherein in short space he so much profited, that he not only spake Latin very elegantly, Spanish, French, Italian, German, Hungarish, and Bohemish, but also very perfectly attained to the knowledge of the sciences, particularly the mathematics."— Pedro Mexia, p. 687.

§ Maximilian was now Governor of Spain; to which office he had been promoted by Charles the Fifth, during the absence of Philip, the Prince of Spain.

by making him his gossip,* thinketh somewhat to augment his courage, if any lack thereof be in him, whereby he pretendeth particular amity ; meaning nothing else but the singular commodity of himself and his realm.

" The *Diet* began the 10th day of July, and goeth as yet very slowly forward, for that the Emperor himself was the first man that arrived there of such whose presence are required in the same. The others, for the substance of them, declare by their little haste the small will they have to come thither.

" Men think, whatsoever he [the Emperor] outwardly pretendeth, a great piece of this assembly shall be for the advancing of his son, and for the matter of Piedmont ; and it hath been told me secretly, that he mindeth to move th' Empire to send unto the French King, as of themselves, certain ambassadors to the number of ten, to be chosen out of sundry quarters of Germany, to require such places as he holdeth in Piedmont and Savoy to be delivered as members of the empire, and in case of refusal to tell him that all Germany have concluded to do their best for the recovering of the same by force of arms. This may fortune to be but a dream ; and yet, because he that told it me is a man that may fortune hath heard

* The object of Henry the Second, in making Maximilian gossip or godfather to his son, who was about to be christened, was avowedly (if we believe Masone) to do honour to Maximilian and Charles the Fifth, but really to widen the breach between them.

somewhat whereby he had occasion this to tell me, I have not thought it amiss to advertise your Lordships what I have heard in this matter. Time will bring this and all other things out of doubt.

" The Emperor hath largely of late recompensed such Cardinals as were of his faction at the election of the Bishop of Rome, amongst whom he hath given Pole two thousand crowns by year in pension out of the bishoprick of Toledo; by whose example the French King hath done the like to such Cardinals as were of his faction. *

" Here is very little speech at this present of the COUNCIL. The new Nuntio, who lately arrived here, had access on Tuesday last, who they say hath commission somewhat to treat of that matter. He is Bishop of Tolon, and of the house of Trivultii; his predecessor, named De la Tour, hath taken his leave and departeth out of hand.

* It is strange that Julius the Third, "this every way licentious man," (to use De Thou's words,) should have obtained Pole's warm approval; but the two thousand crowns' pension throws some light on the business. Pole himself, if we may believe Beccatelli, was actually chosen Pope, but it was *at night;* and he declined accepting the dignity until the election had been made in a regular and canonical manner in the morning, at the hour of mass, and not in darkness.—Beccatelli, translated by Pye, p. 75. In the morning, however, (such are the fluctuations of Papal as well as of other elections,) the Cardinals had changed their opinion. Pole's conduct and scruples are very unaccountable. He refused the Popedom because his own election was made *in the night;* and he himself willingly voted for and approved of the choice of the Cardinal di Monte, who was chosen by *adoration* about *ten o'clock at night.*

" I wrote in my last letters that he had lately very often access to the court. The occasion was, as I am informed, for that the King, since his coming unto the crown, hath given sundry promotions in Provence; the disposition of which, by sufferance of French Kings in times past, hath always appertained to the Bishops of Rome. The King had thought to have broken that custom; but finally he is entreated to yield, and hath remitted that liberty again to the said Bishop, according as the use hath been heretofore. Marry, now the great question is touching such as already be in possession by the King's preferment, which the Bishop wills in any case to be dispossessed for the saving of his title : herein they be not yet agreed, and I trust the unreasonableness of the Bishop will drive the French King to remember that he is a King, and that the country wherein the said Bishop taketh upon him to have a doing longeth unto the crown of France. But there are so many Cardinals and so many *she Papists* who bear no little rule, as, without God's evident working hand, there is little hope to be had of the diminishing of this wicked devotion to the Romish See.*

" Jeffrey Pole † was lately in Paris, and I was at that time informed by an Irishman who purposely came hither to bring me tidings thereof, that he was

---

* It is amusing to contrast these ebullitions of Masone under Edward the Sixth against "*men's wicked devotion* to the Romish See," with his tirades (under Mary) against the pernicious sect of the *new Gospellers*, meaning the friends of the Reformation. † The younger brother of Cardinal Pole.

even then come out of England, and was returning
to Rome; whereupon I sent Mr. Barnardyn thither
to espy his doings, and to learn me as much as he
could what he intended. And suddenly I understood he was come to this court, and by-and-by I
was told he was at my chamber door, whom causing to enter, I demanded what he had to do in
these quarters: he told me his continuance was in
Liege, and, having nothing else to do, he minded
to pass this summer in riding up and down to see
countries, and, having occasion to go this way to
Roan, he thought it his duty to visit me the King's
ambassador. He told me he had been with Mr.
Hobby, who had written in his behalf, but as yet
could have no answer. His desire, he said, was to
return, having not offended any otherwise, but that
he departed without licence out of the realm. Yes,
quoth I, you have been with the unnatural man your
brother.* True, quoth he, and how well I contented myself there my short abode may well declare. I
asked him what entertainment he had, and how
he lived abroad; he told me he had forty crowns a
month of his brother, and that the Bishop of Liege
was very good to him besides. This notwithstanding,
he much desired to return to his country, and prayed me I would write on his behalf; I told him I

---

* Compare Masone's censure of Cardinal Pole, " that unnatural man," with his fulsome panegyric of him four years afterwards, when the Cardinal was on his way to England: the unnatural man of 1550 was, in 1554, " such a one for virtue and
godliness as all the world seeketh and adoreth."

would so do if I might be sure he would be a good
and true subject.   And thus, after a few more tri-
fling communications, he took his leave, and went
forth his journey to Roan; minding, as he said, from
thence to return to Liege.

" Order is taken that neither legionaries, neither
any other men of arms, shall live any more at discretion upon the poor people.   And to the intent the
said men of war may be the better able to live,
having this liberty taken from them, the King hath
appointed to every man of arms, yearly, above the
wages they were wont to have, two hundred franks,
which is double to that they were wont to be paid ;
and every archer two hundred franks, which is six
score franks above their ordinary.   The captains
and officers are increased in entertainment accordingly.   There hath been some matter between the
Emperor and the French King about the taking of
the castle in Champagne, whereof I have written
once or twice; but in the end the French King hath
promised to rase the same, and so is that quarrel
ended.   The party that [ought] owned it, was a very
unquiet man, and, having intelligence with certain
snaphaunces, did much mischief in those parts ; and
therefore is he moaned on neither side.

" The tarrying for the return of Dandelot * hath
made the King to defer his journey to Roan, so as
I think he will not depart from hence all this month

* Then on a mission to Spain.

of August; making his account to make his entry into Roan the 15th of next month.

" I was in hand with the Prior of Capua, upon his departing, for a letter to be sent from him to Marseilles to his officers there, to permit my messenger to peruse the galleys, to see whether any Englishmen remained there. He seemed somewhat to be offended for that I gave no more credit to his words, assuring me eftsoons that I should not find one Englishman there. If I did so, he bade me to account him hereafter " le plus meschant homme sur la terre." Nevertheless, for my satisfaction he was content to write me a letter, which he sent me accordingly.

" In his company goeth sundry young gentlemen, but none of name that I can hear of. Monsieur de Thermes cometh from Scotland in the company of the Queen. The French King hath sent to the Regent for a safe-conduct for the galleys both going and coming, which the Constable telleth me is granted.

" And thus, &c. From Poissy, the 3rd day of August 1550."

The author of the laborious life of Burleigh in the Biographia Britannica, and Dr. Nares in his recent and most colossal volumes on the same subject, have adopted contrary opinions regarding Cecil's promotion to the office of Secretary of State. The first writer believes that he was appointed Secretary previous to 1550; Nares conjectures that his appointment was in 1550. In following this great statesman through the earlier and obscurer parts of his career, and in attempting to fix some points in his life hitherto unknown or misunderstood, it has been already shown by positive evidence that Dr. Nares' conjecture is correct,—that he was secretary and principal adviser to the Protector previous to 1550, but certainly not Secretary of State.*

We have now, however, reached the period of his promotion to the office of Secretary of State, and fortunately it can be fixed on undoubted evidence to a day. In the MS. Privy Council Books of Edward the Sixth, under the date of the 5th of Sept. 1550, is this entry :

> " This day Mr. William Sicile was sworn Secretary, instead of Mr. Wotton ; and Mr. Wotton, by the King's order, appointed still to remain of the Council."

---

* Supra, pp. 71, 73, 290. Previous to this he is sometimes addressed as *Master of Requests*, sometimes as *Agent* for my Lord Protector's Grace,† sometimes as *attending* my Lord's Grace,‡ sometimes *Secretary to my Lord Protector's Grace*,§ and sometimes simply " *Master Secretary ;*" all of which various styles exclude the notion of his being Secretary of State.

---

† MS. letter, Orig. St. P. Off. Mr. Gorge to Cecil, 14th April 1548.

‡ MS. letter, Orig. St. P. Off. Thomas Fisher to Cecil, 17th Aug. 1550.

§ MS. letter, Orig. Sir. E. North and others to Cecil, 13th July 1548.

The two following letters were addressed by Sir
John Thynne and Sir John Masone to the new Secretary, congratulating him upon his appointment.
Thynne, as we have seen, had been a sufferer in
Somerset's *first* disgrace.   His letter contains another proof of the Duke's confidence having been
continued to Cecil.

SIR JOHN THYNNE TO CECIL.

Orig. St. P. Off. *Domestic.* 13th Sept. 1550.

" Being as glad as any friend you have this day
living that you be so placed as ye are, I shall desire you to make reckoning of my small friendship as far as my power may extend, which shall be
ready during my life, when ye shall like to use
it ; praying you if you shall, at any time before
my return out of the country, have occasion to commune with my Lord's Grace of me, that you will
use your old accustomed friendship towards me in
my late suit, which ye know I have made to leave
mine office of Stewardship, which standeth me much
upon for many causes, as you partly know ; and I
shall be glad to serve you faithfully to the uttermost
of my power in any other service his Grace will appoint me during my life, and in this I can never
serve with goodwill.   Further, I pray you to remember my Lord Edward to Mr. Coss before Michaelmas ; for, if that matter sleep, it will be long or he
shall have anything.   His whole trust is in you.

Thus most heartily fare ye well, with like commendations both to you and your bedfellow.

" From Reading, the 13th September 1550.

" Yours assuredly to my little power,

" JOHN THYNNE."

" *To mine assured friend, Mr. Wm. Cicill,*
Esquire, one of the King's Majesty's two
principal Secretaries."

SIR JOHN MASONE TO CECIL.

Orig. ST. P. OFF. 14th Sept. 1550.

" MR. CECILL.—I am right glad to understand your preferment to the office of the Secretary, both for that I know what service you are able to do therein unto the realm, and for that also I trust of the continuance of your friendship, which in that place may stand me in much steed ; which as divers ways I may fortune to be driven to use, so shall the special point thereof be to help to get me honour. You know my weak body, which, sith my coming hither, is not at all amended.

" Your man, Lord, hath painfully and truly served me ; and, in case I were in any hope of my short return, I would yet borrow him of you for a time, having presently no man to whom I would gladly commit his charge. Marry, rather than the tarrying with me should either hinder him or be any lack to you, I will send him to you, as ill as I may spare him. I pray you send him your mind by the next, to the intent I may have some time to provide for the supply of the place he serveth me in, in case you

want to have him to make any haste: you have
surely a *jewel* of him; an honester or a truer man
of his sort is there not within the realm.   And thus
most heartily fare you well.   I pray you have me
commended to your wife : her brother, having been
these two months among the physicians, is, as he
saith, much amended; and, indeed, it appeareth by
the state of his body that he is so.   I mind now to
send for him, and, in case the amendment do continue, to keep him with me till my return; for the
shortness whereof, *omnes Sancti et Sanctæ Deo
orate pro nobis!*

    " From Poissy, the 14th day of Sept. 1550.

        " Your own most assuredly,

            " JOHN MASONE."

Original.
" *Sir John Masone to Mr. Cecill.*
    Poissy, 14*th Sept.* 1550."

I know not that I can better introduce the following letter, than by a passage epitomized by
Strype, from a letter of the learned reformer Bucer, in which he describes the miserable state of religion in England in 1550.   " That which weighed
with him most," he said, " was, that the sinews
of Anti-Christ bore such sway; he meant, that
church-robbers did still hold and spoil the chief
parish churches, and that commonly one man had
four, or six of them, or more; and that many patrons bestowed two or three upon their *stewards,* or

huntsmen, and that upon condition that a good portion of the profits should be reserved to themselves." Is it at all surprising, that this abuse grew to a destructive excess, when we find the Princess Elizabeth intreating Cecil, the newly-appointed Secretary of State, to bestow a parsonage on her " *Yeoman of the Robes?*" The yeoman—parsonage holder—was obliged, indeed, to provide a curate ; but he generally looked out for the cheapest he could find, and the cheapest was another term for the worst. " The curates," says Strype, in speaking of the state of the reformed church under Edward the Sixth, "were both ignorant, and scandalous for their lives. * * They (the people) would ordinarily say, our curate is naught, an *asse-head,* a *dodipot,* a *lack-latin,* and can do nothing. Shall I pay him tithe that doth no good, and none can do?"† In another place, the same author, whose judgment upon such a point must have been completely unbiassed, takes occasion to quote a sermon preached before Edward at St. Paul's, on the same subject, and which describes the courtiers defending the ignorant curates whom they had placed in their livings. " They [the courtiers] say, the curate ministereth God's Sacraments; he saith his service, he readeth the *homilies.* But the rude *lobs* of the country, which be too simple to paint a lie, speak foully and

† Memor. vol. ii. part ii. p. 143.

truly as they find it, and say, ' he ministreth God's Sacraments, he *slubbereth* up his service, and he cannot read the *humbles.*' " *

THOMAS PARRY TO CECIL.

Orig.   St. P. Off.   *Domestic.*   22nd Sept. 1550.

" Sir.—Her Grace hath commanded me to write unto you her most hearty commendations. And being desired and sued unto by one of her old servants, John Renyon, the Yeoman of her Grace's Robes, for his preferment to the parsonage of East Harptree, in the county of Somerset, being now in your hands and disposition, to send unto you for the same ; her Grace hath likewise, upon his said suit, commanded me to say unto you, that if it may please you for her Grace's sake to let him be your tenant, doing unto you therefore as another will, and as shall appertain, her Grace will upon your desire, in case like, gratify the same to your like contentation, whereof her Grace prayeth you to answer her by your letters.   And herewith her Grace hath also sent you the man, to be considered of according to her suit, with a most hearty farewell.

" Her Grace hath been long troubled with rheums, but now, thanks be [to] the Lord! meetly well again, and shortly ye shall hear from her Grace again.   Outred is well occupied in her business, who, I assure [you], doth very honestly.   Thus

* Strype's Memor. vol. ii. part i. p. 412.

leave I to trouble you, as he that is assuredly yours, and most glad to hear of your good calling; wherein I pray the Lord as well to speed you as ever He hath done any. To Him I commit you! At Ashridge, the 22nd of September 1550.

> " Your own assured to command,
>   " THOMAS PARRY."

Among the congratulatory letters addressed to Cecil, on his appointment as Secretary, he received the following from his friend the Duchess of Suffolk. It is, as is usual with the epistolary effusions of this noble and notable lady, humorous, lively, and kind-hearted. It contains, also, another proof that the Secretary had been sent to the Tower.

DUCHESS OF SUFFOLK TO CECIL.

Orig. ST. P. OFF. *Domestic.* 2nd Oct. 1550.

" I DID never mistrust that you should alway live by your change, but at length change for the best and come to a good market. I have ever thought your wares to be so good and saleable: but you must consider the exchange goeth high now-a-days; and, tho' it were painful for you to go as far as the Tower for it, thanks yet be [to] the Lord that in the end you are no loser.

" I am contented to become your partner as you promise me, and will abide all adventures in your ship, be the weather fair or foul; and tho' I cannot help you with costly wares to furnish her, yet I shall ply you with my woollen stuff, which may serve her for ballast. If you marvel how that I am become so cunning in ship-works, you shall understand that I am about the making of one here by me at Bostons', or rather the patching of an old one; which gentle recompense I had for my wines, wherewith the Honor victualled the rebels in Norfolk the last year; so that now I am become a merchant vinter. Thus, many ways beggars seek their thrift; which having sought, and cannot find by land, I mind now to try my luck by water; and if I speed well, I promise you as liberally to divide with you as you promise me.

" I thank you heartily for your news from abroad, and rejoice they be so good. If Nauntun's cause really be no better considered, with much ado, I hold my peace, and threaten to think the greater unkindness. And so fare you with Mistress or my Lady Meleryd," &c.

Masone, in the following letter, throws, as is usual with him, a rapid glance over the state of Europe. The preparations of the French King for his approaching struggle with the Emperor, the intense interest Charles took in the re-opening of the Council of Trent, and the commencement of his war with the Turks by the taking of Africa or Mahadia in Barbary, which was defended with much obstinacy by Dragut Rey the famous corsair, are the graver subjects touched upon; whilst we have some light

talk on the Court pageants, and the Duke D'Aumale's anxiety to have his promised portrait of
Edward the Sixth.

SIR JOHN MASONE TO THE COUNCIL.

Orig. St. P. Off. *Rouen.* 6th Oct. 1550.

" It may like your good Lordships to be advertised, that the French King arriving very nigh the
town of Roan, the 25th day of September, which
was the day appointed for his entry, was desired, for
that the said town was not yet in readiness, to pass
his time till the 1st of October, and to lie in the
mean season in an abbey prepared for him, half a
mile out of the town, which he was content to do ;
and yet in the mean time, for that in the said abbey
there was no convenient place to keep the ceremonies of the order which he useth always to keep at
the feast of St. Michael, he appointed to keep the
same within the town, and at night returned to the
abbey. This feast he kept very solemnly ; the
ambassadors being present, and called thereunto.
And, under the cloth of estate, on the left hand of
him, were the arms of the Emperor, of the King of
Denmark, the King of Sweden, and the King of
Navarre ; at the which feast there was none new
made of the order but the Rhingrave, albeit there
were four places void.

" The first of October he made his entry, which
was so brave and so rich, as the like, by the common
report of this court, hath not been seen. Among

sundry pageants that were represented therein, the plots [models] of Boulogne, and all those pieces, were carried aloft upon long poles.* The next day the Queen made her entry in the same sort thoroughly, and with like solemnity as the King had done the day before; saving, that by the commandment of the King, the representation of Boulogne was omitted.

" There was both the days a fight upon the river between two ships, the one garnished with white crosses, and the other with red; and both the days the red-crossed ship had the worst, and was burned. Many thought, and so did I, at the beginning, the same had been made for an English ship; but it was afterwards known that it was a representation of a fight between the Portugals and the French about the old quarrel for the Isle of Brazil, which appeared openly, for that to the defence of the Portugals' ships came many naked men, their bodies all coloured with red, in which sort the saying is the people used to go abroad in that country.

" Since my coming hither, I have been in hand with the Constable touching my last communication with the King, which was concerning the quarrels that the Scots pick daily with us, the liberty of the Scots of St. Andrew's, and the commissioners to be appointed for matters of depredation. For the Scottish quarrels I am answered that the

---

* The recovery of Boulogne from the English was a subject at this moment of great triumph to the French.

master of Erskine is now at the court of England, and is looked for here within three or four days; at which time the matter shall be weighed and considered, according as may appertain to the continuation of the amity.   Touching the Scots of St. Andrew's,* the Queen hath not yet been spoken with therein, but shall be very shortly, trusting that I shall have therein a good answer.

" * * * I have this day visited the Queen Dowager of Scotland,† who, being accompanied with a great company of Scottish gentlemen, arrived here the 25th of Sept. and was received with much honour.   I used to her such general words of the King's rejoicing of her safe arrival, and of the trust he had of her forwardness to the continuation of the peace, as methought were most meet for the time. She took the visitation very thankfully, and prayed me most humbly in her behalf to yield thanks therefore unto his Majesty, who was, both by reason of his most gentle passport, and the good entertain-

---

* By these Scots of St. Andrew's we are to understand the Scottish prisoners who, on the taking of St. Andrew's by the Prior of Capua, in 1547, were carried into France, and confined on board the galleys.   Among them was the celebrated Knox, besides Norman Lesly, William Kirkkaldy of Grange, and others of the murderers of Cardinal Beaton.

† Mary of Guise, widow of James the Fifth and Queen Mother of Scotland.   She was highly popular at the court of France; and Mason, in another of his letters, describes her as almost worshipped as a goddess.—23rd Feb. 1550-1.   She was accompanied by De Thermes, La Chapelle, and other French officers, and by many of the Scottish nobility.

ment which by his commandment she received by
the way in his ports, the only occasion of her safe
coming hither.

" Africa was taken by assault the 20th of Sept.
with the loss of many men.* In the town were
slain above the number of four thousand, one and
other.   These men make as though they were glad
thereof, but it is thought to be but from the teeth
outward. The Constable told me yesterday, the town
was nothing of importance, having no port, or any
sure defence for the number of more than five or six
galleys.   The haven that importeth altogether is
called Zerbes, and is fifteen or twenty leagues off.
If they get not that, they have by his saying made
a small conquest : others make it a marvellous gain
to Christendom, whereby the Mediterranean seas
are opened, which before, by reason of that hold,
were never clear of pirates.   And as for Zerbes,
truth it is that the open haven is there ; but,
Africa being taken, there is no doubt, say they, of
the long holding thereof.

" At my coming to this town I found our merchants much amazed, and no talk was there among
them but that we should out of hand have war
with the French.   The occasion whereof, as I have

---

* The expedition against this town, one of the strongholds of
Dragut Rey the famous corsair, was commanded by Andrew
Doria, and John de Vega, Viceroy of Sicily ; an immense booty
was taken. The French undervalued the victory, as it was gained over the friends of their allies, the Turks.

learned since, came from our merchants being in
Flanders and Calice, who, upon the bruit raised of
the departing of the commissioners upon the frontiers without conclusion, were straight entered into
such a fear, as some of them, having children and
kinsfolks at Orleans, and Paris, and otherwhere, sent
in post to them to come away, and to put themselves under my protection.

" Such a fearful beast is the merchantman! howbeit, reason it is that the brent child dread the fire.

" Your Lordships shall herewith receive the
names of the principal Scots that are here arrived
with the Dowager of Scotland, who with their
bands fill all this court; and such brawling, chiding,
and fighting make they here for their lodgings, and
others' quarrels, as though they lately came from
some new conquest.* It is thought the King will
tarry here yet eight or ten days. From hence he
goeth to Dieppe, and so to the rest of his havens and
fortresses upon the sea-side ; minding, as he goeth,
to see the musters of his garrisons. A great part of
his study at this present is to make his bands fair,
and to be well furnished of all necessary armour ;
to whom, as he giveth much more wages than any

---

* The principal Scottish nobles who accompanied the Queen
Dowager to France, and whose brawls for lodgings seem to
have offended the gravity and decorum of Masône, were the
Earls of Huntly, Cassillis, Sutherland, and Marshall, with the
Lords Hume, Fleming, and Maxwell; and the Bishops of
Caithness and Galloway.

of his predecessors have done in times past, so chargeth he them with much furniture, as with chafferons, crigneux, and barres of buff.*

" The Emperor is still hot about the Council,† and, whatsoever the matter is, the Pope's Nuntio hath had of late often access to this King; and once or twice the Venice ambassador hath gone with him in company. Some think it is touching that matter, and others think it is some secret practice to withstand the greatness of the Emperor, who is thought, when he shall return into Italy, will pass that way like a conqueror.

" The Duke D'Aumale‡ is much desirous to have a portrait of the King's person, which he says the King himself promised him at his departing out of England. He hath been in hand with me twice or thrice herein, praying me in my next despatch to desire your Lordships to put his Majesty in remembrance hereof. If any shall be sent unto him, this is a very good time therefore, while yet he remaineth in Roan. He speaketh very much honour of the King and of the realm, and hideth not the courtesy that he found the time of his being there.

---

* Henry the Second was preparing for his great struggle with the Emperor. Hence, his attention to his navy, musters, garrisons, and the training and arming of his bands.

† Charles was eager to press on the re-assembling of the Council of Trent; but the high tone assumed by Julius the Third in the Bull, by which he re-assembled the Council, gave much offence to the German Protestant Princes.—Sarpi, par. Courayer, vol. i. p. 498.   ‡ See Note i. p. 1.

He is, as your Lordships knoweth, of right good estimation, and therefore the remembering of him in
this his request cannot be but well bestowed. And
thus, &c.

" From Roan the 6th of Oct. 1550."

I may introduce the following letter, which is
highly characteristic of the class of men to which
the writer belongs—the Puritan ministers, by Fuller's striking passage on the rise of Non-conformity.* " Come we now," says he, " to the sad-
dest difference that ever happened in the Church of
England, if we consider either the time, how long
it continued, the eminent persons therein engaged,
or the doleful effects thereby produced. It was
about matters of conformity. Alas! that men
should have less wisdom than locusts, which, when
sent on God's errand, did 'not thrust one another,'
Joel, ii. 8. Whereas here, such shoving and shoul-
dering, and hoisting and heavings, and jostling
and thronging betwixt clergymen of the highest
parts and places. For now *Non-conformity*, in the
days of King Edward, was conceived; which after-
ward, in the reign of Queen Mary, (but beyond sea
at Frankfort,) was born; which, in the reign of
Queen Elizabeth, was nursed and weaned; which,
under King James, grew up a strong youth, or tall
stripling; but, towards the end of King Charles'
reign, shot up to the full strength and stature of a

* Church History, vol. ii. p. 229.

man, able not only to cope with, but conquer, the
Hierarchy, its adversary.

The writer of the letter was DR. WILLIAM TUR-
NER, who, in 1548, held the place of physician in the
family of the Duke of Somerset, and became afterwards Dean of Wells; a witty, as well as a learned
man, says Strype.* He was the author of a " Dialogue against the Mass," in which the speakers, in
old Bunyan's fashion, are Mistress Missa, Master
Knowledge, Master Freemouth, Peter Preco the
Crier, Palemon the Judge, Master Justice of Peace,
Dr. Porphyry, and Sir Philip Philargyry; and which,
after these personages had delivered themselves of
a sufficient quantity of argument, concludes in the
banishment of Mistress Missa, with all her alleged
abuses, from the realm of England. I command
thee, says Palemon the Judge, to " pack thee out of
this realm with all thy bag and baggage, within
these eight days, and go to thy father the Pope
with all the speed thou canst, and say that here is
in England no more place for him, neither for any
of his generation." Mistress Missa remonstrates,
and implores the priests to find her, if possible, a
place of refuge in the Bible :

> " I pray you heartily, if it be possible,
>   To get me a place in the Great Bible."

The letter is strongly characteristic of the sect of
the Puritans ; honest and sour, ironical and argu-
mentative. Cecil, now the courtly secretary, had

* Memor. vol. ii. part i. p. 216.

been offended, it appears, with Turner's bluntness, and his application to Master Partridge, probably Sir Miles Partridge. Turner endeavours to conciliate him; but his sarcasms against the *" Christians of the court,"* his prayer that the secretary may be guided by *" his old divinity,"* his counsel to him to be patient under other men's judgments, were probably more sincere than palatable advices.

The concluding determination to get his "living by his science, and to set off with two small horses for Germany, where he might correct the English translation of the New Testament, finish his Great Herbal, and at small cost drink nothing but Rhenish wine," are not the least amusing parts of the epistle.

TURNER TO CECIL.

Orig. St. P. Off. *Domestic.* November 1550.

" Grace, mercy, peace, and the continuation of godliness be unto you. Both by your letter, and by that you said that you were almost weary in my matter, I perceive that you were offended with my importunity; and by your words and writing I gather that ye were displeased with my letter which I sent unto Master Partridge, for the which I have a reasonable excuse, if it will please you to hear it.

" Divers about my Lord have promised to put my Lord's Grace in remembrance of my poor state; but, I seeing that they did not, I thought it best to essay what Master Partridge would do for me. If that ye reckon that I meant *of you* when I made mention of the *small boats*, ye were deceived, for I have ever judged that, since the first time that ye came into office, ye both did and would do more than Master Partridge, and yet I know he would do for me what he could.

" As for Maudlin College, because there are no laws to depose the masters, and the fellows should be forsworn if they chused me, which was never fellow there; and the King cannot, by the strength of his visitation (as all learned men say) put out the Master of Oriel College, that I might be placed there; God forbid that I should be the cause of perjury, or desire any of my friends to put any man out of his room, either without or against right and law! Take therefore, I pray you, no more displeasure for me in labouring for either or both : as touching the archdeaconry, God forgive me, which laboured to come into it by the window, and not only by Christ; whilst I laboured to come by it by friendship, as very thieves and murderers now-a-days enter into Christ's sheepfold. Let him that is most lawfully called to that office take it. Therefore, I pray you, sue no more for it at my request; but leave off labouring for all benefices with cure for me.

" The Papists will live out their time in the colleges and benefices, and get yet more promotions, whether ye, and all other good men that would the contrary, will or no; the law of man is so much of their side. And when they are dead, perchance some *Christians of the court,* for their long service, shall succeed in their rooms; except they, being in point of death, resign their offices to some of their *brother Papists,* as Haines did unto Smith, his successor, now Master of Oriel College.

" He that giveth me the advowson or presentation of a benefice giveth me no living, neither rewardeth me for it that I have done, but burdeneth me and putteth me unto a new labour. For a benefice, that is the office of a bishop, parson, or vicar, is a great burden, and a laboursome work. If I do my duty in my benefice, I am worthy my whole wage; then why should I thank any other man for that living which I have earned and deserved myself? If I do not my duty, why should I receive of the poor husbandmen, artificers, and poor widows, my living, and then thank a gentleman for it, who never sweat one drop for it? Why should he, that ought freely to give out the advowson or presentation of a benefice to the best that he knows, claim service of me, or think that he rewardeth me for my labours taken with him, or his, in giving me the advowson or presentation of a benefice; seeing the living that I have of the benefice cometh not from him, but from the poor husbandmen, poor widows, and handicraftsmen, for my pains taken, and to be taken, in feeding of their souls? Is it meet that Christ's mystical body should give me 40*l.* in the year, for th' intent that

I should three ways feed it, and that I should take that living for doing service in a gentleman's house? Let Christ's body be unsevered. I think no; and I trust you think so likewise. Therefore I intend to sue no more for any benefice; neither to take any in such condition. When Christ's church needeth me, it will lawfully call me without any of my labour.

" In the mean time, if that I had my health, I were able to get my living with my science, not only in England, but also in Holland, Brabant, and many places of Germany; although some think it would not be in England as yet, till I were better known. Wherefore, if my foolish importunity hath not utterly quenched out all the favour that you have sometime borne towards me, I pray you heartily, seeing that I cannot have my health here in England, and am every day more and more vexed with the stone, help me to obtain licence of the King's Majesty and the Council that I may go into Germany, and carry two little horses with me, to dwell there for a time; where, as I may with small cost drink only Rhenish wine, and so thereby be delivered of the stone, as I was the last time that I dwelt in Germany.

" If that I might have my poor prebend coming to me yearly, I will, for it, correct the whole New Testament in English, and write a book of the causes of my correction and changing of the translation. I will also finish my great Herbal, and my

books of Fishes, Stones, and Metals, if God send
me life and health. I pray you answer at your
leisure, and interpret all things that I have written
into the best part, as ye would other men should
interpret your sayings and doings; for ye must
sometimes abide other men's judgments, whether
ye will or no. God keep you, and grant that your
old Divinity may bear alway the chief authority,
and govern and lead your policy as an handmaid,
more to the setting forth of God's glory than the
advancement of any worldly kingdom!

> " Your friend to his power,
>
> " WILLIAM TURNER."

" *To the Right Worshipful Master Cecill,*
    Secretary to the King's Highness,
    be this letter delivered."

Untainted motives or perfect purity in public
men are rare, perhaps impossible virtues, in all
times. Under Edward the Sixth, the venality of
judges and councillors was extreme, and there
was little affectation about the matter. Latimer,
who in his Sermons " spared no arrows," in speaking of an evil judge, proposes that his skin should
be hung up. " It were a goodly sight," says he,
" *the sign of the Judge's Skin.* It would be Lot's
wife to all judges that follow after."* The custom
of suitors presenting gifts, appears to have been
then universal: nor do we find that the severe

* Strype's Memor. vol. ii. part ii. p. 134.

ideas of Burleigh, even in the first freshness of his
accession to office, drew back from the *propine* * of
" a piece of French wine," as a prelude to something more worthy the sending.

We may easily imagine the feelings which
would be generated in the bosom of a Secretary of
State now-a-days by the arrival of a " pipe of cla-
ret" at the door of the Home Office, with a letter
entreating his good help and furtherance for the
augmentation of the living of some titled suitor.
So completely are times changed, and so infinitely
more delicately are things now done !

SIR GEORGE SOMERSET TO CECIL.

Orig. ST. P. OFF. *Domestic.* 23rd Nov. 1550.

" AFTER my right heartiest commendations.

" Whereas I have presently written, by Mr.
Winter, unto my very good Lord, my Lord of Somerset's Grace, for the augmentation of this my
poor and small living on this side, in such sort and
manner as this bearer shall more fully declare unto
you ; I humbly beseech you therein, of your accustomed gentleness, that, as my good hope and trust
is, I may have your good help and furtherance :
and as a testimony of my poor heart and duty,
whereas I could come by nothing else worthy the

---

* An antiquated word, now only used in Scotland, meaning
a present or gift; but singularly applicable to a present of wine,
as it comes from πρo πινειν, to drink before,—a glass given
previous to a bargain or treaty.

sending, I have presently sent you by long seas *one piece of French wine ;* praying you not to esteem the small value thereof, but rather my good-will, and so take and accept it, until time may serve me to send you *a better thing.* And thus as one most bounden to wish you long continuance in welfare and prosperous success. At Rysebanke, the 23rd of November 1550.   Your assured poor friend,

"GEORGE SOMERSET."

" To his loving friend Mr. Cycyll, Secretary
unto the King's most Honourable Majesty."

Neither Smith nor Turgot could have expressed themselves more clearly on the subject of free trade, and the wisdom of leaving commodities to find their own unrestricted prices and level, than Sir John Masone, the shrewd political economist of the time of King Edward the Sixth, in the conclusion of our next letter. The folly of fixing the prices of articles of consumption by the legislature, is more pithily and truly stated in these three lines than if the argument were diluted into three chapters. " Nature will have her course, etiam si furca expellatur ; and never shall you drive her to consent that a *pennyworth* of new shall be sold for a *farthing !* " Yet in deference to the grave noblemen of the " Privy Council," who had judged otherwise, he adds, " See what a babbling I make, being clean ignorant of the case !" It may be suspected that the old fox was laughing in his sleeve.

SIR JOHN MASONE TO SECRETARY CECIL.

Orig. St. P. Off.   Dec. 4th, 1550.   *France.*

" Gentle Mr. Cecil.   I have received your letter of the 14th of November, and thank you most
heartily for the good comfort you put me in of my
short return, and for the travail yourself hath taken
in the same.   I have written letters of thanks to
my Lords of Somerset and Warwick, of whose good
agreement I do rejoice even at the bottom of my
heart; for in so doing consisteth their own healths,
and the upright administration of the commonwealth.

" Many there be abroad, yea, and at home also,
that let not to whisper the contrary, because they
would gladly have it so.   The only keeping of our
commonwealth standeth in the good accord of such as
God hath committed the ordering of the stern thereof [unto].   *Concordia p[arta], res crescant.*   When
all the horses draw one way, the cart sticketh not
lightly in the mire.   And wheresoever disagreeing
is, there is the Devil, who is ever the author thereof.   If we may once be Christian men, as we say we
be already,—and that we do once expel out [of] our
realm rancour, envy, malice, partialities, covetousness, and bribery, with the which kinds we are in
outward parts sore charged,—then would I not doubt
of the short recovery of our commonwealth; otherwise we must be assured, God will not be mocked.

He knoweth his sheep, and to others he will say,
Nescio vos.

" I most heartily thank you of your good advertisement of my Lords' acceptation of my doings to
the best part; which, as it is most comfortable unto
me, so proceedeth it only of their goodness, being
in me no earthly thing other than, God will[ing],
in any point to satisfy their expectation.

" I hear here a great bruit of the discontentation
of our people upon a late proclamation touching
cheese and butter; of a little thing we make here
a great matter. And surely, if there be no other
thing than I do see in the thing, the matter might
even as well have been spared. I have seen so
many experiences of such ordinances; and ever the
end is dearth, and lack of the thing that we seek to
make *good cheap.** Nature will have her course,
etiam si furca expellatur; and never shall you drive
her to consent that a *penny*-worth of new shall be
sold for a *farthing*. If *good cheap* follow this device, then hereafter will I think it were good the
like were still used; but this I am sure, the thing
shall not be so plentiful as it was, and then I report me to you whether it will be better cheap.
For who will keep a cow that may not sell the milk
for so much as the merchant and he can agree
upon?

" See what a babbling I make, being clean igno-

* " A bon marché :" a Gallicism.

rant of the case! I doubt not but my Lords saw
what they did, and therefore I may hold my peace
like a fool. * * *

  " From Bloys, the 4th day of December 1550.

    " Your own most assuredly,

       " JOHN MASONE."

 SIR RICHARD MORYSINE, the writer of the following letter to Cecil, was an able diplomatist and
accomplished scholar of these times. He had
been sent ambassador to the court of the Emperor,
in the month of July 1550,† and chose the celebrated Roger Ascham as his secretary. Before
Morysine came into public life, he appears to have
studied for some years in Italy; and several of his
Latin letters, amongst which is one to Winter, the
reputed son of Cardinal Wolsey, will be found in
the Cotton Collection.‡ He afterwards became a
refugee in the time of Mary. In their devotion to
classical studies, he and Ascham were congenial
spirits; and, after the labours of the embassy, employed their leisure hours with Herodotus and De-
mosthenes.§

 It is to be regretted that the gravity of Cecil
should have been offended with Morysine's " *toys,*" as
he terms them; by which he no doubt means that ad-
mixture of anecdote, wit, and gossip about eminent

---

 † MS. Privy Council Books of Edward the Sixth, Sept. 18,
1550.   ‡ Caligula, B. xi.

 § De Vitâ et Obitu R. Aschami, p. 19; à Grant.

men, with the more dry and cumbersome details of
state affairs, for which his letters are conspicuous.
The following letter from the ambassador appears to
be a reply to a remonstrance, upon the part of the
Secretary of State, against the trifles which he had
inserted to relieve the length and tediousness of his
despatches.   Yet, when these *trifles* relate to such
men as Charles the Fifth, Ferdinand, Granvelle,
Philip, or Melancthon, and by a single touch, or
little trait, stamp individuality on character, or
bring vividly before us the minuter and more evan-
escent shades in the picture of the age, we are
disposed to quarrel with the misplaced severity
of Burleigh.   Amongst Ascham's Latin letters, is
one written from Augsbourg to his friend Stur-
mius, dated only two days before this of Morysine.   It describes the intense interest with which
all men's minds were fixed upon the siege of
Magdebourg.   " Nec mirum esse debet, (says he,)
si duo illi *Tricipites*, Cerberus Romanus, et Geryon
Hispanus, [Julius the Third and Charles the Fifth,]
contendunt hanc unam urbem expugnare, cujus si
porta semel fuerit vel fracta vi vel reserata volun-
tate, patet statim aditus et Cerbero in totam Ger-
maniam, et Geryoni in universam fere Europam,
ut nec in religione puritas, nec in republicâ commo-
ditas reliqua esse possit, quæ non brevi aut illius
fœdata habitu, aut istius occupata raptu, fuerit."*

* Aschami Epistolæ, pp. 35, 36.

SIR R. MORYSINE TO CECIL.

Orig. St. P. Off. 17th Dec. 1550. *Germany.*

" Gentle Mr. Cecil.   If I do not give you the thanks which your friendly advices make due unto you, think it is because I can find none big enough, and not that I do love to be unthankful. My trust is, time shall hereafter lend me some occasion to gratify you some ways or other.   If any happen, as have [heretofore] as occasion is, I trust to find where to catch and how to hold.   And yet do I know that ye will think your pains fully paid, in case you see your advices gladly received, and willingly followed.   As ye see me amend that is thought amiss, so think me worthy your farther instructions, as faults and leisure will serve you.   I, deceived, thought my letters (which were long and tedious, as might happen to some when plenty of matter past,) had bred some weariness already, [and] did need some *toys or other*, and that length might have made some piece of mirth's excuse.   I will do on more *gravity*, and keep *mirth* where I have more need of it.   I hope also to be plain in my writing, and make my letters with less labour to please a good many more than they now do.   I made them a piece of my exercise, and thought it my gain to lose some labour in writing them.   I will amend this too.   And yet you do not well mark my long talk with the Emperor, which charge me with vehement words against the   *   *   *   *

*　　*　　*　　*　　*　　*　　†

where, indeed, I spake neither good nor bad of him. Master Hoby, when I had done, sayeth somewhat unto him, which I thought both truly said, and warranted by the instructions that the letters, whereunto your hand is, brought unto us. If the letters be laid together, I do think we may better be shent for saying too little, than want instructions to brave a good deal more than we said. But, howsoever it is, I give you thanks as hearty as I can, that I do learn how I may content whom I utterly mind to please; and therefore, tho' ye see I cannot acknowledge a fault, not mine, for mine, yet, as ye can, I pray you let me now and then have a few lines from you. Ye can no way do me so great a pleasure as to lay my faults before me.

" Fair words, when friendly admonitions are required, trim talk in the place of true counsel; sweet soothings, where sour sentences are the safer, can content but such as know no difference between seeming friends and friends indeed.

" Your letter was welcome to me. I fear nothing but that it shall be [alone] here, and have no more of yours to bear it company. I may mar, but I will compare with the best: he liveth not that would fainer do that he ought. I used no cipher, for that I am borne in hand my letters, being wrapt in shores till they come to Antwerp, come unseen. My fear is I shall rather take some harm here, for

† Illegible.

that ye have too many clerks' men to lay up letters there at home. Good Mr. Secretary, let mine come in as few hands as ye can, for I may else fortune to have here but a short time of service. And thus my wife, knowing how much I am beholden to you for this friendly part, sendeth you her hearty commendations; and, if she could write English as well as you can write Greek, I dare assure you my Lady your bedfellow should little a needed to receive a † * * commendations from her at your hands. Now you must take as good as you can think, and give my Lady as good as ye take. And thus I rest at your commandment. From Augusta, the 17th of Dec.

" Yours assuredly as his own,

" RICHARD MORYSINE."

To whom this letter of the Princess Mary was addressed does not appear, there being no superscription; nor is the year added in the body of the letter, but supplied conjecturally by a pencil note on the back. It is curious, as giving as her own account of the illness with which she had been long afflicted, and marking its recurrence to be always at the fall of the leaf.

THE PRINCESS MARY TO ――――――

Orig. St. P. Off. *Domestic.* 23rd Nov. 1550.

" MY LORD, I most heartily thank you for your gentle and kind letters. And where it should seem

† Illegible.

to you and others, my friends, that the soil and air of this house might be occasion of my sickness, for the recovery whereof you think good that I should remove from the same; my Lord, the truth is, that neither the house nor air is herein to be suspected, but the time of the year being the fall of the leaf, at which time I have seldom escaped the same disease these many years; and the rather to prove the air not to be evil, I have not at the present (thanks be to God!) any of my household sick. Notwithstanding, I had made my proviso's at Wanstead and St. John's two months past, where I intended to have lien all this winter; and by occasion of one departed at Wanstead of the plague, who was buried in the churchyard, being very near to the gate, I was driven from that house; and then my disease coming upon me so sore, hearing also that the air at St. John's was not clear, I durst not venture to take that so far a journey, the stay whereof was a grief to me, because my chief intent of the same was to have seen the King's Majesty.

" So, having no house near hand of my own, I thought it not meet to make any more provision in any other house, but determined to rest here till Christmas was past, and caused mine officers to make provision accordingly. Moreover, where, for the better amendment of my health, you so gently offer me the choice of any of the King's Majesty's houses, or, any other man's else being meet to be had, you would give order for the same; my Lord, your gentleness in this, or in any other thing touching my causes, hath and doth appear to be such unfeignedly, that I have just occasion to think you my very friend ; and, being not otherwise able to recompense it, I shall pray for you ; and hereafter, if I shall espy any house meet for my purpose, shall be bold to require your favour therein ; minding, if strength and health will suffer me, to change the air and house here, for the cleansing of the same, and borrow my Lord Chancellor's house for ten or twelve days, who very gently hath offered me the same. And thus, with my most hearty commendations, I wish you well to do as myself.

" From *Beau lyeu,* the 23rd of November.

" Your assured friend to my power,

" MARYE."

We have already observed that Ireland was always one of the chief cards played by the Romish party in Europe against England. The discontented Romanists in that country, whose cause was wonderfully strengthened by the cruel and absurd policy pursued towards it by the English government, not only carried on intrigues with France, with the Papal court, with the Romish party in Scotland, but, as is affirmed in the following letter, with Wales. It appears, from the terms used by Masone in his next letter, that George Paris, the messenger of the Irish insurgents, a personage with

whom we have already met,* "had very good countenance both of the King and Constable;" but,
although he boasted that they should "shortly hear
the Dauphin proclaimed King of Scotland and Ireland," there seems no doubt that Henry, although
willing to keep up the hopes of the disaffected Irish,
declined giving them any direct encouragement.
His hands were too full of business with Maurice
the Elector, the Protestant Princes, and his approaching war with the Emperor.

The minute and accurate information transmitted by Masone regarding the state of parties in
Scotland, and the intrigues of Mary of Guise, the
Queen Dowager, for her promotion to the regency
in that kingdom, show how faithfully and ably
England was now served by her ambassadors at
foreign courts.

The affair of Parma, at which the Emperor, in
Masone's expressive phrase, "*snuffed*," or took um-
brage, proved eventually the cause of the renewal
of the war between Charles the Fifth and Henry
the Second in Italy. Octavio Farnese, son of Pietro Luigi Farnese, (who was himself the son of Pope
Paul the Third,) succeeded to the duchies of Parma
and Piacenza, with which the Pope had invested
his father. Charles the Fifth, however, had long
coveted the possession of Parma : it was the door
by which the French could always secure an en-
trance into Italy, and the Emperor was anxious to

* Supra, p. 292.

keep the key. On the accession of Julius the Third,
the Pontiff intrigued to recover Parma; but, finding this impossible, he secretly advised Octavio to
throw himself and the defence of his little kingdom
into the hands of France; foreseeing, as it ulti-
mately happened, that this bone of contention
would accelerate the war between Charles and
Henry.

At this moment, however, as we learn from Masone, Charles, solicitous to avoid an open quarrel
with France, turned his resentment against the
Pope, who, by one of those counter-reaches of Italian
policy then so frequently practised, affected extreme
displeasure with Octavio and Henry the Second,
and solicited the Emperor to assist him against
their aggression upon his rights in the duchy of
Parma.*

It is interesting to notice in this letter the court
paid by the Emperor and Henry the Second to the
merchants, and the privileges and immunities bestowed upon them by these princes; they looked,
we see, to be remunerated by the loans and advances of money, which might enable them to continue their wars when their own resources began to
fail. War, in itself so infinite an evil, had thus one
bright side, in raising up a body of men whose
wealth and privileges became a check upon the

* Sarpi, Histoire du Concile de Trente, par Courayer,
vol. i. p. 504.—Ascham's Works by Bennet, 4to. p. 14.

power of the King and the feudal tyranny of the nobles.

I need not point out the diplomatic ability which Masone displays in the following letter ; the facility with which he places us on a pinnacle from which we have a bird's-eye view, not of Europe only, but of Christendom; and the rapidity, yet distinctness, with which the actors pass before us, from the Irish envoy to the Sophy of Persia.

MASONE TO THE COUNCIL.

Orig. Draft. St. P. Off. April 18th, 1551.

" IT may like your Lordships to be advertised, that lately is arrived here with letters, one George Paris, an Irishman, who this last summer, as once or twice I have signified the same unto you, lay here as a solicitor for the rebels of Ireland, and was with a good reward despatched from Blois in the month of December last past. He hath brought in his company another joined in commission with him, who they say is a great gentleman, whose name I have not yet learned. His letters contained nothing but credence. The credence was, as I am informed, the offering of the rebels' service, with their country, as much as in them might lie, to the French King's devotion and subjection; with request that it might like him to send them some aid to defend *his own*, if it pleased him to accept it. In which case they assured him that Wales would also stir, with whom they had such intelligence, as, if they might have hope of any foreign aid, they would not fail to show themselves in the field. Their quarrel was the maintenance of religion, and for the continuance of God's service in such sort as they had received it from their fathers. In the which quarrel they were determined either to stand or to die.

" The order of the aid they referred to his own device, whether he would send the same straight to Ireland, or else (which they wished rather) he would invade the realm of England; which if he did, they thought he should find an easy enterprise, so willing would the people be in that quarrel to receive him. He set forth with many words how often the realm had been conquered, whereof he made a long and particular discourse; concluding, in the end, that never outward enemy attempted there to land, that it was driven back again, and that it was never so easy to be done as at this time. The reasons whereof he set forth at length, omitting nothing that he thought might serve to the helping forward of his lewd message and the advancing of the said rebellious request.

" He was well heard, and had very good countenance both of the King and of the Constable; and had for the first answer, that these demands should be considered, and thereupon should they receive such final answer as they should have reason to be contented. This George Paris seemeth a man of cankered malice, and therewithal a man of light behaviour. He hath told his credence to sundry

Scottishmen, and hath made divers of them who he taketh for his secret friends believe that he is utterly promised aid at the King's hands. And furthermore hath said, that if there come no greater force out of England than yet is talked of, which is the number of six thousand men, he will warrant they shall not much prevail, trusting to hear shortly the Dauphin proclaimed King of Scotland and Ireland at the least; and with these brags, and such others, he filleth every man's ears that he chanceth to talk withal.

" The Bishop of Rome's ambassador hath since his coming been twice or thrice at the court, and it is thought that it is about the same matter; which is the rather conjectured, for that the said George Paris repaired incontinently to him, as soon in manner as he was from his horseback, and since hath sundry times resorted unto him, and at every time hath had long talk with him. Alate [of late] he hath not been so brag; and, as I am secretly informed, he is in the end answered, that they shall look for no aid from hence; and yet I am told by others that the Scottish Queen laboureth to have them holpen underhand, which she would have done by the Earl of Argile and James Kennalt, (I cannot tell whether I hit the name * well,) but it is thought that they shall have none aid of this King, at the least openly.

---

* The name he means to hit is James M'Connel.

" John a Barton is also come to this court, who hath brought advertisement that the Governor* in this circuit hath ridden to keep the Courts of Ayer, as they call them, [and] hath made a strong party of all the nobles and gentlemen of Scotland for the keeping of him in dignity of Governor until such time as they shall have a King. These tidings are nothing pleasantly taken; for the Queen † mindeth utterly to bring herself to the whole government, or else to settle therein some Frenchman of her house. But it is likely that she shall be able to compass neither the one nor the other. Corax ‡ is of opinion that this matter will alter many devices; thinking that, had not that been, this King, for all his fair words, would have aided the Irishmen: and what he will yet do, he doubteth; but he saith, thereof you shall have a great conjecture upon the proceeding of the Commissioners upon the frontiers, who if they go forward roundly, and enter not before the conclusion into some new request which they may think you will not agree unto, it is likely that for this year, at the least, they mean to be still.

" The Scots be here very ill satisfied, having so impoverished themselves as the number of them may for these three years *fast*, for any profit they are like to have of their lands, having eaten up the same beforehand; which is thought to have been done of purpose, to the intent that, being

* The Earl of Arran.   † The Queen Dowager,
Mary of Guise.   ‡ Sir William Kirkaldy of Grange.

brought to extreme need, they may be compelled upon hope of relief, like slaves, to hang upon the Queen, whom, in that case, she will so feed as that they shall not have occasion to be too high therewith.*

" The Earl of Huntley hath obtained some piece of his suit, which is the Queen's consent, when she shall come to age, for his having of the earldom of Murray.† This King hath bound himself by writing thereunto ; but the custody of the *band*‡ he will have to remain in the Dowager's hands.

" The rest of the whole band of the Scots, and especially the Earls of Southerland and Cassills, be against him herein ; and in case it be so meant as the said Earl of Huntley trusteth, it will breed a great stab among them.

" The Archbishop of Glasgow hath long been like to forego his archbishoprick, upon recompense, at leisure, but now he trusteth to continue in the same ; being, nevertheless, bound to forego it at any time it shall please this King to appoint. The Queen is all for herself and for a few other of her

---

* The result showed this to be a shrewd conjecture of Mason's ; for it is certain that the Queen Dowager, Mary of Guise, obtained the support of the chief Scots nobility in her design to supplant the Governor Arran, by bribing them to vote as she wished.

† This promise formed the great ground of quarrel and jealousy between Huntley and the Lord James, afterwards the Regent Murray.

‡ A Scottish word, meaning a contract or agreement.

friends; whose partiality, showed more to some than
others, maketh a great heart-burning among them.
The Lord Maxwell, at his departing, had a chain
worth five hundred crowns. Drumlanrick, who departed at the same time, had nothing. He used
at his leave-taking very rude speech to the Queen,
and, entering into the ship, it chanced him to break
his leg, wishing that that chance had happened at
the going out of his house hitherward.

" Order is taken here for two thousand ton of
all kinds of victual to be sent presently with the
Dowager into Scotland, and partly to be sold, as the
pretence is, to sundry noblemen and others in divers parts of the realm, for the furniture of such
countries where most need shall be found. This is
the bruit, but whether there be herein any other
thing meant I cannot tell ; but good it were to *cast*
the worst. I hear no more of any force that she
shall have with her; but there are in a readiness to
march, upon one hour's warning, twenty-eight enseignes of footmen, and certain men of arms. Whether they shall go yet, it is not known.

" The Emperor *snuffeth* at this alteration of
Parma, but he turneth all his outward displeasure
towards the Pope, who he will not believe but he
hath been a worker therein ; and in his choler he
said lately, " Si je me demasque, je le monstreray
que je ne suis personage à qui il se doibt jouir." It
seemeth that he hath no fancy to be doing with this
King, by whom he hath been so pricked lately, as, if

he had any mind thereunto, he could not have kept his patience. He hath lost by stealth, in Piedmont, Berghes, and another place which this King hath stolen from him. This King hath also gotten another place in like sort upon the limits of Lorain, and finally hath won Parma from his devotion. The Rhingrave hath been, by his sending, in Magdebourg, both to encourage them of the town, and to deliver unto them also some furniture of money, with promise of the continuance of ten thousand crowns monthly so long as the siege shall last; and yet there is nothing between them but " *vostre bon frere et cousin.*" The said Emperor, all this notwithstanding, hath sent commission to his Ambassador to talk of a marriage between the King's eldest daughter and the Duke of Lorain, which I think on this side will not be much embraced.

" I have received advertisement from Mr. Dudley, that the two Englishmen of Berwick, of whom I wrote to your Lordships in my last letters, be come to this court. I have made all the search possible to learn the truth thereof, but hitherto I can find out no such matter ; and in case there be any such thing, they are kept secretly in some village, which practice these men use very much. Howsoever it be, I doubt not but your Lordships to have a good eye to that town, so as it may be able at the least to hold out any sudden enterprise that may be devised against it.

" This King continueth wonderfully th' augment-

ing of his credit with the merchants, which kind of
men he maketh very much of; and, to allure them
more and more into the realm, he giveth them such
privileges and exemptions from the ordinary payments, as they come from all parts daily hither to
inhabit.   This is reckoned a notable policy to avoid
always extremities that may come by lack of money.
This policy have they learned partly of the Emperor, and partly by divers other inconvenients that
they have suffered for fault of present sums of
money.   This way is it thought they shall be able,
being entered into a war, to continue and go
thro' withal; which, whensoever they begin, they
utterly mind to do.   A prince, trusting only to his
own treasure, and the only aid of his subjects, cannot at all times be able so to do.

" Here is a great bruit, (I trust it is untrue,) that
the Emperor hath stayed a great treasure of our master's in Almain; and hereupon, the tale going from
mouth to mouth, it is also talked that he mindeth
to have war with us.   The ship, whereof I have
written once or twice, is finally departed towards
Scotland, charged with sundry kinds of munition.
The Scots say it is to furnish a fortification at a
place called Kirkway,* in Orkney; which Orkney
the King of Denmark maketh a claim unto, as they
say, alleging that it was gaged by his predecessors
for a certain sum of money, which he is ready to
pay.   Now, say they, that this King will fortify the

* Kirkwall, the capital of the Orkneys.

place, to resist such attemptates as the said King of Denmark may make for the recovery thereof. But I doubt there be some other meaning in the matter.*

" The Scottish Queen's shipping is hasted very much, and it is thought she shall embark sooner by a whole month than it was determined. Some say the ill agreement between the French and the Scottish is the occasion thereof; and especially this late confederacy between the Governor and the rest, for the continuance of his government. Others think it is, for that this Queen's belly much encreaseth, the King desireth so to bring the Dowager to her passage as he may return in due time to place her where she shall be brought a-bed, which it is thought shall be at Blois. The Admiral is now come to the court to devise upon the manner of her transportation.

" There are general musters presently a taking thro' the realm, wherein all the men of arms are appointed to have their horses barbed; and therefore are they commanded to bring to the musters no jennets, neither other kind of horses but such as shall be found able for that purpose.† Here is a talk that Monsieur Daumale and Monsieur De Roche-sur-Yon, with divers other notable personages,

* Mason's conjecture was correct.

† Barbed horses were horses clothed in mail, which the light breed, or jennets, could not carry. It required the strong powerful breed to bear the weight.

shall conduct the Dowager into Scotland; but as yet I can find no certainty thereof.

"I see not that these men make any great haste to send unto the place appointed for the General Council,* albeit the day approacheth very near. The Emperor's ambassador hath sued out a passport, for such as for that purpose are appointed to be sent out of Spain to pass thro' the realm of France. It is lately ordained here, that all spiritual persons, as well cardinals, bishops, as all others, shall be resident upon their promotions at the least six months in the year, notwithstanding any dispensation heretofore obtained to the contrary. By this ordinance the court is gayly rid of a great number of that sort, who were so wont to swarm there, as no man could have room for them.

"The bruit of the Turk's army to come to the recovery of Africa, waxeth daily less and less; and it is now thought that, if he send any army at all, it shall be nothing so great as at the beginning it was noised. The Sophy is upon the field, who is like to be a great stay of this enterprise. The King's ambassador with the Turk, who lately came from Turkey in post, (it is not yet known with what commission,) returneth shortly thither again. The galleys of Marseilles, who were not long since

---

* Henry the Second was too intent on his preparations to humble the power of the Emperor, to think much of the General Council; and so little was he troubled with religious scruples, that, as we have seen, he entered into alliance with the Turks, with the design of weakening Charles on the side of Hungary.

disarmed, are commanded to be put in order again ; and for that purpose the Prior of Capua is gone thither.

" The frontier of France upon Spain is straitly kept, and no man passeth that way without passport.   The pilgrims, that have used ever that way to Compostella without let, are now sent back again as fast as they come to those said frontiers, and are not suffered to pass the town of Bayonne. Hereof many men conjectureth diversely.

" The King of Navarre hath been in some danger of death, but he is now in likelihood to recover. The Duke of Vendosme is ridden to him in post, who I think can be content good to give him leave to depart when he will.

" The Lady Fleming departed hence with child by this King ; and it is thought that, immediately upon the arrival of the Dowager in Scotland, she shall come again to fetch another.   If she so do, here is like to be a combat, the heart-burning being already very great. The old worn pelf* fears thereby to lose some part of her credit, who presently reigneth alone, and governeth without impeach.

" I am advertised that the town of Abingdon sueth unto your Lordships for a corporation, and for the farm also of the house and domain of the late Abbey, whereof during my time I have the keep-

* Diana of Poictiers, mistress to Henry the Second, then in her forty-fifth year.

ing, and am steward of the town, wherein I was also born. There is no one thing that more continueth a daily hurt to the realm than corporations; neither was there ever any privilege of that nature sued for, but for an ill intent.* Nevertheless, if your Lordships shall see such considerations as you shall think their request in this matter meet to be hearkened unto, I beseech your Lordships so to pass the thing, as respect may be had to the continuation of my poor interest.

"I hear yet nothing of Mr. Pickering, to my great marvel and greater discomfort, whose tarrying from hence much longer than he faithfully promised me he would have done hath so disappointed me, as never had poor man more cause to complain of the breach of another's faith. Upon trust whereof I have not only sent away a great part of my stuff, which I thought for so little a time I might well have spared; but suddenly also, for lack of provision in time and place, am clean destitute of money, being entered into such a country, as I know not, God be my record, how to make any kind of shift for the supply of my lack. My

---

* Mason's tirade against corporations is amusing, and easily accounted for. In the scramble for church-lands he had accumulated large estates; and amongst others, he had possessed himself of the house and domain of the late Abbey of Abingdon. The town sued for a corporation, and for the "farm" of the Abbey; therefore there was, in the opinion of the worthy knight, "no one thing that more continueth a daily hurt to the realm than corporations."

charges so much increase, what by the vileness of our money, and what by the dearth of things here, as a man will hardly believe it if he see it not. And to help forward my grief withal, I have not heard these eight whole weeks out of England any kind of word, which I am ashamed to report when I am here asked the question, and therefore am I forced to use the best means I can to dissemble mine ignorance in that behalf. Thus, between hope and fear, comfortless, accompanied with sorrow, sickness, and poverty, I commit your Lordships to the keeping of Almighty God! From Amboise, the 18th day of April 1551."

The following letter from Hoper, Bishop of Gloucester, to Cecil, in which he describes so feelingly the misery brought upon the poorer classes in England by the high prices of provisions, forms a natural introduction to the curious paper which succeeds it on the causes of " the universal dearth of victuals in the realm." Fuller characterises Hoper as the " sternest and austerest" of the Marian martyrs : * of such feelings there at least appears nothing in the kind remonstrance to Cecil on the universal distress of the poor, suffering under the " extreme evil of hunger, and seeing their little cottages and livings decaying daily."

Hoper was inferior to many of his Protestant brethren in learning, and his obstinate and length-

* Church History, vol. ii. p. 399.

ened controversies with Ridley and Cranmer, against
the use of the episcopal vestments, betrayed a nar-
row though conscientious understanding: but his
charities were extensive and unwearied; his hospitality generous and noble; his manners simple; his
piety unaffected and profound; nor can any one
read the account of the exquisite sufferings of his
last moments, without admiring the admirable
courage of the man, and lamenting the cruelty and
fanaticism of which he was the victim. He was
educated at the University of Oxford, but fled from
England during the persecution under the Six Articles; and remained at Switzerland, chiefly at Basil
and Zurich, till the death of Henry the Eighth.
In Edward's time he returned, and was made Bishop of Gloucester. In 1555 he was burnt at the
stake.

BISHOP HOPER TO CECIL.

Orig. St. P. Off. *Domestic.* 17th April 1551.

" After my very hearty commendations. Altho' I
have no great matter to write unto your Mastership
of, yet duty and bondage requireth me to show myself mindful of your old and accustomed friendship
towards me, and to thank you for the same, with
hearty desire you so always continue towards me.

" As for the success and going forthward of God's
word, praised be his holy name! every day the number doth increase; and would so do more and more,
in case there were good teachers amongst them
for the furtherance and help thereof. I pray you,

and in God's name require you, that ye stay what ye may, that no man obtain licence to have two benefices, which is a great destruction to this country,—dangerous before God, as well to the King's Majesty that giveth it, as to the person that receiveth.

"For the love and tender mercy of God, persuade and cause some order to be taken upon the price of things, or else the ire of God will shortly punish.   All things be here so dear, that the most part of people lacketh, and yet more will lack necessary food.   The body of a calf in the market 14*s.*; the carcass of a sheep at 10*s.*   White [wheat] meat so dear, as a groat is nothing to a poor man to be sowing any kind of victuals.   All pastures and breeding of cattle is turned into sheep's-meat, and they be not kept to be brought to the market, but to bear wool, and profit only to their master.   Master Secretary, for the passion of Christ take the fear of God and a bold stomach to speak herein for a redress, and that the goods of every shire be not thus wrested, and taken into few men's hands. If it continue, the wealth and strength of the realm must needs perish.   What availeth great riches in a realm, and neither the head nor the greatest part of the members to be the better for it ?   You best know.*   .   .   .   apud Justinian. non prosunt .   .   .   .   quoniam non ad commodum reipublicæ sed ad labem detrimentumque pertinent, inquit.

* The MS. is here illegible.

"So much as have more than enough, buyeth when things be *good cheap*, to sell afterwards dear. God amend it! It is my bounden duty, and all other true men's, to persuade and teach obedience unto the people; and, thanks be to the Lord! I can perceive none other here but love and reverence among the people to the King's Majesty, and to the laws; but, Mr. Secretary, it is the magistrates, and their own doings, that shall most commend them, and win love of the people. Ye know what a grievous and extreme—yea, in manner unruly—evil hunger is. The prices of things be here as I tell ye; the number of people be great, their little cottages and poor livings decay daily; except God by sickness take them out of the world, they must needs lack. God's mercy give you and the rest of my Lords wisdom to redress it, wherein I pray God ye may see the occasion of the evil and so destroy it.

"May it please you to be so good as to desire a licence of the King's Majesty for me to eat flesh upon the fish days. Doubtless, my stomach is not as it hath been. In case it were, I could better eat fish than flesh; but I think it past for this life. There is also here a wise and sober man, one of the elder men of the town, a good and necessary subject for this little commonwealth here, called John Sanford, that is a weak and sickly man, desired me also to be a suitor to you for him in this case; and, doubtless, we will so use the King's authority as none, I trust, shall take occasion for liberty and contempt of laws by us.

" Thus praying you to commend me to Mistress Cecil, and to good Mr. Cecil your father, my singular good friends, I commend ye with all my heart and whole spirit [to God], who keep you always in his fear, and give you wisdom and strength to do all things in this high business, troublous and perilous, to his glory. Amen! 17th April 1551.

" Your bounden for ever to his little power,

" JOHN HOPER, Gloucestr. Episc.

" If I dare be so bold of your gentleness, commend me to all my very friends that be of the Robes, who have used towards me always, from my first coming to the court, a singular and painful friendship in all business I have had to do."

CAUSES OF THE UNIVERSAL DEARTH IN ENGLAND.

Orig. ST. P. OFF. *Domestic.* 1551.

" THESE be the things that be the cause of the universal dearth of victuals in the realm.

" The first is lack of breeding and rearing of poultry ware, for it is not possible to have that *good cheap* that is not.

" The second is regrating, when the most part of victuals be gathered into a few men's hands who may defer to sell but when they see their most profit. And the third is the King's provisions,—when victual is taken from the poor people that be the

breeders, against their wills, and [they] have neither ready money for their wares nor yet so much
as it is worth; which discourageth the people to
breed, and causeth the price of all things, because
there is not plenty of them, to be increased.

"Lack of good laws and statutes is *not* the cause
of this hurt that cometh by provisions, for there be
laws sufficient for that purpose; but because they
cannot be put in execution, the let whereof is lack
of money. So that if we mind to have no more
provisions made as they have been,—that is, without
the consent of the seller, without money, and for
less price than other men pay,—we must of necessity
provide that the King may have money and his revenues increased.

"His provision of money must needs be had, albeit the provisions cease not; for we see the King's
charges daily increase more and more: for that he
selleth the same; so that the more he selleth the
greater at length shall be the burden of the commons, for whose defence it is sold, and who must
be compelled to satisfy that lacketh; so that our
policy ought to be first to consider how much the
King's charges surmount his revenues, and to devise
and imagine how his Grace's revenues may be increased with the least burden of his subjects.

"We must also consider that, as the King's revenues be greater than any of his predecessors, so be
his charges far greater in his household, and also in
his wars, than ever any King's of England were
before.

" If some of his predecessors have had more in respect than the King hath, albeit they had neither monastery, college, nor chantry lands ; then must it be considered *how* the same was greater, and where that revenue is become, and whether the thing whereof it grew of yet remaineth or is utterly decayed.

" It appeareth, by the records of the Exchequer, that Edward the Third had more revenue yearly, by the custom of the staple, than the King that dead is had by all customs of the staple and cloth, by sixty thousand pounds at the least.

" To show what hurt cometh by provisions to the poor men, it shall not need ; experience doth make it but too plain.   But, for example :—The purveyor alloweth for a lamb worth two shillings but twelvepence, for a capon worth twelvepence sixpence, and so after that rate ; so that after that rate there is not the poorest man that hath any thing to sell but he loseth half in the price, besides tarrying for his money, which sometime he hath after long suit to the officers, and great costs suing for it, and many times he never hath it ; so that he is driven to recover his losses by selling dearer to the King's subjects. And, therefore, far better were it for men to give some certainty yearly, not to be cumbered with this yoke of provisions, than daily thus to be tormented, and never to be in certainty of their own.

" This certainty might be thus gathered, that

the King might have yearly of every sheep kept in
the common fields one penny, of every cow and
lamb kept in several pasture twopence, and of every
other shore sheep kept in pasture three halfpence.

" Suppose there be in the realm at this present
the number of thirty hundred thousand sheep,
whereof fifteen hundred thousand to be kept on the
commons and rated at one penny the piece, it will
amount to vi^{m.} ccl^{li.} [6250*l.*] and vii. hundred and
fifty thousand ewes with lambs rated at twopence
the ewe and lamb, it cometh to vi^{m.} ccl^{li.} [6250*l.*]
and vii. hundred and fifty thousand other pasture
sheep rated at i^{d. ob.} [one penny halfpenny] the piece,
it cometh to iiii^{m.} vi^{c.} lxxxvii^{li.} x^{s.} [4687*l.* 10*s.*] :
summa totalis xvii^{m.} clxxxvii^{li.} x^{s.} which is thought
will do somewhat, albeit not sufficient, towards the
provisions of the King's household.

" Now since the wools grow daily, and be converted into cloth made within the realm, that were
wont to be carried unwrought over the seas, whereby Kings of England in time past have had so
great revenues in the customs, and the commonalty
have been less charged with subsidies, the King's
charges daily increasing more and more ; to the intent the King's Highness should have the less cause
to trouble his subjects with requiring any subsidies,
and that noblemen and gentlemen, which be otherwise charged to serve his Highness, be not double
charged, and the poor men that be not able to pay
therewith charged, reason it were that an imposi-

tion were put on cloths, to be paid by the makers
thereof, and by the merchants that carry it over the
sea, after this rate; that is, of the clothier, for a
broad-cloth, five shillings, and a kersey xx^d. and of
the merchant double custom.

" This doth nothing agree with the rate of the
custom of the staple, which is xl. sh. the sack, but
is about half the same custom.

" The clothier can have no loss thereby, for he
will recover it in his sale, which is after the rate of
twopence in the yard of cloth.   And so selling
it, either to the King's subjects or to strangers, they
must bear the burden; which, being so light, they
shall easily do.

" The merchants, if they have the cloth justly
and truly made, shall be great gainers; and so
shall all others that wear cloth, when one garment,
being made of good and true cloth, shall last twice
as long as garments do at this time.

" These things granted,—that it will please the
King's Majesty that his officers, after Christmas
next coming, shall take nothing against the owner's
will, but pay ready money, and as much as the common price is in the market.   And that all manner
of carriages, as well by sea as by land, shall be rated
at such prices as others his Grace's subjects pay."

The reader will, I trust, not be sorry to see a
second letter from Dr. William Turner, which
paints in lively colours the opposition with which

the Romanists in heart, though not in profession, received so strict and stern a Puritan amongst them.
The picture he gives of his " *belly-brethren*," as he
terms them, must, however, be received with some
diffidence. To be penned up in a single room, with
all his servants, children, and household goods about
him, where he had neither comfort nor quiet; to find
study impossible, from the constant squealing of his
babes; and complaint useless, from the perverseness
and power of his enemies ; to have no stall for his
horse, no rations for himself, no assistance in
preaching, no thanks when he preached; to be kept
out of his lawful living by Master Λεπτος,* the Romanist, on one hand, and Signor Σαυρος, the atheist,
on the other,—would have tried any temper and
coloured any complaints.

TURNER TO CECIL.

Orig. St. P. Off. *Domestic.* 22nd May 1551.

" Grace, mercy, and peace be unto you from
Almighty God, Amen ! Here came of late unto
me one Ακανθινος, sometime schoolmaster unto your
bedfellow, as he saith, and desired me to help him
unto the schoolmastership of this town ; to whom,
for your sake, I am ready to do the best that I can.

" We have a schoolmaster here, a man of a very
corrupt and evil judgment ; yea, a man of naughty
life ; who was a year in the Marshalsea for Pa-
pistry, and he, delivered by the King's general par-

---

* Λεπτος, acutus—perhaps Mr. Sharp.

don, as yet hath not recanted his false doctrine, but, as I am informed, defendeth privily the same : wherefore Master Cardmaker, our Chancellor, by the virtue of his office, intendeth to put this man out and to receive in your friend, so that the King's letter be sent unto the Chapter that Akanthinus may be chosen ; without which letters we shall be able to do nothing, for they are all against Mr. Cardmaker and me, whom they handle as wards.

" I have preached eight times since Easter; but I could not make one of them preach, saving Master Cardmaker, who preached once, and hath read oftimes.

" Master Goodman was set into a house by the Chapter, because the same was granted unto Goodman in his letters patent of his deanery ; but, because there is no mention of the house in my letters patent, my belly-brethren will not admit me unto the house except they have the King's letter to command them in the same : the which thing till it be done, I must be pinned up in a chamber of my Lord of Bath's, with all my household, servants, and children, as sheep in a pinfold. I pray you, if there be any remedy in this matter, that I may have your speedy help; for now I cannot go to my book for the crying of children, and noise that is made in my chamber.

" Furthermore, whereas I have in such chantry lands, by the reason of the deanery, I cannot enter into one foot of land, neither one close to put a horse in; whereas the former dean occupied the last year thirteen closes. I can have no help of any man here to set me into my land, and my Lord of Somerset's chief servants are the greatest enemies that I have here, and no man maintaineth Goodman's friends, which hold me out of all possession, so much as they do; and, namely, Master Λεπτος and Master Σαυρος, of the which, the one is all whole ρωμαιος, and the other, as far as I can perceive, αθεος. Goodman hath iii cotidianes and iiii dividentes granted him, until the provostship or the archdeaconry fall; but Goodman hath sold that both from himself and me for viii score pounds, which he received of the canons: so that I have nothing but my bare cotedian, and not my whole divident, and nine pounds in the year besides. I pay ix$^{lib.}$ for my first-fruits and xx$^{lib.}$ for my entering into my residence; besides that, I pay the tenth of my cotidianes and dividentes. "Oportet episcopum esse hospitalem. Qui propriæ familiæ non prospicit, fidem abnegavit, et est infideli deterior,"—and I cannot do, therefore, as I should do, but I trust that God will hold me excused. I pray you commend me to your bedfellow. Farewell! From Wells, the 22nd of May.   Your own,

"WILLM. TURNER."

"*To the Right Worshipful Master Cecill, Secretary unto the King's Majesty, be this letter delivered.*"

War had now broken out in earnest in Italy. The Pope having in vain cited Octavio Farnese to ap-

pear before him at Rome, and finding it equally
fruitless to remonstrate with Henry the Second,
who refused to abandon his hold upon Parma, required the assistance of the Emperor, who willingly
joined his forces to those of the Supreme Pontiff,
and with their united strength besieged Mirandola,
then in possession of the French. The Marshal
Brissac at the same time commenced the campaign
in Piedmont, and the Dukes of Nevers and Vendosme in Flanders. The following letter of Chamberlayne gives us some interesting details of the
state of affairs at this crisis.

SIR THOMAS CHAMBERLAYNE TO THE COUNCIL.

Orig. St. P. Off. *Brussels.* 7th June 1551.

" Please your most honourable Lordships to be
advertised of the receipt of yours of the 26th of the
last month, whereby it hath liked you to participate
unto me the estate of things there with you, which,
God be thanked! are in much better order than, by
the common bruits here, it should seem that some
would wish them for to be.

" Concerning the marriage, the same hath been
here in men's mouths a good while, which I wist
not what to make of, considering the King's Majesty's right and title to the daughter of Scotland,
and that realm : which I did assure myself not to
be forgotten of your Lordships, like as I do now
well perceive the time reserved, that you write of;

in the which Almighty God may work much for our purpose.*

" The French ambassador did once enter talk with me about the same, saying that they here did commune of like matter, not much liking the same, which he for his part, he said, would wish to be so ; for that the same were the way and mean to knit our master and his together, in straiter amity, for the better preservation and safeguard of both their estates, the Emperor's proceedings considered : which was all the talk we had of that matter.

" Here are still preparations for war, and carrying all kinds of munition and artillery to all their frontiers, as well by sea as land ; insomuch that, two days past, the common waggons that ordinarily do serve to conduct merchandize from Antwerp upwards into Germany and Switzerland, were all arrested, and such as were laden discharged, (as men think,) for to carry ordnance, but to what place is not yet known.

" I have answer out of Zealand, that only four ships are there presently a rigging, of two hundred and fifty ton the least ; but, as I am informed other-

---

* The modesty of Sir Thomas Chamberlayne's ideas upon this point is worthy of notice.   Edward the Sixth, according to him, had not only right and title to the *daughter* of Scotland, but to the *realm*.   The tone of the Privy Council seems to have been, that they had not forgotten their claim, but waited for a better time to renew it.   The marriage alluded to is that of Edward to the Princess Elizabeth, the daughter of the French King.

ways, there are many more pressed besides, for to
serve when they shall be called upon; and some
will say, that Monsieur de Aremberg * hath taken
up men in his government of Friseland, for to furnish the same.   In Holland, it is said that twelve
ships are preparing; which to be sure of, I have
sent one expressly there, and have yet no answer.

"There goeth a bruit in Antwerp, that there
should be a strait league lately made between the
King's Majesty, the French King, and the King of
Denmark, which I do guess for to rise by reason
that a certain councillor of the King of Denmark
(as it is told me) did pass hereby this other day
homeward, coming out of France, and would not
be known in this town who he was; saying, one
while, that he came out of England; another while,
out of France.

"We have news that Gonzaga, † at Milan, doth
take all the Spaniards, that were thereabouts in
garrison, for to make an army in the field, and putteth in the lieu of them the Italian inhabitants of

* Daremberg, Governor of Friseland, under Charles the
Fifth.

† Ferdinand Gonzaga, Governor of Charles the Fifth in the
Milanese.   The Marechal Brissac and Monluc, with the flower
of the French nobility, the Duke D'Aumale, the Duke D'Enghien, and his brother the Prince of Condé, the Duke De Nemours, and others, were at this time carrying everything before
them in Piedmont.   Gonzaga was unable to make head against
them.   His soldiers had become mutinous for want of pay, and
all his affairs were in confusion.—De Thou, Book viii. anno
1551.

the duchy of Milan; and this by reason that the
French King hath sent unto Mirandola, Petro
Strozzi with thirty captains, Sampiero Corse with
two thousand footmen, and John De [Allegre], with
one thousand : besides that, all the bands of Italians that the French King had in Piedmont are
sent also to Mirandola, in small troops there, for to
make an army to empesche [restrain] such as would
have to do with Parma.   It is told me that there
is great provision made at Makelyne, [Mechlin,]
among other munitions for war, of vessels for to
bake and brew, which hath not afore this been seen
that the Emperor, for any of his wars past, did prepare the like, which the people do marvel at :
wherefore I have one lying in the same town for
to view and see all things, and the sending forth
thereof, and what way it goeth; whereof I shall
not fail hereafter to advertise.

" I hear say, that the Bishop of Rome, being
moved of some one not to let Parma slip so into
the French King's hands, made answer that he had
no money to make war with.*   The poor people

* There is, in the British Museum, a letter from Sir Richard
Morysine and Dr. Wotton to the Council, (Galba, B. xi, p. 52,)
which confirms this report of Chamberlayne's regarding the poverty of the Pope, and describes the artful manner in which the
Emperor, by lending him large sums of money, obtained so
much power over him that he swayed and directed his decisions as to the Council of Trent. Wotton had been sent by Edward the Sixth (the 10th April 1551) on an embassy to the
Emperor, to remonstrate against the interference of Charles on

about these frontiers towards France, do already draw them with their bag and baggage to the towns and holds.

" Here is taken lately, in a wood beside Gant, twenty or twenty-five persons, Anabaptists, keeping

the subject of the Lady Mary's religion, who had been interdicted by Edward from having mass in her household.—Carte, vol. iii. p. 256. Unfortunately, the letter is included in one of the volumes which have been injured by fire, and there are many lacunæ. A short extract from it may be interesting.

Orig.   " Augusta, 11th August 1551.

" The [Emperor say the ambassadors] seeth this time not unfit for his purpose. The Bishop of Rome is poor ; and, as things stand, must needs have money. The Emperor hath lent him more than he shall be able to repay him this good time. One practice may help two at once. The Bishop may be forgiven that he oweth, and Bulla Aurea may be . . . th' Emperor's will. The Electors be poor, and like . . . . Long diets have brought them to mean fare . . . . and then they make reckoning that poverty may . . . . foul play; being all sought to by an Emperor, by a Pope, and by a General Council, which is like to show the Emperor the favour they can. Howbeit, if France send not hither,—if Denmark, if Swetia, if the most part of Germany keep themselves at home, as all men know England will,—this will be taken rather for an unlawful assembly than thought a Council General.

" The Prince Doria goeth into Spain again to fetch Maximilian and th' Emperor's daughter. If he be not already gone, he goeth within a day or two. The Duke of Alva goeth also into Spain. His family and household stuff is gone into Flanders, and from thence goeth in all haste possible into Spain. He himself, with a few, rideth in post to Genoa, where he taketh his passage. * * The Emperor is gone in solace to Monaco, and hunteth ; meaning, whatsoever his . . . . to seem careless."

there their assembly, most part young men, and
but two women. Were it not for the strait laws
here, this country should be well troubled with the
like; and, as your Lordships do write, I fear me
they run too fast from thence into our country; for
the which, God be praised! you have taken good
order, for, indeed, malicious and evil-disposed people do not let to say that England is at this day
the harbour for all infidelity.

"It appeareth not here, (under correction,) that
the calling down the money with you doth help the
exchange; for, since the same was known of, the exchange is fallen from fifteen shillings to fourteen
shillings for a pound of our money which is far
from thirty shillings of this money that I have
known delivered for twenty shillings of ours;
whereby it may well appear that the exchange is
but merchants' practice; with how little they regard
the common weal, for advancement of their private lucre, I think the world doth see.

"A merchant stranger here did ask me wherefore the exchange should be forbidden in England,
which, he said, he had [heard] say that your Lordships jointly with the calling down of the money, took
to be the remedy for dearth of things as well within
the realm, as also of foreign commodities brought
there. I answered him, that I knew nothing thereof; but I asked him whether, speaking uprightly,
he did think the same necessary, or not; wading
so far in communication with him thereof, that I

made him confess unto me that the one without the
other were no redress; and besides, he said plainly,
that heed must be given, in the mean while, whilst
the money is so called down by a little and little,
that great sums of the like, forged and counter-
feited in foreign parts, be not secretly conveyed
into the realm; for then, he said, the commodities
should be never the better cheap, by reason that
the bringer in of the said testoon or grote should
advance so much by the paying thereof, that always he might give 60*l.* for a pack of our cloths,
and sell the same here again for 50*l.* or 48*l.* and
yet be gainer, and so still until such time as the
money were called down to the very value in ster-
ling silver which is in each piece thereof. And so
made discourse unto me what gain was had by the
testoon or grote put out for 12d. and 4d.; and what
yet will be now, putting them forth for 9d. or 3d.,
yea, and tho' it should be at 6d. or 2d.; for that, he
said, one of our testoons of the latest coin, tried
here in the Mint, was not found to be worth 3d. of
this money in silver. So that of this communication
I have thought good to advertise your Lordships;
not doubting, for all that, but you have already considered as much as is needful in that behalf.

"And truly it is strange to hear that at this day
the strangers, as well as our merchants, do sell here
of our commodities for 50, and 52, and 48, that cost
60 and upwards; as appeareth by our merchants,
that take the shilling for 12d. and the grote for 4d,

that he is not able to go through with such loss as to buy for 60 and sell for 50, for daily they play bankrupt; therefore, there must be some mystery in the matter. I pray God it may be discovered, to the weal of our realm.

"We say now that the Emperor's departure from A—— hitherward, is retarded until the 12th of this month. His son is departed to the Prince of Piedmont, and the [Duke] of Holsten, besides other. This is the sum of our present occurrents; and therefore I will leave to trouble your most honourable Lordships, beseeching Almighty God long to continue the same in health and honour! From Bruxelles, the 7th day of June 1551.

" T. Chamberlayne."

" Postscripta.—Skyperius being lame, using two crutches, and skant able to go with the same, was three days past sent with diligence into Zealand; where, as still I do hear, great preparations to be made to seaward, and in Holland, and Flanders, but as secretly as may be; and about Bois le Duc, as I am informed, men are pressed and taken up. I pray God Skyperius have not a like voyage into England as he had this time twelve-months, when I would wish him to speed no better than then he did.* Here hath been almost these

---

* Skyperius, the Lord Admiral of the Emperor's fleet, had threatened a descent upon the English coast in July 1550, his object being to carry off the Princess Mary.—Edward's Journal, in Burnet, Appendix, vol. ii. p. 18. The same alarm was now felt, and precautions taken against it.

fourteen days, every second day, terrible tempests of thunder, lightning, hail, wind, and rain, which hath overthrown trees and houses, and transported houses and other things from one place to another so strangely, as the report goeth, that I am afraid to write thereof. The Queen, upon Friday last, in the beginning of a sore tempest, (having seen the beginning and likelihood or ever she took horse,) rode three leagues off a hunting, meaning to lie at a cloister, as she did ; and on Saturday arrived an extraordinary post from the Emperor with letters, which the Master of the posts carried to her Majesty with all speed. Upon receipt of the same, she retired to her chamber, and no ink'ling can be had of any news at the post's hands. Now she is returned to this town, and departed towards Tournehault for five or six days, to see what the storm hath wrought there with her trees and things, wonderful by report."

EDWARD THE SIXTH and the Emperor had been on distant terms since the time that the Spanish ambassador had so peremptorily demanded for the Princess Mary the free exercise of her religion. This estrangement, and the high tone assumed by Charles the Fifth, led the English monarch to cultivate the friendship of France, and to seek a marriage with that crown. Henry the Second, on the feast of St. George, was chosen a Knight of the Garter ; the Marquis of Northampton, with a splendid embassy, was sent over to invest the French monarch with the ensigns of the order; and, in conjunction with the Bishop of Ely, Sir Philip Hoby, Sir John Masone, Sir Wm. Pickering, and Sir T. Smith, was instructed to treat of the marriage. With the Marquis of Northampton we have already met. "His delight," says Lloyd,* "was music and poetry, and his exercise war; being a happy composure of the hardest and softest discipline."

Northampton's account of his embassy in the following letter is interesting, and abounds with little touches and anecdotes which bring before us the gay Court of France, its monarch, its statesmen, warriors, carpet knights, and beautiful dames, more vividly than any account of the embassy to be found in the general historians or contemporary memoirs of these times.

There is considerable similarity between the characters of Henry the Second of France and our own Charles the Second: both good-humoured and kind-hearted, courteous, agreeable in conversation, and with no contemptible talents for business and state affairs when they exerted them; but both profligate, extravagant in the money bestowed on their favourites, devoted to pleasure, and utterly unprincipled. The corruption of the Court of Henry the Second, and its loose and licentious manners, (imported during the two former reigns from Italy,) present us also with a parallel to Eng-

* Lloyd's Worthies, p. 187.

land under Charles.   The tone of the literature in
France under Henry forms another point of resemblance to the loose morality which distinguishes the
dramatic and poetic school of Charles the Second.
Speaking of Henry, we might, says Mezeray, be
inclined to praise his love of letters, " si la dissolu-
tion de sa cour, authorisée par son exemple, n'eust
tourné les plus beaux esprits à composer des romans
pleins de visions extravagantes, et des poesies las-
cives, pour flatter l'impureté qui tenoit en main les
recompenses, et pour fournir des amusemens à un
sexe qui veut regner en badinant."*   But the most
disgusting and painful points of resemblance between the two courts remain to be noticed in that
infidel spirit which infected both, and the blas-
phemy and profaneness to which it led.

THE MARQUIS OF NORTHAMPTON AND THE OTHER AMBASSADORS, TO THE LORDS OF THE COUNCIL.

Orig.   St. P. Off.   *Chasteau Brian.*   20th June 1551.

" PLEASE your good Lordships.   Since the last
despatch unto you by Francis the post, we have
been very highly entertained ; first, of Mons. Chastillion, who not only made us a great supper the
night before our departure out of Nantes, but also
feasted us all the way to the court, making us such
cheer (at his own charges) as was not to be looked
for in Bretagne, where, besides the scarcity of good

* Abrégé Chronologique, vol. vi. p. 722.

victuals, everything is extreme dear; and yet was his provision such as made us to wonder in that place to see it.

"About four of the clock at afternoon on Friday last, we arrived here at Chasteau Brian, where Mons. D'Enghien and the Duke de Montpensier* with better than one hundred horse of gentlemen, met us half a mile without the town, and brought us straight to the King's presence, booted and spurred; the King abiding our coming in his chamber of presence, with his nobility and guard about him. Assuring your Lordships that we cannot too much commend him for his benign receiving of us, for he embraced every man, to the meanest gentleman that came in our company; and that with so good a countenance, and so courteous words, that the greater could not be wished.

"That done, and due salutations made by me the Marquis, I declared unto him that the King, my master, understanding the good love and zeal that he bare unto him, was willing, for his part, to show the like good-will again; and had now sent me with his Order unto him, as a token of honour and a manifest declaration of his semblable affection; that, further, he was bent to do and to nourish of his part those things that might be honourable and benefi-

* Louis de Bourbon, Duke of Montpensier, son of Louis de Bourbon, Prince of Roche-sur-Yon; who was head of the second branch of Montpensier, by his marriage with Louise, the sister of the famous Constable Bourbon.

cial for the wealth and unity of themselves and of both their estates : and so I delivered him the King's Majesty's letter concerning the Order, which he opened and read himself, yielding great thanks to the King his good brother, with many gentle words of amity.

" And having a certain space devised with me of the King our master's health and welfare, and of his good towardness, with such like, he caused me to be conveyed to a lodging prepared for me within the court; in the which two cloths of estate were hanged, one in the outer chamber, and the other in my bed-chamber; and further, two mess of meat ordinarily furnished for my table, with such officers of attendance as are marvellously diligent to see that we want nothing. The rest of us, and the company, are lodged in the town, as well as the strait room of so little a place may bear ; the substance of this court being lodged in the villages to give us place. And, for our better furniture, the King sent unto every one of us that were noted to be commissioners, six pieces of wine for our provision.

" The same evening, after supper, the King sent for me the Marquis, praying me to bring some of the young Lords* with their bows into the garden to

* The Earls of Worcester, Rutland, and Ormond, the Lords Lisle, Fitzwaters, Bray, Abergavenny, and Evres, with many other knights and gentlemen, added by their presence to the magnificence of the embassy.—Hayward, Life of Edward the Sixth, in Kennett, vol. ii. p. 318.

pass the time with him; where we shot for his pleasure at the butts with him and his other Lords, until it was late. Then he brought us and all the company to the Queen's chamber, where we found her, with the old and the young Scottish Queens,* and a great company of ladies, at whose hands we had also such good welcome as might be had; and so the King fell to dancing, and drove forth the night to bed-time.

" On Saturday, after dinner, he, with certain noblemen, played at tennis, and sent for me the Marquis, and those gentlemen that were with me, to look upon him; which we did all the while he played.† After supper, he brought the Queen and all her train into the fields, where my men wrestled with certain Brittons and had the better of them. That done, we returned in; and the King fell to dancing as he did the night before, causing some of our younger Lords to dance for his pleasure. Then he had us into his bed-chamber, where we heard his musicians sing, which he delighteth wonderfully to hear. And when all was done, he told me that the

* Mary Queen of Scots, then a child of nine years old, and her mother, Mary of Guise, the Queen Dowager.

† Henry the Second was particularly fond of showing his address in all manly and athletic exercises; indeed, his taste for these at last proved fatal to him. It was strange that, after a reign spent in real war, he should be slain by the lance of Montgomery in a mimic combat. " *Quem Mars non rapuit, Martis imago rapit,*" says Stephen Forcadel, in one of the many epitaphs composed on him.

next morning he would be ready to receive the Order ; and so took leave for that night.

" Yesterday morning, being Sunday, the Duke D'Aumale and Mons. de Rohan, a great baron of Bretagne, came for me the Marquis, to my chamber, and so brought me to the Queen's great chamber, which was advoided, [cleared of company] and kept for me to put on my robes.   I was no sooner there but the Constable came ; who, before, offered to do what I would will him touching this ceremony, and there put on his robes also, and so together we were brought unto the King's Privy Chamber ; where I the Bishop of Ely, after the commission read, made such a brief oration in Latin as methought meet for the purpose ; at the end whereof the Cardinal of Lorain seemed to expound the effect of it to the French King, and of him to receive the answer.   Which answer he made in Latin to this effect :—' That the King, his master, highly thanked his good brother ; was contented to receive the Order, with a singular desire unto perpetual amity.'   Whereupon I the Marquis put on the King's garter, and consequently the rest of his robes ; to the doing whereof the Constable aided, he and I both being, before we entered the Presence Chamber, apparelled in our robes.

" Then went the King into the Church, where he heard mass and offered : and after being returned to his lodging, dined in his robes ; having at his table the Cardinal of Lorain, the Constable, and I ; I being placed highest of the three. And a little before we were set, the Constable called Mons. Chastillion to him, and willed him in any wise to take us, the Bishop of Ely, Sir John Masone, Sir Philip Hoby, and Sir Wm. Pickering, with the Earls of Worcester and Rutland, and make us dine at his table with the Cardinal Chastillion and Mons. De Guyse, and the rest of the noblemen, of whom we were very well entertained.

" After dinner, for that we had sat all the dinner time in our robes, the weather being very hot, the King thought not good to hold me with any long talk ; advising me to retire myself into my chamber, whither, after he had a while devised with me, I was conducted by Monsieur Le Grand Prieur of the Rhodes,* who is brother to the Duke of Guise, and the Prior of Capua. And scant were my robes off, when a gentleman of the King's Privy Chamber came unto me by his commandment, praying me, if I had ever a little George, to lend him one for that day. I sent him in the prettiest I had, which cheerfully he put about his neck.

" About one hour after this came to me Monsieur de Chastillion, and inquired of me whether I would that afternoon speak with the King ; saying that, in that case, he had commission to bring me unto him. I thought not meet to lose any occasion for the doing of such commission as I had in charge of

* Leo Strozzi, brother of Pietro Strozzi.

your Lordships; and therefore I answered, if it
were his pleasure, I would straight wait upon him.
And so, taking with me my colleagues, I was conveyed unto him by the Prior of Capua, and the said
Monsieur de Chastillion; and finding him in his bed-
chamber, accompanied with the Cardinals Lorrain
and Chastillion, Monsieur de Guise, D'Aumale, and
the Constable, I the Marquis approached unto
his person; to whom, after some words of office, I
delivered the King my master's letter of credence,
and, following the order of my instructions, I
declared to him at good length, in such sort and
with such words as I thought fittest, the King my
master's inclination and affection towards him, his
great desire of the continuance of the increase of
the amity, and finally the devise of some good mean
for the perpetual establishment of the same, following thoroughly the tread and direction of our instructions.

" This done, I called unto me my colleagues,
whom the Constable had in the mean season entertained; to whom, in the King's presence, I declared
briefly what to the King I had said at more length
touching the premises. Whereupon I Sir Philip
Hoby, whom for that purpose we thought all (for
divers considerations) most meetest, declared in like
state the King our master's earnest mind and desire, not only to the continuance and preservation
of this amity, but to the augmentation of the same.
The King, thanking his good brother of this good af-

fection towards the perfection of a straiter amity, declared at great length his *reciproque* desire, sparing
no kind of speech whereby he might do us to understand the same, joining his countenance and his
words so together, as greater demonstration could
not outwardly appear of his like desire, which he
grounded upon divers reasons, and specially for that
the love had been many years so great between the
two fathers; which albeit in their latter time, by
such means as we were not ignorant of, was in much
blemished, yet was he sure that for his fathers,
[part he] unto the dying day, could never remove
the love of the King from the bottom of his heart;
which natural affection as he had received from his
said father as it were of inheritance, and would not
fail to embrace and cherish the same during his life,
so to this, his father's love, which was in him of
nature, he would join his own and double it. All
which discourse he had made privately unto me the
Marquis, before I called my said colleagues unto it.

" He declared further, how commodious a strait
amity should be unto them both, who, being so
nigh neighbours, might easily always the one be
ready to aid the other; adding, that there were
abroad that bare no good-will to any of them,
whereof he thought that I Sir Philip Hoby, could
tell somewhat; but, being joined in such amity together as he trusted they were and should be, no
malice towards them was to be feared. How constantly, with what sincerity he had hitherto pro-

ceeded with the King his brother,—how desirous he had alway showed himself of his friendship,—he took record of me the Ambassador here resident. And whereas there had been some wars at the beginning between them, he sware he never enterprised thing with worse will, neither that more was against his stomach; but that, he said, thanks be to God! was at an end, and he trusted for ever: intending from henceforth to omit no occasion whereby the world might understand his assured good mind towards the King his brother, so as thereby all tokens of the contrary, which had chanced in times past, might utterly be defaced.*

" After he, with very many words, had said unto us th' effect hereof, I the Lord Marquis entered into the first branch of my commission, and in as good a sort as I could, following in all points the order of mine instructions. I made the overture of the Queen of Scots, setting forth unto him how far the Scots had therein proceeded with us; being ready, if it so liked him, to show presently the authentical records thereof; declaring unto him how thereby all controversies might be taken away, so as the amity between them, being builded upon a

---

* The speech of Henry the Second, although somewhat long-winded, justifies Mezeray's observation that this monarch " avoit une merveilleuse facilité de s'exprimer aussi bien en public qu'en particulier." (Abrégé Chronologique, vol. vi. p. 722.) But it is singular how often we find weak men (and Henry was governed by his mistresses and favourites) possessing this easy flow of elegant language.

most sure foundation, might, by the aid of God, last and continue for ever : the most earnest desire whereof on the King my master's behalf caused him this to require at this present, and to use this kind of frank proceeding with him.

" Hereunto he made no direct answer,* but thanking the King his brother that it liked him to use this frankness with him, the like whereof he would in all points follow for his part, he said he would, against the next day, appoint certain commissioners to treat with us, who should so proceed with us as we should not have any reason to find ourselves discontented.   We desired him that they might be such as were known to be thoroughly given to the good of this notable amity ; he bid us not doubt therein : and thus, after he had caused us make collation (as they call it here) with him, he dismissed us ; and I the Lord Marquis was again brought to my chamber by the two personages above named.

" The same evening the King, the Queens, and

* Henry the Second must have been somewhat puzzled with this demand of the young Queen of Scots, as her marriage with the Dauphin was already fixed.   The French King had made the proposal by Montalembert, the Sieur D'Esse, in 1548, and the Scottish Parliament had unanimously agreed to it.   It was not wonderful, therefore, that he avoided a direct answer.   Yet it appears by a letter from Sir John Masone, 10th May 1551, (Orig. St. P. Off.) that there had been then a great consultation regarding the marriage of the Scottish Queen to the Dauphin, which the Constable Montmorency and the Chancellor were anxious should be deferred.

all the ladies, supt in the park ;* unto the which I the Marquis, with all the Lords and young gentlemen of my company, were bidden. The place was very pleasant; but the good countenance, and great cheer that we had both of Lords and Ladies, exceeded. After supper we rode all into the heath beyond the park, where certain red-deer were entoiled, and standings made for the ladies to see the coursing. The King himself caused horses to be brought for divers gentlemen of our company to gallop the course, which indeed was both fair and pleasant. In effect, the entertainment that we have had at the King's own hands hath been very great ; for at all times of our access unto his presence, in all places and in all companies, he hath used us so familiarly and friendly, that it is impossible for him to show us in his own person greater demonstrations of love and amity than he hath showed openly, as this bearer can more at large declare unto your Lordships, who not only hath seen it from time to time, but also is therein sufficiently instructed by us; wherefore it may please you to give credence unto him.

---

* This rural supper, given by Catherine of Medicis and her ladies, in the park of the Palace, is described *con amore* by the Marquis, who was more of a gallant carpet-knight than a warrior or statesman. The pleasantness of the place, and season,— a sweet evening in June,—the great cheer, where the tables were spread beneath the green-wood tree, the hunting scene after supper, the store of Lords and Ladies galloping over the heath, or sitting in groups to see the sport, would have formed a charming subject for Paul Veronese or Watteau.

" On Monday, after dinner, Secretary Aubespine came unto me the Marquis, and declared that,
whereas the King had the day before accorded to
appoint certain commissioners to meet this day
with me and my colleagues, he was sent to show
me that the said commissioners were in a readiness,
so as, when I should think good, I should be wellcome to the place which was appointed for the
assembly. Whereupon I and my said colleagues
were conducted thither, where we found the Cardinals of Lorrain and Chastillion, Monsieur de Guise,
the Constable, the Bishop of Soissons, Bertrandi,
now entitled Le Garde de Sceau, and Monsieur
de Cheneis, one of the four Generals of France ;
who being set on one side of the board, and we
on the other, the Constable, being the mouth of the
rest, declared that the King had showed unto
them what communication had been yesterday between him and me the Lord Marquis, with the rest
of my colleagues, and had appointed them according unto his promise to treat with us, as well in
such things as had already been talked of, as in
many others that we would desire to be heard in,
requiring us to declare unto them such matters as
we had to commune and to treat of.

" Whereupon I the Marquis answered, that
albeit I had yesterday opened an overture unto the
King's Majesty, and had declared unto him reasonable matter to induce him to consent unto it, as I
doubted not but, weighing the justness of the re-

quest, he would devise for his good brother's satis-faction therein; yet, forasmuch as it seemed they required to hear the same again, I would tell the same tale unto them as I had done before unto the King; which after I had done in such manner as I was led by the instructions,* and as I had in effect done before unto the King, it was first answered that the King would be ready to show unto his good brother all the signs of amity that honourably might be demanded; and, forasmuch as for our parts it was alleged that we had certain sealed in-struments whereby might appear the consent of the realm of Scotland and the Council of that realm, they [required we should] communicate [such] unto them, and thereupon such answer should be given unto us as reason should require.

" It was again said unto them, that th' instru-ment was ready to be showed; marry, we would gladly know whether, in case by the viewing thereof our request should seem reasonable unto them, they

* These instructions, (endorsed 17 Maii 1551,) though with-out date in the body of the deed, are still preserved in the State Paper Office. — Sir John Williamson's Collection, vol. xix. p. 299. From their tenour it is evident that the English had no expectation that Henry the Second would listen to any proposal regarding the young Scottish Queen, which seems to have been made as a matter of form. In one part of the in-structions, the ambassadors are directed to inform the French King that, on the 12th of October next, Edward the Sixth would be fourteen years old; and to request that the marriage may take place within three months after the Lady Elizabeth shall have attained the age of twelve years.

minded to proceed with us in that matter to any good effect; wherein we prayed them to use such frankness with us as we had used, and intended still to use with them.

" After they had one of them looked a time upon another, ' By my troth,' quoth the Constable, ' to be plain and frank with you, seeing you require us so to be, the matter hath cost us both much riches and no little blood, and so much doth the honour of France hang hereupon as we cannot tell how to talk with you therein, the marriage being already concluded between her and the Dauphin; and, therefore, we would be glad to hear no more thereof.'

" I the Marquis answered, that we were come to treat of no matters but such as might be thought to tend to the perfection of the amity between the two princes, and to the contentation of them both; and whereby, as before was said, all *piques* and quarrels might be taken away for ever. And albeit that the King my master, by the advice of his Council, thought the marriage of Scotland might best have brought that to pass, and therefore could have been contented to have in marriage, specially at this King's hands, the Scottish Queen; who, besides the promise made by the whole realm, had spent also for her both blood and riches; yet, for that it shall appear unto them that the King doth prefer the joining of amity with his brother before all other affections, I had commission, forasmuch

as the other overture pleased not, to demand in
marriage the Lady Elizabeth,* eldest daughter
to this King; whereunto the said King my master,
was the more moved, first, for the good affection he
had particularly to his said good brother, whereof, being daily about him, I could be a good record; a great ground whereof was the daily good
report made unto him by his ministers here, and
others also, of the semblable good inclination
and like good-will and affection of this King towards him: secondly, for the good report of the
likelihood and towardness of the young lady; and
so forth.

"After I had so much said in this branch as I
was taught by the common instructions, the Constable made answer in the name of the rest, that,
if a mean Prince should make request to have a
King's daughter, it could not be but well taken,
for that at the least it must needs be a declaration
either of some virtue or quality that he esteemed
to be in the party; or else of the coveting of an
alliance that he was desirous to have with the
Prince. Much more then must this request, made
of so noble a Prince,—a Prince of such puissance
and of such virtue,—be with all thanks hearkened
unto; and therefore he did us to understand, first,
that the King his master most heartily thanked
the King our master; and that they would most

* Elizabeth became afterwards the wife of Philip the Second
of Spain.

gladly, according unto his commandment, treat with us in this matter, when, and at all times that they shall be required.

"Here we fell to the particularities of the commission; first, touching no contract to be made before the gentlewoman come to the age of twelve years, for such reasons as we could gather out of our said instructions. After some reasoning, we asked them what they could be content to give with her. They answered, they had no commission to offer any thing; but what we would demand should be reported unto the King, and thereof should we have speedy answer. We demanded 1,500,000 crowns,* (xv C^m crowns). 'Frankly demanded!' quoth they, laughing: we alleged such reasons as we thought might serve for the persuading of them to think this sum reasonable.

---

* In the instructions so often alluded to, the clause regarding the portion to be demanded with the French Princess would have done honour to the diplomatic powers of the sharpest Jew or money-lender in Christendom. It is said, "Item, the said Lord Marquis and his colleagues shall demand of the French, for the dote [dower], 1,500,000 crowns French; and in the next degree to descend to 1,200,000; and in the third to a million, and there to rest." Notwithstanding this *"resting at a million,"* the Lord Marquis, by the last instructions sent him, (Sir John Masone's Letter Book, p. 385,) was directed to *descend* first to 800,000 crowns; then, if that was resisted, to 400,000; then, if that was still refused, to 300,000; and lastly, rather than break off the marriage, to agree to a dote of 200,000 crowns, the transportation being at the charges of the French King.

They said, they had married daughters in times past to divers places, and had also daughters of other realms married unto them, and therefore it was the more easy thing to know what sum were meet in this case. In the end, they prayed us to deliver unto them our particularities in writing, whereof they would make report unto the King, and at our next meeting we should thereof have such answer as, in reason, we should have cause to be contented. Hereunto, for the better speed of the matter, we thought good to condescend.

" In all this conference they referred all things to be reported first unto the King, and at his hands answer to be fetched. And yet, in the principal point that we doubted most of, it seemed by their countenance that for their parts they might be induced to consent thereunto without great sticking. If any difficulty there be, it will be in the greatness of the sum required for the dote, and the smallness of the penalty, and especially in the sum of the dote ; wherein it may like your Lordships to send with speed your pleasures whether, rather than fail, you mind to add any thing to the one and to diminish any thing of the other.

" Your Lordships, we trust, will consider the great distance of the place from you, how long it may be after our despatch before we can have answer again ; how we remain here a great number without horses, and how this King useth often to remove from place to place ; and therefore, to avoid the length of our tarrying here, to send, with all the speed that may be, your resolute determination herein.

" In what sort, and with what gentleness, we are here entertained, we refer, as before we have done, to the declaration of Sir William Cobham, whom at this present we send to your Lordships expressly for that purpose. I the Lord Marquis most heartily do desire your Lordships to remember, with as much speed as may be, Mr. Pickering's despatch; which I do the more earnestly require, for that I have promised Mr. Masone he shall no longer tarry here than I.

" From Château Brian, the 20th of June 1551.

" W. North'.   T. Ely.   J. Masone.

" Philip Hobby.   Wm. Pickering. T. Smith.

" D. Oliver."

It was to be expected that Charles the Fifth, encumbered and perplexed as he was at this moment with the management of the Council of Trent, the war with France, the coalition of the Protestant Princes, and the ill success of his schemes for the aggrandisement of his son, should have viewed this projected matrimonial alliance between England and France with much jealousy. That he did so, we learn from the following passage of a letter from Chamberlayne, the English resident at Brussels, to the Lords of the Council.

" The arrival of my Lord Marquis at the French

court, and his honourable entertainment there and
depesche from thence, hath been here commonly
talked of, and nothing at all liked that such em-
bracing of amity and likelihood of perdurable
friendship should be between the King's Majesty
and the French King.   The common people do talk
much thereof, and say plainly that a marriage is
concluded; which talk, in my opinion, neither doth
nor can do hurt, nor the agreement between us and
Scotland when it shall be known, but perhaps divert
some of Cæsar's purposes, and make him a better
neighbour." *

In the mean time, when England had fortunately
composed all differences with France on the one
hand, and Scotland, her near and troublesome
neighbour, on the other, the country was afflicted
by a grievous scourge in the shape of a distemper,
called the English disease, or sweating sickness,
which carried off multitudes of people.   On the
10th of July a hundred people died in London,
and next day one hundred and twenty were carried off.†   Soon after, some in the King's court
were infected, and Edward was hurried to Hampton Court, although an ambassador was daily expected from France, to whom Warwick and the
Council were solicitous to pay all possible honour.

* Orig. St. P. Off.   Brussels, 11th July 1551.

† This fatal disease first appeared in England in 1486, then
in 1507, then in 1517, then in 1528, and lastly, now, in 1551.
—Herbert's Life of Henry the Eighth.   Kennet, vol. ii. p. 99.

It was found necessary, however, to order all the noblemen and gentlemen who had been appointed to receive the embassy to return in haste to their homes; and a letter was addressed to the Bishops, which, as it has escaped the industry of Strype, Burnet, and Fuller, I may give from the original.

Orig. St. P. Off. *Domestic.* 18th July 1551.

" EDWARD.   " By the King.

" RIGHT REV. FATHER IN GOD.—Right trusty and well-beloved, we greet you well: and being not a little disquieted to see the subjects of our realm vexed with this extreme and sudden Plague that daily encreaseth over all, we cannot but lament the people's wickedness, through the which the wrath of God hath been thus marvellously provoked; for the more we study how to instruct them in the knowledge of God and of his most holy Word, that consequently they might follow and observe his laws and precepts, so much the more busy is the wicked spirit to alienate their hearts from all godliness; and his malice hath so much prevailed, that because the people are become, as it were, open rebels against the divine Majesty, God, after one plague, hath sent another and another, encreasing it so from one to one till at length, seeing none other remedy, he hath thrown forth this most extreme plague of sudden death.

" And because there is no other way to pacify his fury and to recover his grace and mercy but by prayer and amendment of life; considering the cure and charge committed unto you, we have thought good to call upon you to use all diligence possible throughout your whole diocese, as well by yourself as by good ministers, to persuade the people to re-sort more diligently to common prayer than they have done; and there not only to pray with all their hearts in the fear of God, as good and faithful men should do, but also to have a better regard unto their livings, and specially to refrain their greedy appetites from that insatiable serpent of *covet-ousness*, wherewith most men are so infected, that it seemeth the one would devour another without charity, or any godly respect to the poor, to their neighbours, or to their commonwealth; for the which, God hath not only now poured out this plague for them, but also prepared another plague that after this life shall plague them everlastingly; wherein you must use those persuasions that may engender a terror to reduce them from their cor-rupt, naughty, and detestable lives. But as the body and members of a dull or sick head cannot be lusty or apt to do well, so, in many cures of this our realm, as well the chief as the particular ministers of our church have been both so dull and so feeble in discharging of their duties that there is no mar-vel though their flocks wander, not knowing the voice of their shepherd, and much less the voice of their principal and Sovereign Master.

"We trust ye are none of those; but, if there hath

been such negligence in your jurisdiction, we exhort and pray you, and nevertheless charge and
command you, by the authority given us of God, to
see it reformed, encreasing also amendment in that
that already is well begun, in such sort as your diligence may declare you worthy of your vocation, and
the effects thereof yield unto God an obedient, faithful, and fearful flock, as we wish to God we may
shortly see.

" Given under our signet, at our Honour of
Hampton Court, the 18th of July, the fifth year of
our reign.

" E. SOMERSET.	J. BEDFORD.
" T. HUNTYNDON.	T. CHEYNE.
" G. COBHAM.	J. GATE."

The King's stamp-signature is prefixed to this
excellent letter. The sin of covetousness had infected the higher ranks still more than the people;
the desire for amassing large estates out of the
plunder of the church being one of the most striking features of the times.

The diplomatic service, even in its highest stages,
seems to have been little sought after in the reigns
of Edward, Mary, and Elizabeth; and yet nothing
is more striking than the ability, zeal, and intimate
acquaintance with European politics of the men
who acted as resident ambassadors, and watched
over the interests of England at foreign courts.

Their correspondence, preserved in the State Paper Office, is a noble monument of their talent and indefatigable activity : but never were genius and devotedness more parsimoniously rewarded ; all of them make the same complaints,—their *Diets*, that is, their quarterly allowances in money, are ill paid, their debts heavy, their ambassador's plate worn out and shabby, the advances necessary to be made out of their private fortune intolerable, their desire to return home extreme. From the conclusion of the following letter, addressed by Sir W. Pickering to the Council, we find he was in the same predicament as his brethren, needy and home-sick. He spent *fourteen* French crowns a day, and the King only allowed him *seven*. As to his abilities, the letter speaks for itself. It gives us a masterly sketch of the policy of France and England at this period in relation to the great enterprises of Charles the Fifth, and the condition of Italy and the empire.

It is curious, and not uninstructive, to mark the effect which the political opposition of the Pope to Henry the Second produced upon the religious opinions of that country; so little did they deem themselves dependent as a church upon Rome, that at one time they were beginning to talk of choosing a Patriarch.

Pickering became afterwards a principal favourite of Elizabeth, possessing every quality which this princess loved and valued,—" he was an able statesman, a ripe scholar, an elegant and magnificent courtier, and an uncommonly handsome man, of a tall stature and dignified presence."

SIR W. PICKERING TO THE COUNCIL.

Orig. St. P. Off. *France. Melun.* 4th Sept. 1551.

" PLEASETH your good Lordships to be advertised, that upon Tuesday last, being the 1st of Sept. I received your letters of the date of the 28th July, so that they were a month on the way.   Immediately I sent my man to the Constable for the knowing of the King's pleasure for my repair to his presence.   His answer was, The next day if it so pleased me, and from henceforth that there should need no such ceremonies of sending ; since the King had willed me in nowise to use myself as a stranger in that place, where I was no less welcome than in the King my master's house, and that all the doors in the court should be as open to me as to him that was most priviest about the King.

" I repaired the next day, according unto the Constable's appointment, and was bid to dinner with him; where there dined also Monsieur Guise, Cardinal Chastillion, and his brother newly arrived in post with news from the frontiers.   What they were, I could not so suddenly learn.   As after dinner the Constable demanded what good news I had from England, Very good, Sir, quoth I, for the King my

master is in good health, and the sweat is well
ceased, thanks be to God! He seemed right glad
thereof, and prayed God long continue his welfare.

" After I had declared to him part of my charge,
and some news likewise that touched his master's
affairs, newly arrived out of Italy, that came the
same morning to my hands, he brought me to the
King's presence; unto whom, after I had declared
the King's Majesty's commendations, I showed him
that I had received a packet out of England, which
albeit it had been long time since despeched, yet had
the evil luck thereof been such, by reason of some
negligence, that it came but then to my hands. The
effect whereof, I told him, was, how thankfully the
King my master took the honour done unto him in
his Majesty choosing him into the noble Order; which
I assured him the King's Highness took in such
good part as nothing could have been devised more
for his contentation, and that therefore his Majesty
had sent him his right hearty thanks.

" And here, according to your Lordships' commandment, did I set forth as well as I could the
great honour and virtue of Monsieur Marechal,* pre-

---

* In the beginning of July, Henry the Second sent over to
England Monsieur le Maréchal St. André, and other French
commissioners, not only to treat of the marriage, but to
present the young King with the ensigns of the order of St.
Michael, into which his good brother of France had elected
him. Edward was solemnly invested with the order at Richmond on the 17th of July; " the King walking to the chapel

senter thereof, with the good behaviour and qualities likewise of such gentlemen as accompanied him into England; excusing as it were the small entertainment that he had there found by reason of the sudden plague of the sweat, the extremity whereof I said was such that the King could not keep his train about him for the receiving of the said Marechal, as he prepared and thought to have done. Moreover, the manner of the disease was so sudden and dangerous that the King's Majesty, with a very few of his chamber, was fain to withdraw him from all company.

" Here he seemed right sorry for the danger that the King was in ; and yet rejoiced at the good news that the plague was clearly rid out of England, and well arrived, as he heard say, in Flanders. I declared unto him likewise, how the King's Majesty

between the Marechal and Monsieur de Guise, who after the communion both kissed him." On his departure, (August 3rd,) St. André received in reward three thousand pounds; besides a diamond, taken from the King's finger, esteemed worth one hundred and fifty pounds.

† Hayward, in his Life of Edward the Sixth, (Kennet, vol. ii. p. 319,) denominates this sickness " a new, strange, and violent disease ; for," says he, " if a man were attacked therewith, he died or escaped within nine hours, or ten at the most. If he took cold, he died within three hours; if he slept within six hours, as he should be desirous to do, he died raving; albeit in other burning diseases that distemper is commonly appeased with sleep. It raged chiefly among men of strongest constitution and years, of whom one hundred and twenty perished in some one day within the liberties of London ; few aged men, or women or children, died thereof."

had given me special commandment heartily to
thank him for the good news out of Italy that of
late he sent him by the said Marechal; which were
so much more welcome unto his Majesty, by as
much as the good beginning of that enterprise promised as it were a good success unto him, whereof
the King would no less rejoice than if the cause
were his own; assuring him that the King my master wisheth the same good fortune at all times unto
his Majesty in all his affairs as he desireth unto
himself: And this is, Sire, quoth I, that I have on
his Majesty's behalf to say unto you.

" First, he thanked the King's Majesty for his
gentle recommendations, seeming no less to rejoice
of his healthful estate than glad to hear that he had
so thankfully received the honour done unto him of
the Order; wishing occasions daily to be offered
wherein they might better show their great affections and dear friendships one to other. And as
for the Marechal's entertainment, he said he was
right well assured, as well by his own report as
otherwise, that it was very honourable;* and de-

---

* " The feastings were exceeding sumptuous; and at their
return they were wafted over the seas by certain of the King's
ships, by reason of the wars between the Emperor and the
French King."   In the MS. Privy Council Book of Edward
the Sixth, sub anno 1551, July 21st, letters are directed to be
addressed to the Lord Admiral, advertising him that " the Marshal St. André will pass by land to Dover, and from thence cut
over to Bulloign, requiring him to prepare two rowing pinasses
and two other great ships to waft him."

clared how much he was beholden to the King's Majesty, his good brother, for the great honour he used at all times unto all those that came on his behalf to visit him.

" Sir, quoth I, your Majesty may be well assured that there can none come from you to the King my master that can lack at any time good receiving. Here he said that he had a quarrel to me for my long absence ; charging me in nowise from henceforth to use myself like a stranger, but like a familiar, and one with whom he would communicate all his causes, for so required the assured friendship between my master and him.   I required him pardon for that was past, excusing myself that my long abode at Blois, for the doing of my duty to the Queen my mistress,* was partly the occasion thereof, with a grudging of a fever wherewith he heard before that I had been lately troubled ; but that I was now and at all other times at his Majesty's commandment, and ready to obey his will and pleasure according to my duty, and to the charge I have in that behalf from the King my master.

" Among other familiar and friendly questions, he demanded if I had heard any news of his affairs beyond the mountains.   Sir, quoth I, I have received a packet from a friend of mine that came lately out of Italy ; the effect whereof I have already opened to Monsieur Constable, which I am sure

* The Lady Elizabeth, betrothed to Edward the Sixth.

you have long before now, if they be true. The news I send your Lordships here inclosed, which I was so much the gladder to declare to the King, as I thought thereby to increase my credit, and to be more acceptable to him; for, though they were of no great importance, yet they came right well to purpose, as the time required; and the King took them very thankfully at my hands, and showed me that he had received some part of them five days before, and other more which he would participate with his good brother; and for my good-will, declared at large herein, he gave me his hearty thanks.

"Sir, quoth I, in showing myself at all times to be your good servant, I know to serve my master best, since the King my master taketh his things and yours for all one; and therefore, in uttering any thing that may advance your service, I shall do but my duty, which I trust never to pretermit when occasion serveth.

"Now, Monsieur Pickering, quoth he, for requital of yours, my news of Parma be such, and report them for certain to the King my good brother. Peter Strozzi hath taken one Camillo Castilione, a gentleman sufficient to redeem any prisoner they have of mine, and a man of great credit and charge with them. He was expressly sent from Don Fernando to the Pope with instructions of importance for the order of their whole determination both of Parma and Mirandola. My men have also [routed] a band of Spaniards coming from Milan towards Don Fernando's camp ; * the captain taken, but his name could he not remember : his towns, he said, there, were victualled for two years, and lacked nothing requisite for towns of war. Among the rest, I noted much how he brought in Magdeburg, which he assured me to be in better case than ever it was.

" Sir, quoth I, these be good news indeed, and I dare assure you the King my master will be right glad to hear them. He somewhat lamented that Don Fernando had enclosed some part of his gentlemen that were prisoners in Cremona ; that he had bought them to raise their ransom ; but he doubted nothing, or the year went about, to be even with him.

" After many discourses of th' Emperor's evil malicious mind against him, he showed me that Marillac,† his ambassador there, whom he com-

---

* *Don Ferdinand Gonzaga,* Governor of Milan under the Emperor. The troops of the Pope, under the command of Dumont and Alexander Vitelli, had joined the army of the Emperor, and acted against the French ; his Holiness pretending to be incensed that Henry the Second had espoused the quarrel of Octavio Farnese, who had thrown himself into the arms of France. The Pope's policy was to withdraw quietly from the contest after he had set the Emperor and the French King by the ears ; hoping thus to weaken both.

† *Charles de Marillac,* son of William de Marillac, Comptroller of finances to the Duke de Bourbon, was born at Auvergne in 1510. His abilities attracted the notice of Francis the First, who employed him in many negociations ; and, after the death

mended to be wise and diligent in his office, had advertised him that the Emperor had been so extremely sick that he would not suffer the most priviest in his affairs to come near him, and, as he thought, he was unable to escape the danger thereof. Sire, under your Majesty's correction, quoth I, it was wont to be an old practice of his when he studied most mischief to feign himself most ill at ease. —Well, quoth he, Pullyn my man, who, ye know, hath been before time in England, hath taken fourteen or fifteen ships of his, three of them laden with artillery passing towards Spain.—He hath well eased them, Sir, quoth I, of a long voyage, and I am right glad thereof.

" He entered into a long discourse of the Turk's army, being in number one hundred and fifty gallies, which, he said, had been of late at Malta, where they were valiantly repulsed, notwithstanding that they had burnt a place called Augusta; and that they had been likewise before Africa, and had reviewed the town, without further attempting the same; which news, he said, were advertised him by a small vessel of his own that lately had been near those parts. In the end of his news, he required the King's Majesty very gently, that if the Scottish Queen* (whom he thought almost ready towards

of this monarch, he was equally in favour with his son Henry the Second, who made him his resident ambassador at the Emperor's court. He was the intimate friend of the Chancellor de l'Hôpital; he died in 1560.

* Mary of Guise, then about to sail for Scotland.

her passage,) were driven by adventure of tempest or otherwise either that for her pleasure she did take landing in England, that it would please his good brother she might be well entreated.

"Sire, [said I] I shall advertise the King's Majesty hereof, and your Majesty need doubt nothing that she shall be so honourably received as her state requireth, and as the commodity of the country will serve for. Thus, after much familiarity and friendly fashion, with his request to be affectionately recommended to the King his good brother, I took leave of his Majesty, and was brought to the Constable's chamber, where I tarried his return from the King.

"Among other communications with him, he entered very frankly with me, opening, as the King had done before, the evil and naughty disposition th' Emperor had towards the King his master; alleging that it had been his part much rather to have prepared him against the Turk, that was already entered Christendom, than against a Christian prince.* But be you well assured, Monsieur l'Ambassadeur, that he shall find us awake and ready, come when it please him.

"There is no doubt therein, Sir, quoth I; but now you may perceive his ambition to be such, as he

* This argument came somewhat awkwardly from Henry and the Constable, who had called in the Turk to attack Christendom, and threaten the dominions of Ferdinand, that he might prevent him from co-operating with his brother the Emperor.

would willingly the whole world were his tributaries, and without doubt his ill-will proceedeth of a horrible rancour and malice towards the King, specially in attempting matters against him in these his latter days, when no man that looketh upon him will almost promise him three days to live.*—That is most certain, Monsïeur l'Ambassadeur, quoth he, for our ambassador hath written unto the King that he was never so feeble and near his grave as he hath been of late.

"Yea, Sir, quoth I, I take him many times sickly and ill-disposed, and in those times mindeth he commonly most mischief.—Well, quoth he, then mischief come to him! Ye see likewise, he said, Monsieur l'Ambassadeur, what revel the Pope maketh, and how he stirreth against the King.— Sir, quoth I, tho' I be partial† in Popes' causes, (being a true Englishman,) yet I cannot judge of two evils, which is the worst. But would to God ye knew Popes so well as we do in England, then do I nothing doubt but that you would have the same opinion that we have of them.

"In some things, quoth he, peradventure we esteem him for worse.‡—Yea, Sir, quoth I, yet

* Yet Charles survived this prophecy of Pickering nearly seven years. It is amusing to read the scene of gossiping congratulation over the sickness of Charles the Fifth; nor is the digression of Montmorency to the bustling animosity of the Pope, and the shrewd remarks of the English ambassador, the least interesting part of the picture.   † Partial—biassed.

‡ A singular and candid admission from Montmorency, and yet none more bitterly hated the Hugonots.

not ill enough, nor for so ill as he will deserve
at your hands before these matters be ended;
but, at a venture, I would ye had them in like
estimation in all causes as we have.—Well, Monsieur l'Ambassadeur, quoth he, I trust we shall
well enough provide for them both.—There is no
doubt thereof, Sir, quoth I; I pray to God ye may.
After this manner was our talk. Your Lordships
may perceive what way these matters will shortly
weigh.

"I have moved the Constable again for the Scottish gentlemen that served the King's Majesty in
his wars, according to your request made to the
King by my Lord Marquis at Angiers.

"He required their names. I said they were
not many, and therefore required him to have their
pardon and restitution in general; whereof I gave
him a memorial, which, he said, should straight be
sent to the Queen: and here, ready to take my
leave, he showed me how good a servant he was of
the King my master, as some of his ministers were
well able to report; and as he had been, so would
he still remain, knowing so best to serve his master,
standing in the terms that presently they do, whereof he trusted never to see the change. I told him
that he was so esteemed, and that I would report no less to the King's Majesty and your Lordships, seeming to me as he craved the same at my
hands. Here he assured me that the presenter of
my Lord Marquis' reward should be chastised, as he

had well deserved, for he had failed in his duty
therein.*

" The Emperor's ambassador showed me, three
or four days ago, that he found the King very ill-
disposed against his master.†

" Here is a bruit raised that the Switzers will not
aid the French, since the peace is broken by their
occasion, and the league serveth only in cases of th'
Imperialists breaking first. Two of the principal
cantons are out of the league; nevertheless, there
is no doubt that he shall be served at his pleasure
at all times, and with so many as he lust to have.

" Monsieur de Nemours, the Great Prior, Monsieur le Beuf, and many other gentlemen, are upon
the depesche towards Parma. The Rhingrave, with
his bands, likewise repaireth with speed towards
those parts. The principal of the nobility, temporal and spiritual, be presently at Fontainbleau, for

---

* This alludes to the present given by Henry to the Marquis
of Northampton on leaving the French court. It was, (Kennet,
vol. ii. p. 320,) only worth 500*l.*; the present from Edward to the
French ambassador being worth 2000*l.* Hence the apology of
Montmorency.

† He might have assured him, with equal truth, that his
master was ill-disposed against the King. The marriage treaty
with England raised the animosity and jealousy of Charles the
Fifth; and he secretly commanded his sister, the Queen of
Hungary, Regent in the Low Countries, to arrest the French
ships in her ports. This led to reprisals on the part of Henry
the Second; and, although appearances were still kept up, it
was evident to all that watched the times, that war was on the
point of breaking out. The affair of Parma was the spark
which kindled it.

the establishing (as the voice goeth) of their Religion, and likewise of the perpetual stay of all payments that were accustomed to be had from hence to Rome. The Papists fear lest this open denial of the Pope's authority might breed more heretics in these parts than all France were able to suppress.

" Cardinal Chastillion, as I hear, is a great aider of Lutherians, and hath been a great stay in this matter, which otherwise had been before now concluded, to the destruction of any man that had almost spoken of God's word. Nevertheless, the Protestants here fear that it cannot come much to a better end, where such a number of bishops and cardinals bear the swing. They were once about to choose a Patriarch, as I lately writ to your Lordships, but since I hear no more of that matter.

" The trumpets have given warning for all soldiers, upon pain of their life, to repair with speed to their garrisons. Cardinal Tournon, Monsieur Monluc, and the French ambassador at Venice, have solicited the Venetians to set in a foot with them for Parma, persuading the great commodity that in time were like thereby to grow unto them, and what danger it were if the Emperor should recover the same, being already so great in Italy that almost no man durst attempt anything against him. These persuasions avail nothing, for they are wise, and will enterprise no more than they may wield. Then did they descend to lower degrees, and desired place in their towns upon their coasts

to lay in some provision and store, which was likewise denied them; they have only consented, as
the Genoese have done, that his soldiers shall at
all times have free passage thro' their countries.

" The Emperor hath taken a tax in Spain of
500,000 crowns, pretending his cause against the
Turk; but wise men judge the Pope and he will
part stakes. Here is a rumour that Andrea Doria
is dead.*	Other occurrents I have not at this time
to write unto your Lordships, but that I suppose
the King will not far out of these quarters whilst
the spring.†

" Now I must most humbly beseech your Lordships to be my good lords, and to take in good
part mine earnest and needful suit unto the same;
for the which it may please you to call unto your
good remembrance, that what time it pleased you

---

* The well known Genoese admiral; one of the greatest, the
most fortunate, and the honestest men of his time. Francis the
First never committed a more serious blunder than in giving
Doria cause to quit his service; and Charles the Fifth knew his
value too well, not to cherish him with special honour. The
part which he acted in the history of Europe from 1513, when
he was placed at the head of the Genoese navy, to 1556, was so
important, and so full of incident and adventure, that a good
life of him would be one of the most entertaining books that
could be written. The present report of his death was prema-
ture. He survived it nine years; and, after all his battles, died
in his bed in 1560, at the age of ninety-three. Although the
greatest naval commander of his day, he was twenty-four years
old before he commenced the service; but he was loath to
leave it when he once began, and at the age of ninety the old
admiral still commanded his galleys.

† Will not remove out of these parts till the spring.

to command me in the King's Majesty's service,
that then to all your Lordships I did 'knowledge
and allege mine inability in every respect for the
burden of such an office : yet I humbled myself to
your commandment, rather adventuring the name
of a fool for the undertaking of a thing past my
capacity, and [means] than by refusing the same
to avoid the King's Majesty's service; which, as
God judge me, I had rather had been where my
life might have gone in danger, than in such office,
more honourable than appertaineth to my simple-
ness and merit. And now that I have somewhat
tasted this service, confessing still mine inability
in all respects; but specially finding the import-
able charges such, that mine own undoing were
nothing towards the sustaining of the same, I am
forced most humbly to beseech your Lordships, according to my necessity, and to your favourable
promise at my departure, to have me in your good
remembrance for the mending of mine entertainment. And here I most humbly beseech my Lord
Marquis to say what he knoweth herein, or that it
may please your Lordships to command Mr. Masone
to inform you the truth, who knoweth in what state
I am in, and how I may live in this place ; either
that it may please your Lordships to compare the
smallness of my dietts with the ordinary charges
of my house, praying God that the King's Majesty
and your Lordships may never be good unto me if
I spend not, one day with another, thirteen or four-

teen French crowns, and that I have of the King's
Majesty amounteth not to seven crowns the day;
which God knoweth, and I confess, to be far more
than my service deserveth, and yet not half so
much as the furniture of this place requireth.
Thus, wholly referring myself in all things to the
wills of your honourable Lordships, I beseech God
long to preserve the same! At Melun, the 4th
Sept. 1551.

" Your Lordships' most humble at commandment,
" W. PYCKERYNGE."

The three following letters to Cecil, from Parry,
Secretary Petre, and the Earls of Wiltshire and
Warwick, though apparently slight, contain matter
from which a future biographer of Burleigh may
borrow some new touches. The letter of Sir Thomas Parry, the *cofferer*, or treasurer, of the Princess
Elizabeth, demonstrates the early friendship—we
might almost say affection—with which she treated
the Secretary, whose advice, as we have seen, had
already been useful to her in the management of
her domestic concerns. From the sentence of the
Princess, dictated to Parry, it would seem that
scarce a day passed without some intercourse between Elizabeth and Cecil by letters or messages.
She had been ill, and bids Parry say to Mr. Cecil,
" tho' I send not *daily* to him, I am well assured
that, for all that, he doth not daily forget me."

With Secretary Petre we have had some intercourse already.* He was now a victim to the gout —a frequent malady of statesmen—and, being tied to his couch, had waxen " preacher." The text he had chosen was one of universal application in those days—" covetousness," or, as he pithily terms it, " fishing in the tempestuous seas of this world for gain and wicked mammon."

" This summer," says Strype,† speaking of the year 1551, " the King and his Council issued out orders to all the bishops, charging and commanding them in their own persons, and their preachers and ministers in their several dioceses, to preach against the sin of covetousness, which now grew most insatiable amongst the people." This sin, as the same writer tells us, put on various shapes. It would monopolize corn, promote enclosures, and, above all, would tear and rend the substance from the church, the universities, and the hospitals for the poor.‡ There can be little doubt that, amongst the many anglers for the Savoy, whom we hear of in Petre's letter, there were some Christians of the Court, as Turner calls them, who would have shut its door upon the poor men which it supported, and turned its revenues to disreputable uses. It was against these fishers for money, and not for men, that Thomas Lever, a Protestant preacher, delivered a remarkable sermon at Paul's Cross. " Covetous officers," said he, " have so used this matter

* Supra, p. 76.   † Strype's Memor. vol. ii. part i. p. 495.
‡ Strype, vol. ii. part i. p. 495.

that those goods which did serve to the relief of the poor, the maintenance of learning, and to comfortable necessary hospitality in the commonwealth, be now turned to maintain worldly, wicked, covetous ambition. You, which have gotten these goods into your hands to turn them from evil to worse, be ye sure that it is even you that have offended God, beguiled the King, robbed the church, spoiled the poor, and brought the commonwealth to a common misery."*

My object in giving the brief and apparently immaterial letter of the Earls of Warwick and Wiltshire, will be more apparent when I come to make some remarks on the final fate of the Duke of Somerset. It shows us the position and the power held by Cecil on the 15th Sept. 1551, within a month of the apprehension of the Duke.

THOMAS PARRY TO CECIL.

Orig. St. P. Off. *Domestic.* Sept. 1551.

" Sir.—I have enclosed herein her Grace's letters, for so is her Grace's commandment, which she desires you, according to her trust, to deliver from her unto my Lord's Grace; taking such opportunity therein, by your wisdom, as thereby the rather she may by letters again hear from his Grace; and that also she may somewhat understand what time his Grace, unto whom she refers all, shall think aptest for her access.

" Her Grace commanded me to write this:

* Strype's Memor. vol. ii. part i. pp. 409, 410.

'Write my commendations in your letters to Mr. Cecil, that I am well assured, tho' I send not daily to him, that he doth not, for all that, daily forget me; say, indeed, I assure myself thereof.'

" Touching your gentle letters, I think myself most bounden to you, that so gently would participate my service, or the pleasure I may do you; whereof I beseech you to assure yourself ever, not as a young poor friend, but as your own self, as far as ever my power may extend. Your request is [finished] fully; let the party make the report.

" I had forgotten to say to you that her Grace commanded me to say to you, for the excuse of her hand, that it is not now as good as she trusts it shall be; her Grace's unhealth hath made it weaker, and so unsteady, and that is the cause.

" Thus, leaving to trouble you, I desire Christ give you perfect health, and send you one day's leisure to see her Grace, and myself once able to deserve that I have found in you. At Hatfield, this present Sunday.

" She removes not to Ashridge these ten or twelve days yet, for the unreadiness of things there; but then, God willing, she will be there.*

" Your own assured bounden ever,

" THOMAS PARRY."

Addressed.   " *To the Right Worshipful Mr. Cicil, Esquier.*"

---

* Ashridge in Hertfordshire, where the Princess had a stately house; of which Norden gives a description. Nichol's Progresses, vol. i. p. 4.

SECRETARY PETRE TO SECRETARY CECIL.

Orig. St. P. Off. *Domestic.* 14th Sept. 1551.

" After my most hearty commendations. I thank you for your letters, and also for your pains for the Savoy. I doubt not but there be, as you write, good, or rather great plenty of anglers for it. If they do angle for the good continuance of the poor men, and of the house, I like their angling well. And whosoever hath most desire to do so, I would he might take the fish. Marry, I would all things were done in order, and every man called to such places specially, rather of other men's vocation, than of their own labour. At the beginning, the Apostles left their fishing of fishes, and became fishers of men; and now we, which talk much of Christ and his holy word, have, I fear me, used a much contrary way; for we leave fishing for men, and fish again in the tempestuous seas of this world for gain and wicked mammon.

" Thus you see, lying here alone, I am waxen a preacher. I do send you herewith a note of a commission for the visitation of the Savoy. W. Say was not in London, and therefore I did it myself. You may put out as you think good. * * * My leg, I thank God, beginneth well to amend. To-morrow I intend to ride towards my house in a litter. I go the rather to comfort my weak wife, who is somewhat troubled with the death of her young son. * * * Thus, leaving to trouble you, I wish you as well to do as myself! From London, this 14th of Sept. 1551.

"WM. PETRE."

THE EARL OF WILTSHIRE AND THE EARL OF WARWICK TO SECRETARY CECIL.

Orig. ST. P. OFF. *Domestic.* 15th Sept. 1551.

"MR. SECRETARY.—After our hearty commendations. You shall receive herein enclosed a letter sent to me, the Lord Great Master, from the Count Palatine, Otho Henricus. We pray you to cause the pact and convention made with the Dns. Philip to be sought, as [appertaineth]. You may write unto us your advice what answer may be made according to the tenor of the said pact. And so we bid you heartily well to fare. From Chelsea, the 15th Sept. 1551.

"Your loving friends,
"W. WILTSHIRE.   J. WARWYK."

The fate of Bishop Ridley, who fell a victim to the dreadful Marian persecution, and, in company with the venerable Latimer, sealed his convictions with his blood, is familiar to every student of the history of the Reformation, and seldom have cruelty and fanaticism been let loose upon a kinder or more generous heart. When Bonner was deprived, Ridley succeeded him in his see of London; and one of his first acts after entering on possession, was to assure the mother and sister of the extruded prelate, who had been inmates of his palace, that "they should not lose the benefit of the Bishop of London's board. He never failed to send for them to dinner and supper, constantly placing Mrs. Bonner at the head of the table; nor was any difference made even when the Lords of the Privy Council came to share the feast, as they often did: on such occasions, as if he had succeeded to the love as well as to the office of her son, he would then tenderly take the old lady by the hand, and, leading her before the magnates to the head of the board, say, ' By your Lordships' favour, this place, of right and custom, is for my mother Bonner.'"

Regarding the following letter, which the prelate addressed to Cecil, I have been at some loss to form a precise opinion. Is the information it contains regarding the miserable state of Cecil's private fortune at this time real, or is it playful, and meant for wit? The Secretary of State,—the trusted, courted, confidential organ by whom the all-powerful Northumberland conducted the government, — the friend of every influential nobleman about court,—the familiar correspondent and intimate adviser of the Princess Elizabeth,—is here seen, almost *in formâ pauperis,* complaining of his " *poor lame house*," bemoaning the " *sorrowful sight of the bottom of his purse,*" and begging for " *half-a-dozen trees,*" which the Bishop, contrary to his usual practice of resisting " unlawful beggary," is constrained to grant. This is certainly strange;

but, if it be taken seriously, and I am inclined to think it so intended, it is new in the life of Burleigh. There is a passage in a letter written ten years later than this by Cecil to Windebank, tutor to his eldest son, Thomas Cecil, afterwards Earl of Exeter, and then a student at Paris, which seems to me to corroborate the narrowness of Burleigh's early fortune, and to be almost decisive of the view which I have already taken of his origin from the lesser gentry of the country. Thomas Cecil had, it seems, been idle and extravagant; and his father, who was much incensed at his conduct, addressed a letter to Windebank from Hertford Castle, on the 10th Sept. 1561, in which he uses these remarkable words :

" If I see him so untoward and inconsiderate I will revoke him home, where he shall take his adventure, with *as mean bringing up*, as I myself have had." *

BISHOP RIDLEY TO CECIL.

Copy.   St. P. Off.   *Domestic.*   16th Sept. 1551.

" GRACE AND HEALTH. Your preface so prettily mingled with sorrow and gladness, and the sorrowful sight that you had of the bottom of your purse, and your poor lame house, hath so affected and

---

* This extract I owe to the kindness of my learned friend Mr. Thomas Burgon.

filled me with pity and compassion, that altho', indeed, I grant I am blamed because by my fashion,
used towards some, I may plainly seem to condemn
unlawful beggary, yet you have filled mine affections so full, and have moved me so much, that you
have persuaded me to grant unto you half-a-dozen
trees, such as I may spare you and mine officer
shall appoint. I ween they must be pollards; for
other, either few or none, God knoweth, I think
are left of the late spoil in all my woods.

"And, Sir, if you that can move men so migh-
tily to have pity on the decay of one house, if you
(I say) knew the miserable spoil that was done in
the vacation-time by the King's officers upon my
woods, whereby in time past so many good houses
have been builded, and hereafter might have been,
also so many lame relieved, so many broken
amended, so many fallen-down re-edified; forsooth,
I do not doubt but you were able to move the
whole country to lament and mourn the lamentable
case of so pitiful a decay. But, Sir, wot you what
I thought, after I had refreshed my spirit with once
or twice reading over of your letters. Jesus!
thought I, if God had appointed this man to have
been the proctor of a spiritual, that can thus move
men to have pity upon a lame house; who could
have passed by, with a penny in his purse, but
such a man could have wrung it out with words,
altho' the passenger had been never such a *cringe?*

And thus I wish you ever well to fare. From Full-ham, this 6th Sept. 1551.

" Yours in Christ,

" Nɪᴄ. Lᴏɴᴅᴏɴ."

This last part of Ridley's letter, regarding the mi-serable havoc made by the King's officers upon the woods and property of the bishoprick, presents only one amongst a thousand instances of the sacri-lege of those church-destroying days. The Bishop seems indirectly to lament that the same eloquence which in Cecil could so well plead for a decaying house, should not rouse itself to advocate the rights of a despoiled and forsaken church : but here Cecil's own hands, as well as those of his patrons, North-umberland and Somerset, were tainted with the spoil.

END OF THE FIRST VOLUME.

LONDON :

PRINTED BY SAMUEL BENTLEY,

Dorset Street, Fleet Street.